How to Go to Work

The Honest Advice No One Ever Tells You at the Start of Your Career

Lucy Clayton and Steven Haines

PENGUIN BOOKS

PENGUIN BOOKS

UK | USA | Canada | Ireland | Australia
India | New Zealand | South Africa

Penguin Books is part of the Penguin Random House group of companies
whose addresses can be found at global.penguinrandomhouse.com.

First published 2020
001

Copyright © Lucy Clayton and Steven Haines, 2020

The moral right of the authors has been asserted

The list on pp. 216–17 by David Ogilvy is taken from
The Unpublished David Ogilvy (Profile Books, 2012)

Text design by Couper Street Type Co.

Set in 11/13 pt Dante MT Std
Typeset by Jouve (UK), Milton Keynes
Printed and bound in Great Britain by Clays Ltd, Elcograf S.p.A.

A CIP catalogue record for this book is available from the British Library

ISBN: 978–0–241–39946–0

Follow us on LinkedIn: linkedin.com/company/penguinbusiness

www.greenpenguin.co.uk

MIX
Paper from
responsible sources
FSC
www.fsc.org   FSC® C018179

Penguin Random House is committed to a
sustainable future for our business, our readers
and our planet. This book is made from Forest
Stewardship Council® certified paper.

For Kit & Ella – Get a job

Contents

CONTENTS

CONTENTS

CONTENTS

Introduction

I grew up in a house where work was a dirty word. It meant something you'd rather not be doing. It was just a distraction from the better business of living.

My parents were unambitious and unconnected, my dad didn't know anyone else's influential dad, my mum didn't aspire to earn a certain salary or to own a specific kind of car. For them, the concept of aspiration made very little sense because they already had everything they could possibly want: love, comedy, comfort and time to enjoy those things.

But they were grafters.

They knew that if you wanted to protect the stuff that mattered at home, you needed to put the hours in elsewhere. To fund fun time. One of my first life lessons was that if you want treats you have to work for them: those KFC family bucket feasts don't pay for themselves. I really love KFC.

But work is so much a part of how we all live that it doesn't make sense to think of it as just a distraction. Even if you are in the rare situation of working 9 to 5, five days a week, and getting eight hours' sleep a night, you're spending well over a third of your waking hours at work. It takes up too much of your day-to-day to be an afterthought.

How we spend those hours has a fundamental impact on the quality of our lives. The UN's wonderfully titled *World Happiness Report*, which surveys thousands of people around the globe, shows that not only are people who are employed much happier than those who are not, but that managers, executives and officials feel much more satisfied with their lives than people in other roles.[1] The balance between the variety of tasks, our opportunities to choose what we do and the support we get from our colleagues contributes greatly to our happiness.

Our social status and relationships are tied up in what we do for a living. You've probably been asked 'Where do you want to be in ten years' time?' If you're anything like me, the weight of expectation in that question can make you feel pretty inadequate as you trawl through the sudden, alarming void of your mind to come up with something that sounds impressive. Or at least feasible. But remember, anyone who's able to answer that question with total clarity isn't allowing for the fact that our working lives, our adult lives, don't follow a perfect linear pathway from school to retirement. Career is a verb as well as a noun. And actually, it's OK not to have a plan. As this book will demonstrate, many magnificent experiences can come from accidental careers, from unexpected opportunities. Who knows what might happen?

There are around 8 million young people in the UK between the ages of fifteen and twenty-four, and at some point in any given year, many of them will be going to work for the first time. In the US that number is 38 million. But our education systems are doing a terrible job of preparing young people for the realities of the working world. A British Chambers of Commerce survey of 3,000 firms found that nine out of ten thought school leavers were not ready for employment.[2] So often the advice you will be given is based on flimsy or irrelevant examples, like sixth-form uniform policies which insist you wear 'business casual' – ignoring the fact that business casual hasn't been a dress code anywhere since nineteen eighty-something. School careers advisers are over-stretched and under-resourced and at best they can only know a few industries superficially well.

Going to work is an enormous, life-changing thing. You'll never be the same again. You begin knowing nothing and then, very quickly, you can never unknow what it's like to be bone tired from a fourteen-hour shift or the exhilaration of receiving your first pay slip. The experiences you are about to have will change you forever. And yet, no one is really preparing you for them. Or even really talking about it. Beyond the perfunctory 'congratulations' when you get hired, people just expect you to get on with it. There are no manuals to help manage your expectations or to reassure you. Compare that with other life-changing moments such as starting a family – all prospective first-time parents read *What to Expect When You're Expecting*. It's culturally compulsory and deeply comforting because it charts all the approaching unknown territory for you. You begin knowing nothing and then, very quickly, you can never unknow what it's like to be bone tired from a fourteen-hour shift or the exhilaration of your baby's first smile. That book demystifies the otherwise terrifyingly mysterious.

This book will do exactly that for your transition into work – a truly transformational time; moving from student to worker, from childhood, dependency and security to fully fledged, responsible, tax-paying adulthood. Do not underestimate the scale of this change. Work is, for most of us, central to independence, but so is learning to live away from the structures of home and education, integrating into new cities and discovering how you want to live in a world no longer defined by other people's house rules. It's a big deal. And you have to do it all at the same time. It's exciting, exhausting and nerve-wracking as hell.

There are other books that will tell you how to achieve greatness (and there's nothing wrong either with greatness or with wanting it), how to lead or how to win. But there are so many of these books about that we often forget that there is also greatness in simply going to work. In doing a good job and being paid fairly for it. In being keen and challenged and not bored out of your mind. In having something sparky to say when someone says, 'How was your day?'

I've been mentoring young people for a long time and I'm writing this book because there's so much simple stuff that isn't being said. I don't claim to be an expert at working; if anything, my CV is patchy, strangely shaped and features moments of sheer idleness. But I have helped hundreds of people at the start of their professional lives, and talked with many who have made what they do for work a hugely positive part of their lives. I want to share what we've learnt together. This isn't me saying, 'Let me show you how it's done.' This is more a collection of tips whispered in your ear. It's also a healthy dose of perspective, not just from me but also from a diverse collective of people who have been there and done that.

The truth is, whether you're interested in being an apprentice, a novelist or a surgeon, some of the basics stay the same, so we've gathered together knowledge from people with dream jobs, important lifesaving jobs, colouring-in jobs and some rock-solid sensible ways to earn hard cash: the kind of work you really want to do. And we've mixed it together with highlights from some of the most important and useful research about how to perform in the workplace, from leadership theory to project management principles, so that you don't have to wade through those detailed and often contextless tomes yourself.

This book is a guide to how to go to work: the mechanics of turning up, clocking in and contributing. It's what you need to know that no one ever tells you. From what to do before you start your new job, to the questions to ask on day one, to the sticky subject of how to resign – this book will help you navigate the early days of workplace politics, expectations and frustrations.

Whether you want to make millions, make beautiful things or make the world a better place (or, if you're lucky, all three), there are aspects that feature in the daily life of every job, like meetings, presentations and conference calls. To achieve what you want you'll need to understand how to get dressed, build great teams and know where the loos are.

Across your working life, from interning to CEOing, you'll experience moments of revelation and epiphany that range from the mundane through to the game changing. This book gives you a shortcut, taking the collective wisdom from those who have gone before you. But instead of showing off about how we got there, we're giving you honest insights and unfiltered advice.

I wanted to write a book designed to help you show up and do a decent turn. It's not about success, or striving for the top or killing it. This is about going to work and grafting to make that a foundation for a life full of love, comedy and comfort.

This book can't give you the coordinates to every loo in the land, but it can help with pretty much everything else.

Good Luck.

Why We Wrote This Book

This book is for anyone ambitious but apprehensive, tenacious but tentative, overexcited and underprepared. In anticipation of all your fledgling careers, the things you will make, the problems you'll solve and the people you'll become.

We wrote it because we felt that young adults were being set up to fail by a system that was out of touch and old fashioned. Through our work with and alongside excellent people who happened to be younger than us, we've noticed the same things going unsaid, the same misconceptions being perpetuated, and the same strange directions being pointed in. People arrive at work with an awful lot of wonky baggage, which makes them anxious and uncertain, and contributes to their feeling unprepared. Sometimes it's the result of inadequate resources (in careers centres, for example) or a piece of misguided advice (thank you, parents) or just plain gaps in experience and expertise from the people who were trying to help – but so much of our mentoring seemed to be about undoing a lot of unhelpful assumptions. We spent a lot of time recalibrating expectations – raising them up or pushing them further – or challenging notions about careers that seemed to belong to a much older generation or an employment landscape that no longer exists.

So, rather than trying to redress all this one individual at a time, we thought we'd write it down and share. This is a manifesto for your first years at work. It will take you from your Saturday job to fully functioning, proper professional players. Don't feel you need to read it cover to cover or section by section; use the contents pages to match its advice to your experience. It's designed to be your guide for all the basics as well as for some of the bigger questions about who you are at work and where you're going. It's here to support your decision making and offer a different perspective from the official one you're so familiar with (the one we think is failing you).

How We Wrote This Book

This book has two authors and one narrative voice. We wrote it together because we have very different,

7

complementary talents and a shared passion for bringing this idea to life. It's a demonstration of one of the most important pieces of advice in this book (spoiler alert) – that you should work with people who compensate for your shortcomings and allow you to focus on your strengths. That's what we have tried to do in this process. (We hope you think it's full of strengths, or that would be embarrassing, but if you think we've missed things or have a question you wish we'd addressed you can contact us at howtogotowork@gmail.com.)

The spirit of this book is very much unified, but although we wrote it together, we have radically different skills. The 'I' in the pages that follow is Lucy's – it's full of her stories, recollections and observations (they are all real and true) but they are underpinned by hardcore facts and researched insights that are Steven's (they are also real and true).

Beyond our voices, included throughout this text are the contributions of so many brilliant people who all gave us a resounding 'YES!' when we asked to include their wisdom for your benefit. We'll thank them at the end, but this book is a kaleidoscopic, clarion combination of so many conversations between people who share our optimism about your future and who want to help equip you for it (even if *we* will all be dead by then).

Section 1
Starting Out

Where I grew up and how I grew up really affected the way I saw the world. This may be a bit of a generalisation, but I think for most people, having particular dreams, and seeing a way to realise them is a normal thing. It might be something as simple as a dream job, for example, and recognising the steps that need to be taken to get that job. We didn't have that. Where I'm from that doesn't really happen. People might have the skills they need to get their dream job, but they can't see a way to get there.

STORMZY IN *RISE UP: THE #MERKY STORY SO FAR*

Even if you've had good support at home and in education there are going to be lots of things no one has told you about making the transition into the workplace. It's an almost universal rite of passage and yet it's still shrouded in mystery. A lot of this is simply because people tend to forget about the very beginnings of their career once they reach the apex of it – so you hear about Microsoft starting in a garage but you don't necessarily know how they got the garage in the first place. Stellar career success stories rarely mention the Saturday job on the shop floor or the five years of babysitting that paid for the first laptop. But everyone starts somewhere, so consider this section your guide to getting started . . .

Some Myths About Careers Advice

It's not what you know, it's who you know

My grandmother was a dinner lady. She had to be a dinner lady because she was a single mother (my grandfather died young) with three small children. She could only work during school hours. So that meant working in a school. And since she had few formal qualifications, it meant being a dinner lady. It also meant that those three children often ate the same for lunch as for supper, because when money is tight, a school's worth of leftovers are a lifesaver.

'It's not what you know, it's who you know,' was one of her favourite catchphrases. She said it in a doomed tone, with a slow head shake designed to remind you of your place and its fundamental unfairness in a class war she was too weary to fight.

Even as a child I knew this was nonsense.

My grandmother believed that opportunity was something dished out to the privileged and denied to everyone else. She was pleased when my father went to work in the Ford factory in Eastleigh because it was an honest job with a steady wage, although she would have preferred it if he worked in an office. In a suit. My father is as unsuited in skills and temperament to factory work as any human is likely to be. He is good at photography and cooking. He can't fix anything, isn't at all practical and he doesn't understand cars.

Her situation was challenging and very hard work. And I think she truly believed that there was an alternative version for people from a different background who could be hooked up and sorted out in glittering, effortless but lucrative careers with just a few phone calls from Daddy, while the rest of us were destined to settle for a lifetime of double cabbage and drudge.

There is, of course, some truth in her oft-repeated statement. It's not just that young people from well-off backgrounds get a helpful push up the career ladder, they are also less likely to fall too many rungs down.[1] So I don't dispute that parents making connections or leveraging influence happens all the time and benefits those kids who are best placed to exploit all that.

BUT there was always a fundamental flaw in her logic, namely that it is possible to change 'who you know' simply by meeting new people. Interesting people, who do the kind of work you would like to do. You can introduce yourself. And even if the idea of 'networking' fills you with dread, it's worth remembering that you're already meeting new people all the time. Whatever job you choose, you're going to encounter new warm bodies. And some of the people you meet when you're starting work are going to become some of your greatest and most trusted friends. So if you know all the 'what' and none of the 'who', then get busy with the 'who' and you'll suddenly find that opportunity is everywhere.

I've tested this theory. In my career I've had at least three transformative moments when I sought out someone I had zero connections to and ended up with a job. Specifically, a job at the BBC, a magazine column and a fashion CEO role. You've got to get out there.

It's tempting sometimes to imagine that the limits of our immediate experience are hard lines, impossible to cross without a sponsor for safe passage into your dream job. Even if you do have a fairy godmother who is conveniently able to get you work experience at your favourite record label or bankroll the first investment round for your tech start-up, remember that the safe route isn't always the most exciting. And if you don't have parents with connections then please don't ever think that disqualifies you from making them yourself. In my experience, all the best people do.

All you need to do is believe in yourself

People love me. And you know what? I have always been very successful. Everybody loves me.

DONALD TRUMP[2]

You know what? Total self-belief can be a dangerous thing.

Social media bombards us daily with supposedly inspirational messages urging us to find our inner goddess, or to wake up, kick ass and repeat. We're told that everybody is always #nailingit. Personally, this makes me want to nail myself to the floor and bleed out all over the carpet. But of all the dodgy tropes, the idea that all you need is total self-belief is the absolute worst.

It's really possible to stay at home believing in your-self all day while binge watching Netflix and eating Pringles. In fact, I am *most* myself in this exact situation. It's glorious. But doing that isn't going to get you a good job and it certainly isn't going to mean you keep that job.

Self-belief is as important a skill for doing well in the workplace as breathing. If you don't believe you're able to deliver, you'll never get going, let alone see it through.

But self-belief isn't enough on its own. As Harvard Business School professor Rosabeth Moss Kanter puts it, 'it's not enough just to *feel* confident. You have to do the work.'[3]

And sometimes, it can even get in the way. The idea that we have an unwavering, steely core of self-belief that will see us through come what may is unattainable and often damaging. It's also often seen in Donald Trump personality types. Not something to aspire to.

It's perfectly normal to want what you don't have, to wobble when you're tested, to think you might not be good enough, to be intimidated by the polished person next to you, to falter when you're out of your depth or to panic that you are in the wrong place at the wrong time. All of this is healthier than bullet proof self-belief. Because it means that you are paying attention and that you are trying. And I would hire for those qualities over pure confidence every single time.

By all means believe in yourself, but always do so in context. Start by believing that you can get the job done, but know that if you're not good at something initially, you'll work at it. If something makes you nervous, you'll practise until it's comfortable. If you get knocked back, you'll give it another whirl tomorrow.

As Kanter says, 'Confidence grows when you look at what can go wrong, think through alternatives, and feel you are prepared for whatever might happen.' Self-belief means knowing you can improve. It's about honouring your potential. So it's a useless quality without a work ethic to accompany it.

Why not become a funeral director?

When you start to think about your career options, you'll already have lots of ideas and influences in mind. They might feel fragmented or contradictory. You might have long harboured fantasies of a job that's half-astronaut, half-vet, or perhaps you want to become a ballet-dancing firefighter? The good news is that hybrid jobs are everywhere these days (OK, maybe not those exact ones), so there's usually a way of blending your interests to fit your ambitions. (For more about hybrid jobs, see Section 8). Or you might have no idea what path you fancy pursuing. And that's fine too (as long as you're making reasonable efforts to discover something). We'll suggest ways to do that later on . . .

In this book we'll help you find direction, but first it's important to suss out where those first sparks of interest come from and to determine if it's a credible source.

When I was at school we had to do a career-determination test that came on a CD-ROM (yes, I know,

I'm ancient), with snappy, simple questions like 'Do you prefer to work indoors or outside?' or 'Are you happiest in a team or working alone?' Once this pathetic little quiz had finished, the computer would spit out its firm recommendation for the job you were most suited to. Then the careers adviser would turn the lights off in the Portakabin library and go home.

My sister Charlotte is today a successful, inspiring and dedicated teacher of primary-aged children. The CD-ROM quiz told her to be a funeral director. Not everything we are told is helpful. Or worth listening to. Even if it comes rubber stamped from the curriculum.

It's no secret that careers advice can be pretty patchy and the careers advisers you're likely to come across don't always have the widest possible range of reference points to guide you in those early, exploratory conversations (especially if what you want to do is niche, or very new).[4] The brutal reality is that they sometimes haven't had careers themselves beyond the school gates. In the worst cases, their agenda can be directly opposed to yours. As one college adviser confessed to me recently, 'I took this job because careers is the graveyard shift and that suits me fine.'

Nothing about that is fine. It's really, really depressing.

Although the technology we use to shortcut massive life decisions has improved immeasurably since the 1990s, it's still not smart enough to provide you with all the answers after a spot of multiple-choice questioning. If you're not going to do some soul searching and investigation yourself, you may as well put your faith in a fortune cookie. Because, let's be honest, apart from being a midwife, there is no job further from funeral director than teacher. Just remember, not all advice is equal.

Saturday Jobs

A Saturday job is worth more than you might think. I don't know a single successful, well-adjusted person who doesn't credit their Saturday job as an important influence on their lives, both at the time and decades later. What usually starts as a simple attempt to earn some money and gain some freedom can often prove the gateway drug to a whole load of more intense, interesting experiences.

The best place to start is at the beginning, which is usually the bottom. Restaurants, shop floors, behind bars (not like that) and supermarket checkouts – from time immemorial these have been the best places to earn your stripes. And that's still the case. Search online for local opportunities, get recommendations from friends and family and take a look on noticeboards and in the local paper.

Any role that requires human interaction with a business model behind it will teach you a ton of stuff you're not going to learn in college. A work experience placement, an employer talk or a careers fair will only go so far. No one sees the whole of a business like an entry-level employee. It's a view easily lost as you move up the ladder in an organization. It's not uncommon for business leaders like TESCO's turnaround CEO, Dave Lewis, who had senior staff join him at the tills in the run-up to Christmas, to get back to the shop floor to better understand their customers.[5]

Here are some of my favourite first jobs:

- **Me:** working in a doctor's surgery when I was fifteen (illegal, but an absolute eye-opener)
- **Beyoncé:** sweeping the floor in her mother's hair salon
- **Warren Buffett:** shop assistant, JCPenney
- **Kanye West:** GAP sales assistant
- **Mick Jagger:** hospital porter

Nothing is beneath you. Rod Stewart was a gravedigger . . . which is more like starting at the end than the beginning, but I digress . . .

Think of a Saturday job as a warm-up – it's not the beginning of a lifelong interest in flogging shoes, or serving ice cream. It's just a start. But it's also a baseline. Once you've been a waiter you can work anywhere in the world. And because your tasks are relatively straightforward in an entry-level job, you've got time to develop your skills without enormous pressure to be perfect.[6] Those skills will be there whenever you might want to call upon them. On your gap year, in your students' association, founding your first business – who knows when?

Once you've done the Saturday job you'll always know what it's like to be on the other side of the table. Since Daniel Goleman's famous book *Emotional Intelligence: Why It Can Matter More Than IQ* was published, a lot of stock has been placed on the skills we need to relate to others, things like self-awareness, active listening, emotional vocabulary, showing empathy and managing emotions. These are vital qualities you'll need in work. They will help you form and lead teams, get the right product or service in the hands of your potential customers, fight ground-breaking legal cases, fill the dancefloor or lead the mission. Keep that in mind when you've got ten plates of food that need to be dispatched in the next five minutes before the next twenty orders arrive. For many people, their Saturday job is their first experience of being under pressure without a support network around them. No form room, no school nurse, no retakes. It's frightening and liberating. And the worst thing that can happen is you get fired. Which isn't terrible in this scenario.

Waiting on tables for a large catering company was how I spent one of the best summers of my life. We were poorly paid, and often tired, but we learnt how to work as a slick team, how to deal with grumpy chefs and drunk guests. How to apologize to customers, how to gauge the energy of the room and how to do a full night's work in a five-inch heel (more on dressing for work later). I swear, I've called upon elements of that experience every working week since.

Three reasons why giving up your Saturdays is a good idea

1. Earning

Instead of £10 it's X many minutes of your time. It buys you a portion of that pair of jeans or these many drinks. And if you save it, your summer will be immeasurably better than just sitting at home staring at a screen or going on holiday with your parents. If you really save hard you can protect yourself, push yourself or parade it about depending on your personal circumstances and lifestyle preferences.

As well as enjoying a taste of financial freedom, try to learn about money. How you handle your own finances is often shaped by your early experiences.[7] The vast majority of young people don't learn enough about money management at school,[8] so get to know how money works now and you'll thank yourself later in your career. See Section 3 for tips about how to manage your money in the early days of work.

2. **Having too much spare time is a bad thing. Particularly when your weeks aren't jammed full of lessons**

    So many young people I mentor made themselves miserable at university because those famous humanities subjects with eight hours of contact time a week, plus weekends, leaves you with a lot of time to fill. And more importantly, it's solitary time. Library sessions, lie-ins, lazing around – it all sounds lovely but it's a lot of hanging about in your own head. And that isn't always a good thing. It's proven that the busier we are, the more we get done, because it increases our perception that we are using our time effectively.[9] So don't always think of a part-time job as a distraction from your studies. Very often, despite it being a completely unrelated activity, working alongside formal education, up to a point, can make you better at your main focus (your studies) and happier overall. A US study found that college students who worked in a regular job up to ten hours a week had higher levels of satisfaction and better test scores,[10] while a UK study found that in the longer term higher education students have better career outcomes if they combine paid work and work experience with their studies.[11]

3. **Doing something outside your immediate circle of home and friends gives you a connection to a bigger world**

Simply by showing up you have improved your chances of doing well in the future. Simply by showing up you'll have more perspective.

There's always something revelatory and gratifying about your first job (if you want to know more about this then listen to the podcast that accompanies this book where we ask a host of people about their teenage Saturdays). From cleaning windows to babysitting, it all counts. The more interaction you have with work, the more you are developing those vital workplace skills that employers prize so highly. Getting paid is a bonus, but there are plenty of other compelling reasons to give up your Saturdays.

A quick point on the law. Although in principle part-time jobs should give you many of the same rights in work as full-time jobs, the law varies considerably depending on country, age, terms and conditions and many other factors. It's worth looking into this through the information on government websites. At worst, contracts can be a bit murky and unscrupulous employers can take advantage, like the time a restaurant manager tried to make off with my sick pay to fund the staff Christmas party. Equally, many employers are understandably cautious about where your priorities will sit between essay deadlines and the evening shift, or they're worried about the legislation that allows them to employ you in the first place. If you equip yourself on these issues then you can make a case for being safely and honestly employed. Just make sure you're clear on the terms of your contract and get advice if you feel you need it from places such as ACAS, Citizens Advice or the US Department of Labor.

Now, if you live in total rural wilderness, or if you have commitments at home that make it hard to work conventional hours, or if for whatever legitimate reason a straightforward Saturday job isn't an option, don't worry. There are other ways to get involved, you just have to be creative. Think about:

- Podcasting
- Blogging, vlogging etc.
- Library assisting
- Charity work and volunteering (charity shops are a good place to start, as are foodbanks)
- Babysitting

- Dog walking
- Making stuff to sell – Etsy and online marketplace platforms
- Remote working
- Teaching music to people younger than you

Don't imagine that any Saturday/starter job is too small or insignificant. It all contributes to your overall employability.

How to Get the Best Out of Work Experience

Experience of workplace cultures is essential. School work experience placements, Saturday and holiday jobs need to be the norm for all young people. Knowing how work environments operate, understanding workplace culture, decision making and hierarchies are key skills for life. This skill should be learnt as early as possible. So my advice is to get experience of workplaces, observe how things happen, how decisions are made, how people behave, the language used, the respect shown and experience being part of the team.

ELIZABETH TAYLOR, THIRD SECTOR CEO AND FORMER HAIR WASHER AT A HAIRDRESSING SALON

Work experience, in all its forms, not only gives you the chance to gain insight into the realities of work but can also be an opportunity to try out an industry that you are interested in. It will help you make connections, gain perspectives and find out about possible future job opportunities.

Broadly, there are four types of work-related learning:

- Workplace visits (which are usually for the day)
- Job shadowing (which is usually a couple of days)
- Work experience placements (which can last one or two weeks)
- Internships (which can last several months)

The benefits include:

- Helping you develop some of the broader skills necessary for employment
- Giving you invaluable visibility into a particular company or industry
- The chance to try out a role in practice, either by observing the day-to-day of people who do that job or getting the chance to do some of the same tasks yourself[12]

Find out if your school or college arranges these opportunities. If not, you will need to organize it yourself by contacting companies you are interested in and finding out what they can offer. Don't underestimate the impact of getting in touch and expressing an interest.

To make the best of your placement you'll need to do some planning:

- Find a role that sounds like the kind of thing you'd want to do, but don't worry too much if you then discover it isn't

- Make sure you're doing it for long enough –
  less than a week generally isn't enough to
  get your bearings, let alone gather any insight
- Find out about the company beforehand, read
  about what they do on their website and take a
  look at who runs the place
- Be clear on what the employer expects and
  make sure the placement has variety, a clear
  structure and purpose – this will ensure that
  you do more than just make the tea (although
  making the tea is important too)
- Remember that if you have a disability or
  require specific support, employers may not
  automatically know to make the reasonable
  adjustments you're used to having in school or
  college, so contact them in advance to put in
  place the support you'll need to do the job

Work experience opportunities vary depending on
where you live and what your school or college is able
to broker.[13] It might not be that you can find your dream
job locally, so it's worth doing some digging about jobs
related to your wider interests.

And most importantly, when you are there, listen. Listen hard. Think of yourself as being undercover; gather
intelligence. By listening, you can gain a sense of the
way an organization works, what their hiring policy is,
who their competitors are, what the future looks like.
Keep a note of what you do and what you learn about
the work and about yourself during your placement. It
might not always seem like it, but the employers put a

lot into offering up these opportunities, so use the time wisely. All of this will arm you for turning your initial interest in a job into a plan of action for a career.

If you're asked to work alongside someone, try to think about what it's like for the person you're shadowing. You are not the centre of their attention; they still have to do their normal work around you. So you might have moments of feeling ignored or invisible. Don't take it personally, I've always said that having a work experience person with you is a bit like having a toddler – you know you should teach them, but it's just so much faster to do it yourself. Having a work experience shadow can be frustrating. Some days deadlines get in the way of politeness, but if you find yourself without a task more often than not, or assigned to a filing cabinet for ten hours, do ask for more. The simple sentence 'I'd love a new challenge today' can get you out of all sorts of stationery cupboards.

Before you go, read Section 3 about starting out in your first job. It's all relevant and should give you confidence going in. Work experience placements are a good, safe place to test how you respond to new situations. The more you engage in all of it, the better equipped you'll be when you find yourself in a real-life version of going to work. Afterwards, talk to your peers about their time, glean as much as you can from the breadth of your year group's experience, and if there's something that sounds interesting, start investigating that as a future possibility.

Finally, *always* ask for feedback. Even if you sulked at Simon on reception and spilt your flat white on the CEO and accidently swore at a customer – ask for feedback. Don't rely on the official system, this isn't about filling in a form and dutifully handing it to your tutor. What you need if you are to learn anything is to get proper, face-to-face honesty from someone you spent significant time with. Those conversations are really valuable; they're where you talk about the things that never make it on to the form.

Which means it might not always be things you want to hear. I once told someone that they consistently rolled their eyes at me whenever I briefed them. Her work was brilliant; it was considered, well researched and on time. But her attitude stunk. I would never have been able to write that down without it sounding like a character assassination, but over a cosy chat at the end of her tenure I was able to say, 'Watch your body language, it really undermines what you produce and it doesn't accurately represent who you are. You're better than that.' When I mentioned the eye rolls she was at first horrified and embarrassed and then very grateful that I had told her. I am certain her eyes have remained unwaveringly front and centre ever since.

So, the day before your last day, ask for a quick chat in confidence and put time in that person's diary. Fifteen minutes max. And prepare questions, for example:

- 'What was I good at and what could I improve upon?'
- 'Did I present myself and my work well or do I need to do it better?'
- 'What would I need to learn to be in a job like this one?'
- 'How did you begin your career and what advice would you give me for starting mine?'

Don't forget to say thanks (in writing – a postcard will do) and, assuming it went well, ask for a reference. At this stage, even a couple of sentences from someone who knows you in a working environment can help you convert the next opportunity into a proper role.

The value of hating your work experience placement

Lots of people have a miserable time doing work experience. Having a miserable time is not the same as a waste of time. I'm a firm believer in the value of hating your work experience placement. Having to turn up on time every day at a place you loathe in order to perform tasks that feel meaningless to you is the best possible lesson in why it matters that you make informed choices about what to do for your career. If that fortnight feels long, imagine what decades look like.

When you're in full-time education, at whatever level, your days are carefully structured to be full of variety and stimulus, society and surprise. This is done by a team of professionals who are paid to expand your mind. That's a gift. But if you're in a job you hate, your days are structured only by doing things you don't care about, on projects that don't inspire you, for bosses you can't relate to. And lunch. And that's it.

So, if you hate your work experience placement, see it as a stark lesson in what to avoid. Analyse what it is that turns you off. And plan an alternative. You might not hate it wholesale, there might just be bits that bore you. Or you might dislike the environment, the uniform or the banter. This is *all* useful. Spend the time recognizing the things that excite you in an otherwise banal set-up. Talk to that person in the other department who's caught your attention, or the one who looks like they might be having a more interesting time than you. If you find yourself inputting data when you'd rather be on the building maintenance team, then ingratiate yourself and ask for a day shadowing them. For the staff who are supposed to look after you, having a work experience kid around when they are trying to get their work done can be a burden, so they're usually very happy to lend you out for a day.

Most importantly, there is a lot of evidence to suggest that a work experience placement does help you make decisions about what kind of job you might want to do long term.[14] And that includes finding out what you definitely don't want to do – there are plenty of cases of people working harder to get good qualifications because they were desperate to avoid the job they glimpsed during work experience placement. I think I'm probably one of them.

I never want to go home

If you got the golden ticket and your work experience placement feels like heaven, then lucky you. Now all you have to do is behave like a sponge. Learn as much as you can about every aspect of the work – different roles, hierarchy, logistics, politics and strategy. You have a limited time with access to all the people in that workplace, so milk it. Talk to them. All of them. Don't hide behind your desk sending emails. Don't spend lunchtime looking at your phone. If you're shy, remember you will probably never see any of these people ever again, so what's the worst thing that can happen? And volunteer for stuff, get your hands dirty. If you show interest, enthusiasm and demonstrate that you have a pulse, you're likely to be remembered, which makes it a whole lot easier when/if you apply for a job later.

There are lots of things a work experience placement won't do. Like actually train you to do a particular job. Don't expect to become an expert in an industry just by hanging out there for a while – the best you can hope for is a broader perspective.

I feel absolutely nothing

This is the trickiest of categories. It's rare to have any kind of new experience and have no instinctive response at all. But if you really have a vacuum of feeling I'm afraid this is an alarm bell about being disengaged from the process.

So many educators and careers advisers have told me that the biggest problem they face is apathy. They worry that young people don't seem to be fired up by the idea of work. The fact is that early career choices matter. How much you earn, whether you are invested in by your employer with skills and training, and your ability to get a new job when the market changes, are all influenced by these early choices.[15] Being in neither work nor education can be hard to escape, leading to many young people being stuck in an abyss between school and employment.

If your work experience is like a prison sentence then view it as one: you have to do it anyway, you can't go home, so you may as well learn some new skills or it's a complete waste of your time.

Speaking of going home, it goes without saying that walking out on your placement is the kiss of death. You'll be judged by everyone around you – your temporary colleagues, your teachers and your peer group. You'll affect the chances of other students being given opportunities in future years. You will feel like you've failed, even if not turning up seems like the best possible option every morning. I don't care if you have to drag your sorry carcass there daily – do it. One day it will be a distant memory. Show up and see.

Interning

I've had interns come in, flop on to a chair and yawn at me, 'Ahhhhhh. Not sure I'm going to get much done today, I AM SO HUNGOVER.'

WILLIAM SMALLEY, RIBA ARCHITECT AND FORMER NEWSPAPER DELIVERY BOY

In gaming terms, interning is a level up on work experience. Internships are usually longer than work experience placements, so they show a prospective employer that you have held down an almost real job for a decent amount of time. During an internship you'll learn vital skills and build your network. But it's also a less protective, trickier space to navigate. Internships might not always mean giving up your whole summer, but some will. They're often competitive and rarely well rewarded financially.

It's important to be conscious that 'internship' can be confused with 'free labour' by unscrupulous employers. Historically, whole industries would operate with a steady stream of young unpaid talent slogging away and being made to feel grateful for the opportunity. As Congresswoman Alexandria Ocasio-Cortez highlighted on National Intern Day in the US, the problem with unpaid internships, especially those that claim you're being paid in experience, is that 'experience doesn't pay the bills'. In the UK alone, it's estimated that there are up to 70,000 internships taking place each year, targeted mostly at graduates. While they should be an opportunity to gain insight and practical skills, an influential UK think-tank found that many internships 'do not offer meaningful learning opportunities, have poor working conditions, and are inaccessible to young people without the connections and know-how to get one'.[16] The fundamental problem of opportunities going only to people who can afford to give up their summer while living away from home has been rightly slammed by the UK's Social Mobility Commission. It's just not fair.

Fortunately, this picture is changing.

If you want to see both sides of the coin, look at the horror stories reproduced on @fashionassistants Instagram and review the new British Fashion Council's guidelines on best practice for internships – a piece of work that aims to lay down the rights and wrongs for employers and interns in what is often a murky situation, in an industry notorious for exploiting young talent. 'As the issue of unpaid internships has been brought to light in the media,' says British Fashion Council CEO Caroline Rush in her introduction to the guidance, 'Her Majesty's Revenue and Customs has made it clear that it will crack down on the fashion and beauty industries where historically interns have unfortunately not been dealt with in accordance with the law.' As the guidance recognizes, 'Even though the term "intern" is used commonly in the industry, it has no legal status on its own. An intern's rights depend on their employment status,' but, continues Rush, 'Our aim is to ensure our industry fosters inclusive environments within businesses where workers are paid at least the National Minimum Wage and staff are supported and protected in the workplace.'[17]

Consider, it's possible that a good, even tangential Saturday job might be better than a bad internship. It's worth weighing that up before you commit to anything.

Paid vs unpaid

In the UK, if an intern is doing real work that would otherwise be completed by a paid employee, they are entitled to payment under National Minimum Wage legislation.[18] In the US, the employer needs to show that the internship does not replace a paid role by demonstrating the value to the intern.[19] In Japan, the law does not distinguish between part-time working and internships. That said, the legislation in all these countries, and most others, is rarely enforced, and the situation regarding not-for-profits and public bodies remains unclear.[20] Your rights and responsibilities will differ depending on which country you are working in, so it's always wise to check before you start.

Getting a good one

The best intern gigs are usually part of an education programme, a year in industry in the middle of your degree, for example, and although they are often unpaid (or near as dammit), they are part of the mechanics of your wider education and the relationships on both sides are nurtured and valued.

The worst are those where you're treated as cheap. Or childish. And they exist everywhere. If you're considering an internship, do your research. Not just about the company but also about the culture. Try to meet previous interns and learn about their experiences.

The better-structured intern programmes tend to be in organizations big enough to have properly thought-out schemes and a system in place to energize intern talent. Equally, if you find an opportunity somewhere small, that has its own advantages (you're likely to get your hands dirtier, quicker; the 'all hands on deck' mentality of a small business can be a massive advantage to an intern). Just be prepared to carve out your role yourself – you might be the first intern they've had, so don't expect your placement to be perfectly stage managed.

The intern is usually the lowest of the low in the hierarchy of any business, and to a certain extent you have to embrace that. No one is expecting you to have any skills yet; making the tea is your job, so do it with good grace (all the best CEOs still make the tea, it's not something good people grow out of).

Also, be wise to the politics of your position. Often you'll be reporting to someone not that much older than you, and it's usually the first time they've ever managed anyone. This is bad news for you as you'll probably feel experimented upon. But be sympathetic; one day it will be your turn.

It's important to make relationships beyond your immediate contact – be sociable, ask questions, insist on seeing all parts of the business, ask to shadow people for a day. By doing this you expand your sense not just of the organization but of the opportunities within it. And by making multiple relationships at the beginning you avoid the risk of being 'kept' by one person who may or may not always have your best interests at heart.

Rinsing the experience

The sparkliest interns do all the things we talked about in the work experience section but with more confidence, more context and more curiosity.

Most importantly, they treat this as a real job. They turn up on time, they don't run from the building at 5 p.m., they volunteer, they share ideas (remember you're often uniquely placed to provide insight from outside; you're fresh eyed and younger than everyone else – this gives you a voice, use it shamelessly), they ask for advice.

When you're given a task, crack on with it. If you can

be relied upon to deliver considered results quickly, then that's about as good a reputation as you can get as an intern. Because no one is expecting your output to be perfectly polished, they'll almost always need to tart it up themselves or make it more robust – so speed on and everyone gets the time they need. Importantly, make sure your written work is simple to read, easy to edit, error-free and unfussy. So often I see interns struggling to get this right. A good way to make sure you're not way off the mark is to:

- Look around you, how do your colleagues present stuff?
- Spend time getting the content right first, so your message is clear
- Spellcheck the shit out of everything
- Ask someone how work should be presented – there is usually a house style, even if it's not formalized

A fundamental lesson for internships and beyond is that if something comes off your desk, it has your name on it. Be proud of the way it looks. Don't use a fuzzy low-res logo. Don't use sloppy spelling or slang. Imagine every email and every document has your name, in bold, at the top.

One of the hardest things about being the intern is managing your time. Unlike a proper job with a well-defined description of your role, targets, direct bosses and clarity on what the hell you're supposed to be doing, interns are often dumped upon. People will walk past, see your eager face and ask you to do the thing they've been putting off for a fortnight, on top of that project you were briefed on yesterday and the meeting you asked to go to this afternoon. Because your tasks can come from all sorts of unlikely places, it can be difficult to work out their order of priority or who trumps whom in terms of seniority. If it's not obvious – ask. A straightforward 'Do you need me to do this before I help with Nigel's research on spreadable cheeses in the Pacific Rim?' will do it. And if it's still not obvious, then frankly I would do the thing that gets you the most attention. A perfectly honed piece of work for the managing director is likely to serve you better than refiling the shared drive for the bloke whose surname you can't remember. That might sound ruthless but you only have a limited amount of time to impress, so divvy it up according to impact.

Your experience will be very different depending on the size of the organization you're camping out in. If there are four or five staff you'll get to do a lot more, but you're reliant on the warmth and trust of your relationship with them. Interning in small companies can deliver great rewards. In a larger firm you might be part of an intern scheme where you have a slick experience, but not much chance to get stuck in. It will, however, allow you to observe an industry working at scale in a way that is hard to imagine without having seen it first hand.

Contribute and then own your contribution: becoming invaluable

Any decent internship will involve a huge variety of activities – sometimes with no logical core. You might feel like you're just doing scraps of things and can't connect them all together, so write a diary of each day and what you contributed. It's really hard to recall at the end of an internship and you'll need to, so jot it down in real time.

Because an intern's time can feel patchy or haphazard it's always a good idea to have an ongoing project bubbling away for moments when there's a lull. This saves you from ever feeling left out or at a loose end and it's something you have total ownership of. Suggest this to your boss at the beginning – a piece of in-depth research, some trend forecasting, some number crunching, whatever it might be that you can usefully work on and contribute to the business at the end of your stay.

Whenever you can, even if you're the youngest, least qualified person in the room, contribute somehow. It doesn't need to be by shouting out impulsive thoughts in the middle of an important meeting, but it can be a tentative chat in the stroll back from the boardroom or the workshop. If you have an idea, share it. Be engaged. There's nothing worse than an intern who behaves like a simpering shadow (or 'Creepy Butler', as someone once nicknamed one of my interns), so be an active, vocal presence. Your ideas might not always be relevant, but you'll learn something from testing them out in this very safe space. You're uniquely placed, not a 'proper' employee, so make sure you discover some things about yourself by speaking up, as well as learning about the business by listening.

★

Then take ownership of your contribution, for example:

- If you've delivered on a task, ask to present it in the meeting
- If you've written the notes, sign it with your initials at the bottom
- If an idea is well received by one person, offer to write it up and email it to the wider team

So often, interns do the donkey work and someone else takes the credit. It's possible to elegantly fix this simply by putting your name to something. And that's good practice for later on too.

If it's dysfunctional, how can you improve it?

If you've approached your internship following all the advice above and still find yourself locked in a cupboard or collecting someone's dry cleaning, what should you do?

Try to fix it before you flounce out. You'll feel like you've conquered and triumphed if, instead, you stick it out and make it work. That's not the same as putting up with everything. Be assertive. Read Section 3, apply all that advice and if things don't improve only *then* consider closing this down.

Being witness to a dysfunctional set-up isn't in itself a bad thing, you'll learn a lot about how not to go to work. There is some value in watching it play out, even if it isn't perfect.

If you're being exploited

There's a line between the opportunity-filled chaos of a great internship and one where you are being genuinely taken advantage of. Much of what you can do to avoid this happens before you start – do some digging, clarify the role and expectations, fix the time commitment and, if it's of a decent length, make sure it's paid. But if it does look like it's turned sour:

- Talk to someone you trust and find out the complaints procedure
- Go to Human Resources or, if it's a small company, the person who has the remit around keeping staff happy, often the COO, and ask for an 'in confidence' conversation (remember you can always take someone with you if you would like moral support/chaperoning)
- Be very clear about what's gone wrong and what you'd like to do about it
- Leave (as a last resort)

If you're concerned about speaking up to your employer, there are helplines and organizations that can help, such as ACAS. Take a look at our suggestions for further reading and resources for sources of support. Most situations can be resolved with some advice and assertiveness. You don't always need to go nuclear in full complaint mode. Take it slowly and try to navigate your way through the problem with the help of an advocate or a mentor.

What to ask for before you leave

If you've completed/survived the internship, you've gained an invaluable insight into the workings of the minds of people who inspire you, you've built up a CV-defining set of experiences and you've filled your phone with new contacts. Now, just like in your work experience placement, make sure you finish the job.

- Write a summary of the skills you've learnt, the projects you've been part of and the ideas you presented – get your immediate line manager to agree it. You can use this material as the basis for future applications and interviews
- Get a written reference (ask for one early, not on your last day in the building)
- Get honest, unvarnished feedback about your strengths and areas to work on
- Write and say thank you, to your immediate boss, the big boss, the guys in the post room – everyone who helped you
- If you think you've made a connection with someone who could become a guide or a mentor, say so; and keep in touch

How to be a good intern

1. *Don't be afraid to let your personality show.*
   I'm not looking for someone who ticks all the boxes.
   The most important thing for me is that they fit
   brilliantly into the team, are interested, invested and

capable. Almost everyone I have employed began their careers as interns.

2. *In the first place try to circumnavigate the Human Resources department and get your application directly to the head of department, as they are rarely aligned on who looks like the best candidate.*

3. *Be yourself. My first boss told me quite merrily that the only reason I got the job was based on my interview parting shot: 'I hope all the other candidates are shit.' While I'm certainly not recommending this as a blanket approach, she and I had already established a rapport and I guess I felt she would appreciate this alternative enthusiastic gesture for the role.*

4. *Weak handshakes. Yes it's a massive cliché but it's very hard to have confidence in someone who can't even shake hands properly.*

5. *The best interns are SO HELPFUL and gently assertive. Don't assume your boss is comfortable asking you to do the mundane things; they might find it mortifying while simultaneously being desperate for a hand, so make it easy for them. One of the most heavenly phrases is 'I'm going to . . .' As in, 'I'm going to book you a taxi,' or, 'I'm going to get that file from reception.'*

6. *Look for the gaps. Sometimes there is a more efficient way of doing something that may seem*

glaringly obvious to you. Don't be afraid to suggest it. It's our interns who generally slap us into organizational shape.

7. *Listen and take notes. Interns who don't take notes make me nervous. It shows you care. It shows you're taking it seriously.*

8. *Overconfident interns who swan in like a twenty-year veteran of Work World are annoying. Unless you happen to be a Class-A raconteur, don't talk endlessly about your career goals/housemates/dinner plans; let other people set the tone and join in, or not.*

9. *Remember your job is to help others, don't start attempting to scramble frantically up the ladder as soon as you arrive. We've had interns marching up to desks interrogating the busy inhabitant about their jobs. This is bad. Save it for the kitchen (hotbed of all decent work chat).*

10. *Understand your job parameters. While your parents may think you're a shoo-in as next editor of Vogue, don't use the internship as a test-bed for your future role. Very few people are charming enough to get away with offering unsolicited advice. If I have a great intern, I am often interested in their opinion. But wait to be asked.*

FROM GABBY DEEMING, CREATIVE DIRECTOR, *HOUSE & GARDEN*, FOUNDER, DAYDRESS, AND FORMER WAITRESS AT JEPHSON'S REGENCY-THEMED CAFÉ

And finally . . .

Internships are what you make of them. The now world-famous and beloved publisher's logo that's proudly emblazoned on this very book was originally sketched by a twenty-one-year-old office junior named Edward Young.[21] Be more Edward.

Apprenticeships

If you want to get straight to work and earn a wage, but don't want to miss out on securing recognized qualifications, then apprenticeships are a great route to take. Furthermore, some apprenticeship providers (like WhiteHat in the UK) are building communities to replicate the university or college experience, complete with socials, societies and personal development events.

The best education schemes invest in you and your career. That's why it's important to make sure both your apprenticeship provider and employer will support you during your qualification. There's plenty out there so be sure to ask questions about the support you'll receive. There's a close link between your effort and the effort an employer puts into you. As you move through the apprenticeship, you can move upwards in the organization. In three to four years you could be managing teams and budgets as well as having gained a qualification, rather than be at the bottom of the career ladder saddled with debt as an entry level graduate. And if you choose to leave, you go with not only a qualification, but experience and transferable skills. What's not to love? Here are some things to consider if you're interested in this route:

- Rather than choose on the basis of your preferred academic subjects, think through how you like to work – in teams, on your own, with words or with your hands – and what jobs inspire you
- Do online research on what the average day looks like in your chosen role. Digital marketing doesn't necessarily mean managing social media or interacting with influencers
- Consider any personal commitments you have and whether a 9–5 job or more of a shift structure would work for you
- Take a look at the range of opportunities offered by employers and on apprenticeship-finder websites. If you can, try to speak to someone who already does that job
- Follow the guidance in Section 2 about how to write a résumé (aka CV) to find out more about how to complete your application form
- Do your research on the employer; think through why you want to work there and what interests you about the apprenticeship you are applying for
- Don't get hung up on the starting salary, but be prepared for lower pay to begin with – apprenticeships can be a smart route to a higher salary in the long run; do also consider your

commute and the amount of time and money
it requires

If you choose an apprenticeship, be prepared to work hard and straight away, but be confident that you have an employer looking out for you. The aim is to work together to make this a mutually beneficial experience.

Volunteering

Few things are more beneficial to yourself and society at large than volunteering. Volunteering has a significant and observable impact on employability skills as well as career readiness. It's the perfect match between the work skills and the emotional literacy that will set you up for success later.[22]

What you learn will contribute to your first résumé, but more than that, the experience may fundamentally change your view of the world. Food banks, care homes, refugee projects will all open your mind to people's lives. If you love sport, volunteer to help your local youth team; if you love the outdoors, help preserve wild spaces; if you love to cook, make a meal from food surplus for people struggling to get by.

Charities and local groups have lots of goodwill but they don't have the time to invest in making your personal experience a perfect one, so, even more than work experience placements, you'll need to find the opportunity, set the structure around it and reflect on what you're learning.[23] Here are some ideas:

● **Work out what it is you want to do and why you want to do it**

What cause matters to you? Would you prefer to help out at your local community centre or fundraise for a global charity? Think about the skills you have that you can offer – it makes it much easier for an organization to match you to an opportunity.

● **Think about what you want to learn**

It might sound a bit selfish to be thinking about yourself before you volunteer, but everything that's set out here about work experience and Saturday jobs is relevant for volunteering too. Plan out what you'd like to learn, write down what you observe about work and about yourself and ask for feedback at the end.

● **Make the time**

Managing volunteers is hard work for charities and local groups – setting up rotas and contacting people, making sure everyone is prepared and equipped. And – apart from the big charities – they may not have people employed to do all this. So don't feel snubbed if they take a while to get back to you, and be prepared to be willing and flexible. Most importantly, though, be honest about the time you can give – would you like to volunteer once or set up an ongoing commitment? Would you like to go overseas for months or just pop in to the community garden when you can?

Employers love seeing volunteering on a résumé because it signifies that a candidate has perspective outside their immediate circle. It shows you're motivated and proactive. A poll for Oxfam found that 80 per cent of employers are more likely to hire a person with volunteering on their CV because they believe volunteers have better social skills, are good team players, and more hardworking and self-motivated than other applicants.[24]

Voluntary work is arguably almost essential to transition into work. Social action can lead to higher wages and increased job satisfaction. Don't take my word for it – these are direct quotes from a study into the benefits of volunteering for getting into work.[25] People are increasingly looking for jobs with social responsibility and employers are increasingly becoming socially conscious with more social enterprises growing all the time. This is a real area of growth and opportunity.

What's more, there is a strong link between giving something back and our sense of wellbeing and life satisfaction.[26] While you're helping others, you're also helping yourself.

A note of caution

Young people, with the best intentions I have to say, often think the thing to do on their gap year is to go and volunteer in an orphanage. They may not realize it, but they are driving what is sometimes a lucrative business model, they are keeping the institution open as a magnet for funding or private donations, they are driving a system that we know from eighty sound years of research irreparably harms children.

J. K. ROWLING, FOUNDER AND LIFE PRESIDENT OF LUMOS, SPEAKING ON THE *TODAY* PROGRAMME ON BBC RADIO 4

If you have been considering volunteering abroad, you may have realized that getting it right is complicated. In writing *Learning Service: The Essential Guide to Volunteering Abroad,* the charity Lumos talked to hundreds of people around the world to try to understand the dangers and pitfalls of volunteer travel, and to offer a process for how it could be done ethically. Navigating the options can be tricky. However they offer some guidance:[27]

When considering volunteering abroad, try NOT to do the following:

- *Seek easy answers. Issues such as poverty and inequality are huge and complex. If there were easy answers, then they would not be such big problems! Embrace the complexity and stay open to learning.*
- *Try to be a superhero. See your role as a small cog in an ecosystem of change rather than as central to the narrative, and reflect this in your communication back home.*

- *Volunteer in an orphanage. Children in residential care are already extremely vulnerable, and short-term volunteering can worsen attachment disorders. On top of this, foreign support for orphanages has been proven to incentivize child trafficking.*

Instead, DO remember these pointers:

- *Learn before you can help. Go with an open mind and be ready to learn from local people. Challenge your assumptions and learn about yourself.*
- *Research your options. Some forms of volunteering are more impactful than others, but the right option for you depends on your skills and experience. Do your own research and ensure that the choices you make match your values.*
- *Learning and serving are lifelong. Solving huge global issues takes more than a short stint abroad. Consider how you can weave social impact into your lifestyle and daily choices.*

Further Resources

Daniel Goleman, *Emotional Intelligence: Why It Can Matter More Than IQ* (Bloomsbury, 1995)

Nikesh Shukla and Sammy Jones (eds.), *RIFE: Twenty-One Stories from Britain's Youth* (Unbound, 2019)

Stormzy with Jude Yawson, *Rise Up: The #Merky Story So Far* (#Merky Books, 2018)

For careers advice, sources include:

apprenticeships.gov.uk
Career Hacker: careerhacker.ai
Careers Wales: www.careerswales.com
GetMyFuture: www.careeronestop.org/GetMyFuture/
National Careers Service: nationalcareersservice.direct.
gov.uk
Northern Ireland Careers Service: www.nidirect.gov.uk/
campaigns/careers
Skills Development Scotland: www.skillsdevelopment
scotland.co.uk

An extensive guide to sources of careers guidance in countries around the world can be found in the ILO's *Career Guidance: A Resource Handbook for Low- and Middle-Income Countries* (International Labour Organization, 2006)

For advice on your rights in work:

ACAS www.acas.org.uk
Citizens Advice https://www.citizensadvice.org.uk/
Department of Labor (US): https://www.dol.gov/

Lumos: wearelumos.org

Section 2
Getting In

Recruitment is big business – an entire profession in its own right. You might even want to become a recruiter yourself. They help organizations get the right people for the job. Sometimes they are external agencies, sometimes they're part of Human Resources departments, advising on job adverts or sifting applications. Whoever they are, they stand between you and your future boss, so you'll need to know how they operate.

The recruitment processes we're familiar with today started around the 1950s when organizations who needed to fill high volumes of jobs started to emerge. To make the process as easy as possible, they asked for statements of skills and experience – which later became résumés.

Today, recruitment is mostly online with sponsored adverts and recruiters scanning and sorting LinkedIn profiles. And the trend towards reliance on technology continues to accelerate.[1] In your case it's very likely that scanning profiles and the early rounds of recruitment will be automated, so it can be hard, given the prevalence of technology in the modern interview process, to remember that this is essentially still a very human process with human outcomes.

A computer might set it all up and narrow down the selection or rank you against your peers, but it's doing so based on criteria written by thinking, feeling people with a beating pulse. Real live human beings; the same ones you'll be working with if you get the job. So however complex or computery the world of recruitment is today, you will at some point be looking at a face and asking them to give you a chance.

We don't hire robots. We like conversation. And laughing. And connections. And critical thinking. And cake.

Don't be Afraid to Show Some Personality

One of the great joys of working is the opportunity to meet new people and form relationships – so when you are applying for a job, don't feel like you have to be joyless in order to seem professional. Don't use language that doesn't come naturally (if you're uncomfortable, we're uncomfortable) and try to be yourself. Or even better, a polished, bright, super-keen version of yourself.

Gimmicks and tricks

We've all heard apocryphal stories about people using body paint and stardust to get the gig. In advertising (the industry I grew up in) there were more than a few of those (I suspect they're rarer in accountancy). Any career with a vaguely creative streak runs the risk of applications full of fluff or bad jokes. Stories of putting your CV on a billboard, offering foot massages (creepy or what?) and standing outside offices with a sandwich board saying 'HIRE ME' (also creepy) are often entertaining, but be cautious if you're considering a similar approach.[2] Remember, the really bonkers ones are almost always urban myths – those people don't exist, let alone stump up for a solid 9–5 at Disney or Apple or Tesla.

These stories are also a massive distraction from the sometimes straightforwardly boring business of getting a job. Filling in forms, doing online interviews, video interviews and tests is a slog. You must gear up for it and stay on task for the whole process. There are no shortcuts. And while it's fun to think that maybe you could bypass an entire recruitment system by knitting a rug with the CEO's dog's face on it, honestly, your time is better spent researching, preparing and practising for the slog itself. Sorry.

Having said that, there is a slither of space between personality and gimmick which is useful. As a teenager, my friends and I sent a joint CV for all three of us, along with a photograph of us smiling together at a party, to every single catering company listed in the back of a glossy society magazine (I hate to admit it but this was so long ago, before everyone had a website). We wanted to waitress and we wanted to do it together. We knew that if we applied as a team we solved the problem not of one waitress but of three. We got a job instantly, despite having zero experience. We spent the summer living and working together in central London – it was all more fun, more cost efficient and logistically effective as a team.

If you have a genuinely ingenious idea for answering a question on an application, then sure, use it. But don't ever stray from the required format for the sake of standing out from the crowd. It might work, but equally it might make you stand out for all the wrong reasons. The golden rule is: substance beats stunts.

Answer the questions and tell them how you will do the job (that's it)

Speaking of straightforward, remember that old adage about reading the exam questions properly? Same here. Read the application form and the job specification, then respond to it with clarity, confidence and a little bit of charm.

In every touch point of every part of the interview process, remember this isn't about passing a test – it's about proving yourself capable of doing the job. Not always already qualified, not always already trained, but *capable*. Full of potential and in possession of a safe pair of hands. In every response, demonstrate how you can and will do the job. So much of this is about being easy to say 'yes' to.

What seems like the horrendous task of writing a covering letter is actually a perfectly straightforward exercise. The good news is that your potential employer has given you everything you need to do it.

A friend gave me this simple piece of advice years ago and I must have told a hundred people, who use it every time they apply for a new job. It's so simple it's almost too obvious, but you'll be surprised how many people don't do this. Here it goes in three easy stages:

1. **Read the purpose of the job and think: do you want to do that job every day?**
   It might be at Google or somewhere you consider glamorous, but if you want to write beautiful prose rather than code, and the job purpose is coding, it doesn't matter how much you want to work for Google, do not apply for that job. If, on the other hand, you do want to write beautiful code, proceed to Step 2.

2. **Tell them exactly how you meet the person specification**
   Cut and paste the section that lists skills, experience, knowledge and so on. Under each line tell them how your skills, experience, knowledge and so on match what they are looking for. Sounds eerily simple? I've sifted thousands of covering letters and résumés. For a competitive job, I've got a couple of minutes for each. The brutal reality is that if you have clearly said how you will be able to deliver exactly what I have asked for, in the order I have asked for it, you make it very easy for me to shortlist you. Put the criteria in bold, put it in bullet points if you want. Many other candidates who have all the requirements but have told me their many merits in lengthy, dense paragraphs will end up in the rejected pile, while your application has sailed on through.

3. Close with a sense of anticipation
Round off the letter with words like 'I would relish the opportunity to discuss this further' and sign off as you would for any formal letter. Don't be overfamiliar, don't start with 'Hey' and end with 'Cheers' – it's disrespectful rather than cosy, the use of casual language has the opposite effect and puts distance between you and the reader.

So what seems like the mammoth task of writing a covering letter is actually just a little exercise in elegantly showing off.

Writing Your Résumé

Junior positions can get lots of applicants. You end up looking for reasons to exclude people rather than keep them. CVs should be succinct and deliver the important information as quickly as possible. Like a three-minute pop song. Don't bore us, get to the chorus.

DR JOE GROVE, SIR HENRY DALE FELLOW, VIRAL IMMUNE EVASION, UNIVERSITY COLLEGE LONDON INSTITUTE OF IMMUNITY AND TRANSPLANTATION, THE ROYAL FREE HOSPITAL, AND FORMER SHELF STACKER AT TESCO

Writing your résumé for the first time can easily lead to a heavy dose of existential dread. How do you write a career summary when you haven't had a career? The truth is that no one is expecting you to have had one. But, wherever you've got to in your education, you have done a lot – perhaps more than you think – that shows you could be a great hire. So this exercise is your chance to demonstrate your vital workplace skills (even if you didn't learn them in a workplace) by succinctly communicating information. And it's easy enough if you follow these rules:

The basics

- **Keep it short**
  In twenty years you'll be cramming a career on to two sides of A4, so there's no excuse for making it lengthy now. Make everything about it short: snappy sentences, brief descriptions.

- **Keep it clean**
  Use a classic font like Arial or Times New Roman, minimum 10pt font. You don't need pictures, text boxes or decorative borders, just vital information and lots of room for it to breathe. This is not a party invitation, it needs to be clear and legible and its job isn't to communicate a sense of fun. Keep your graphic design and typography simple, subdued even.

- **Put your name and contact details at the top**
  My CV has my name, my personal email address and my phone number centre aligned

at the top. This means that whoever is reading it knows who I am and how to contact me.
NB if you have a comedy email address you set up when you were fourteen, this might be the time to get a new one.

The content

The most common format is the chronological résumé. This lists roles, education, qualifications and other relevant experience in reverse order (most recent first). The basic headings are:

- Employment history: job title, dates and a short description
- Educational achievement: institution, course title, grade
- Volunteering and any other achievements

If you have any complementary experience or talents then do share them, but don't overshare. A friend of mine had an applicant who sent pictures of her paintings for a job as a studio production assistant. The paintings were close-up portraits of her vagina. No.

Please avoid ridiculous proclamations about yourself – don't tell us you're a storyteller or that anything is 'in your DNA'. This isn't a dating profile.

There are different schools of thought about including a personal statement at the start. These are usually a maximum of 200 words that set out your stall about the skills you bring. The problem in the early days is that you can waste valuable time with empty statements, jargon and overclaiming. You may be a 'hardworking team player' but no one is going to say they aren't. If you want to take this route, you might want to try a skills-based résumé which starts with a few key skills you want to show off, with a good solid example of when you've demonstrated them.

If you want to include a personal statement, restrict it to a short paragraph that includes:

- Who you are, e.g. a recent graduate, an aspiring events organizer
- A sentence or two on the skills you have demonstrated to date that are relevant to the role you are applying for, e.g. experience in the front line catering weddings
- A bit about your career goals, e.g. that you are excited about starting a career in hospitality

Follow this formula in each sentence you write

The majority of your résumé will detail your skills and experience to date. The legendary senior vice president of people operations at Google, Laszlo Bock, wrote the following formula about how to describe your skills and experience on your résumé:[3]

Accomplished [X] as measured by [Y] by doing [Z]

Here is a real example from a CV:

- Secured the future three years of the project by gaining $11m funding by moving the funding base from a single foundation donor to multiple sources of statutory funding

And if that sounds a bit remote, how about:

- Exceeded standards by receiving 100 per cent positive feedback from customers by organizing my time to manage all requests
- Beat the fundraising target for my local charity by 20 per cent by organizing a series of events to engage the community

At the end, write 'References available on request.'

As with covering letters, you will need to review your CV each time you apply for a job. Show how your skills and experience are relevant to the specific role by speaking directly to the requirements of the job specification. Don't skip this step. If it seems too much like hard work to revamp one piece of paper for each interview, ask yourself, do you really want to apply for this role or are you wasting everyone's time?

And although you may not feel like the jobs you've done to date are relevant, include them. Your Saturday job as a tour guide tells employers a lot about your ability to work with the public, handle responsibility and turn up for a shift. Remember, nothing is wasted.

And a few other points to finish off:

- Read out what you've written to someone who can give you good feedback
- Always check the spelling and grammar
- And, do NOT lie on your résumé; it absolutely stinks if you're caught out

Writing Your LinkedIn Profile

Your LinkedIn profile is not a CV – it is the digital extension of your professional brand.

MANUEL HEICHLINGER, SENIOR MANAGER
TALENT ACQUISITION EMEA, LINKEDIN, AND
FORMER NEWSPAPER DELIVERER

So, how do you start building your brand?

- Choose your photo wisely. We take in a huge amount of information from a picture, so think about the message you are conveying.
- Set up your custom url and connect your online presence across social media.
- Use the Summary to your advantage. This is particularly important in your early career. Set out in two short paragraphs what motivates you, your achievements to date, the skills and experience you have gained and the opportunities you're interested in. Use the rules of résumé writing, but remember you can be more conversational in tone. The first couple

of sentences really count, because the reader will need to click on 'see more' to read the full thing.

- Fill out each section as fully as possible, including your Saturday jobs, volunteering and personal achievements. They may not feel relevant to your career aspirations, but they speak volumes about your willingness to do a day's work to a potential employer.

- Decide on the skills you want your prospective employer or clients to know you for and ask for endorsements from people you know. It doesn't have to be a huge amount – someone you did work experience with is a good start.

- Make connections, starting with the people you know. Don't cast out wildly to boost your numbers, and always send your connection requests with short notes that have a clear reason why you want to connect.

- Search for jobs by setting your keywords, follow employers and groups that interest you and get to know more about potential employers and who works there.

- Build up your interactions, congratulating and endorsing others thoughtfully, publishing some blogs on topics that interest you and commenting on others. As you build your career, this is a wonderful platform to voice your perspective on industry issues.

Social Media and Public Profile: The Power and the Pitfalls

From the moment you approach the idea of entering work, your social media audience changes from friends, family and those soulmates from distant nations who share your love of avocado to include recruiters, colleagues, customers, clients and a whole bunch of other people you hardly know, but who are gathering impressions about what kind of person you are outside of work. Suddenly, it's all wide open.

So, you may need to clean up your act a bit by changing the settings on your personal accounts to private and checking back through your timelines for anything that might be deemed offensive. Think of this as a moment of reinvention, cleanse all your social accounts of anything dubious or inflammatory first, but also consider things that might make you appear juvenile or untrustworthy. If you're not sure, delete it or maybe even close down your old online personas and begin again with box-fresh new profiles.

Because the normal cues of social interaction – like facial expressions or tone of voice – are missing online, we are more likely to post things on social media that we wouldn't otherwise share. There's a perceived distance. Psychologists call it the 'online disinhibition effect'.[4] That photograph might have been hilarious at the time, but how does it look to a harassed middle-aged recruiter in the cold light of an office strip light?

Remember, you can and will use social media to

support your work networks and as a tool for your personal brand, but that can grow organically along with your career. Set up a LinkedIn account and populate it with some content that speaks to how you want to be perceived in your future career. In the meantime, if there's anything lurking in your social media history that might zing out and make you harder to say 'yes' to – get rid of it now.

Psychometric Tests

If you are applying for roles at large employers you're likely to come across some kind of test alongside the application and interview.

Psychometric tests either evaluate basic skills like numeracy or attempt to categorize you in a personality type to assess your suitability for a role. It clearly makes sense to check whether an applicant for an accountancy job is any good with numbers, but classifying a person as an 'INTP' or 'The Shaper' can sound more like tarot cards or astrology.

A quick note on personality types: there are various versions of these based on the original studies by psychotherapist Carl Gustav Jung. His original set are thinking, feeling, sensation and intuition, each having one of two orientations, extroverted and introverted. So 'extroverted feeling' might be the preferred mode of working of someone who is outgoing and sociable with strong values, whereas 'introverted thinkers' might be more likely to use rational, evidence-informed thinking and be happier working intensively alone.

Like any test, finding examples and practising is the best place to start. Remember, these are not tests of knowledge, but of how you think, so you need to understand how they work. Here are some tips:

- Brush up on those verbal reasoning and numeracy tests you thought you'd left behind at school (sorry)
- Check in on the core requirements of the job and any mention of specific programmes or skills, and make sure you have revised those
- Find some good examples of scenario-based questions online and think through what they are asking you to demonstrate in each scenario
- Remember to work carefully and swiftly through each question and pace yourself – the tests are usually timed
- For the personality tests avoid trying to win; say what you really think and be honest
- Always ask for feedback; you're not a lab rat, even though you may have temporarily been made to feel like one

Interviews

At this point employers are hiring you for your potential, not your previous experience. Your résumé needs to get you through the door, and that's when the magic happens.

FELICITY HASSAN, MANAGING DIRECTOR, AUDELISS EXECUTIVE SEARCH, AND FORMER BREWERS FAYRE SERVER

So you've jumped through all the hoops, passed all the tests, been given the green light from the robots and now you're actually invited into a building, to meet people, in real life.

Genuinely, if you've been through the rigour of a large corporation's super-modern recruitment scheme, you do need to take a breath and prepare yourself for turning up and talking to people face to face. This is when it all gets real and you might feel slightly numb to that if you've done everything through a screen up until now.

If you've made it through the door that means you're good on paper. Now you need to show how good you are in person. But don't be anxious, a huge part of doing well at interview is about preparation and logistics.

In advance of the interview

By now, you'll know quite a lot about the fundamentals of the role and the industry. If you haven't done so already, look up the company in detail, read their annual plan and find out about the challenges that they are facing. The people interviewing you will be thinking about this day in and day out, and it's amazing how many candidates forget that. Reflecting on what is front of mind for the person recruiting you in an interview is a simple way to build their confidence that you're the right person for the job.

Candidates can always distinguish themselves by having a broad perspective about industry trends or current conversations swirling about the sector. And that's all easily within your grasp – by following the relevant people and places on social media. Citing examples proves you're super engaged and excited about being part of the wider conversation.

Read a newspaper, listen to the news, get wired to culture. This might seem an old-fashioned piece of advice, but honestly there's nothing worse than appearing disconnected. Do a news search and make sure you're up to date on any relevant stories too. We all want to work with people who are engaged in the world around them. Read an actual newspaper or listen to the *Today* programme, NPR or *Newsday* for weeks before. Seek out the podcasts that juxtapose current affairs with the industry you're applying to. There are loads of them and it's rude not to. And this will give you an edge in interview because you're already thinking wider than the role itself.

If you can, find out who is going to interview you and learn a bit more about them through their company profile or on LinkedIn. Get to know the person behind the interview desk. It may be relevant to your rapport or it may just make you more comfortable in the interview knowing something about them. (NB this is not the same as looking at their wedding photos on Instagram; that's just weird.)

Find out where you are in the process. If you're in a multilayered interview machine be aware that, broadly speaking, those layers represent different considerations in the organization. The first stage or 'screening interview' is pretty standard. A second interview usually gets you in front of the recruiting manager. From there each stage will go into further depth and introduce you to different people from across the business. When I ran grad recruitment for a major agency, our thinking looked something like this:

● **1st Round – Checking you're real**
  Is this person how they seemed on paper?
  Or did their mother fill in the forms?
  This is essentially a chemistry meeting.

● **2nd Round – Checking you can hack it**
  Does this person have the raw potential to
  thrive in this role and beyond? Do they have
  the basic skills, the curiosity and the work ethic
  to enrich this business? Can we coach them to
  become a strong colleague?

● **3rd Round – Checking you fit in (the
  train test)**
  If we were stuck on a train to a client meeting
  for four hours would I want to throttle them?

When you first start out, everything about the interview process seems artificial and agonized. Later in your career that feeling lessens, partly because interviews start to morph into conversations between peers and collaborators, but also just because of practice. In advance of the interview, rehearse. Research potential questions and prepare some answers that get your best points across.[5] Pair up with a friend. Ask your parents. Use a mirror. Perversely, the subject we know most about (ourselves) is often the subject it's hardest to talk eloquently about. You'll be researching lots of new territory in order to be prepared for your chosen job. Both areas are worth rehearsing OUT LOUD. Vocalizing will help you better internalize what you want to get across and help you edit what you say. It might sound fine in your head but speak it, own it, hear your words yourself. Talking out loud is the most efficient way to refine your thinking and to gain confidence. And it's free.

Dress rehearsals

If you've been offered two interviews and one company is far more appealing to you than the other, make sure you go to both. Even if you actively don't want to work at one of the organizations, it's just invaluable practice to go through the motions and you'll learn far more by spending a day somewhere even if you have no intention of spending a second one. Turn up and use the day to hone your proposition and secure the job you want elsewhere; it's a dress rehearsal.

How to arrive

- Turn up fifteen minutes early. Introduce yourself and wait in reception. Please do not sit there looking at your phone. Instead, read the literature on the coffee table, drink in the atmosphere and use this time to calm any nerves. Breathe.
- Dress appropriately. What to wear differs with every industry but broadly you must look:

  clean

  tidy

  like you give a shit

Beyond that, the nuances of dress change for every occasion. For a first interview it's wise to play it a bit safe – as it's never great for your outfit to be more memorable than your personality (I speak as someone who has this problem daily). Consider also the environment – a small room, big aftershave situation is a disaster. Read more on presentation in Section 4 and take your cues from there.

Tell them why you are there

In his book *Find Your Why*, Simon Sinek gives the example of Emily, a graduate interviewing for her first job. The interview panel 'could see from her application that she was bright, but they worried about her lack of real-world experience. More important, they wanted to find out if she would fit their culture and how she would cope under pressure'. Sound familiar? Sinek continues:

'A conscientious student, Emily had prepared for the interview by learning everything she could about the company. But every other candidate had access to the same information. So Emily went a step further. Emily unleashed her WHY.' Sinek's advice is that, before you get into your skills and strengths or how you deal with difficult situations, answer the simple question of why you want to do this job at this organization. If you're interviewing for the role of social media campaigner at a refugee charity, tell them why you care about human rights and how you are passionate about the potential of social media to influence change. If you're seeking your first job as an apprentice in hospitality and catering, tell them why seeing a family coming together for a great evening over dinner makes you feel like you're doing something important. And if you're being considered for a job in a tech start-up, tell them why working for a small company creating something new gets you out of bed in the morning. A very common first question in an interview is: 'Tell us why you want this job?' Think about WHY in the broadest possible terms and you'll be off to a flying start.

When to stop talking

In an interview you will be asked questions about yourself. It's imperative that you're able to answer pithily – and to know when to stop. This isn't a therapy session, or a rambling moment of self-reflection. But knowing when to stop speaking is hard and it's something you should rehearse. Do not underestimate the power of a succinct sentence followed by a full stop. It's so easy when you're nervous to prattle on, straying inevitably further from the point and closer towards things you might regret later. Stop. Breathe again. Keep breathing.

In an interview you're not there to fill the silence. You're there to answer the questions. Get used to the pauses in between, enjoy them. Knowing when to stop talking is a major indicator of emotional intelligence.

The author of *Influence* and professor of psychology Robert Cialdini goes further to say that asking a simple question at the start of an interview, for example 'What was it about my application that interested you?' gives you a greater chance of success by focussing the interviewer on your merits, a technique he calls 'pre-suasion'.[6] It's a nice warm-up trick.

Questions you should ask the employer in a job interview

You might have heard the line 'You're interviewing them as much as they're interviewing you', which is quite obviously nonsense when you're starting out. The reality is that as a young person entering the workplace you probably shouldn't feel entitled to grill your interviewer hard. You are, after all, there to impress.

That said, it is important that you come away with an understanding of the kind of culture at play in the organization and that you like – or at least respect – the people you encounter along the way.

Although it might feel like the interview is over by the time you reach this stage, interviewers will be assessing the quality of the questions you ask. Not asking questions looks either arrogant or disengaged. That said, they may also be running over time and want to finish up. So have a couple prepared, ask one or two and make sure they are relevant and can be answered succinctly.

Here are some examples you can adapt:

- **What are the biggest future challenges facing you/your team/your business?**
  This demonstrates you're engaged in the long term and not just interested in earning a quick buck and getting the bus home

- **Beyond my initial training, what opportunities would there be for ongoing professional development in this role?**
  This shows that you want to learn and that you're ambitious

- **What's your favourite thing about working here?**
  This is an opportunity to form a connection with the person in front of you and to think about what a career in the organization might look like

- **What would you expect the person in this role to achieve in their first few months?**
  This shows you're already thinking beyond the interview, that you are ready to get to work and want to achieve things quickly; it's

also a good opportunity to find out how much
they've thought through the day-to-day detail
of the role

● **Who are the main teams in the organization
I'd need to work with to deliver this role?**
This shows you are aware that you'll need to
work with others to get things done

And at the end of the interview always ask what the
next steps are in the interview process. This gives you
helpful information and gives the interviewers confidence
that you are interested in what happens next.

Questions not to ask

● 'Show me the money' (Or anything about
salary, that's for later)
● 'So, did I get the job?' (Um. Just wait and see)
● 'What's the annual leave allowance?' (You're
thinking of holiday already?)
● Anything personal about the interviewer as
small talk (Disturbing)

The asshole question

Occasionally you'll encounter one of those 'quirky' questions from an interviewer. Generally I find them pretty
obnoxious, and in my view they tend to be used by
people who otherwise find naturally sparkling and interesting conversation eludes them. It's tempting to imagine
that tricky questions are there to catch you out (a UK

study found that a third of interviewees had regretted their answers to these awkward questions[7]) but mostly it's just an attempt to engineer a vibrant discussion, so don't panic. The best job interviews feel memorable and stimulating on both sides without the mention of spirit animals etc. But if you do encounter an annoying question, how do you handle it?

In 2002 I was asked, 'If you were a novel, what would you be?' (This was actually in an interview that consisted entirely of annoying questions and a little bit of sleaze. It's not a great example.) I gave it hardly any thought and responded glibly with '*Harry Potter*, because of the limitless merchandising opportunities.' And that was the end of that little chat.

Surprising questions aren't always there to be slippery; sometimes they are just an attempt to warm you up, so don't assume sinister motives. And don't second guess what you think the interviewer wants to hear – an authentic answer, however flat or fluffy, will always land better than a pretend one.

Polish

In their 2019 BBC Two documentary *How to Break into the Elite*, producer Clare Hix and Journalist Amol Rajan explored the cultural context that can hold young people from working-class backgrounds back in their careers. The film exposes the experiences of young UK graduates who struggle to get hired despite having excellent degrees from excellent universities – repeatedly being told that they lack 'polish' at interview stage.

So what is 'polish'? It's basically code for a whole bunch of soft skills (assertiveness, body language, tone etc.) and often a whole bunch of judgement (accent, outfit, etiquette etc.). More often than not, 'polish' is simply a euphemism for class signifiers; it's classism with a sparkly name. Because the truth is that these things are all taught (subtly, daily) in all private schools and are mostly absent from the crowded curriculum in state education. I know this because I've been to both kinds of school. I remember deliberately smartening up my posture and my accent at my scholarship interviews and hoping that would help. I remember knowing (aged fifteen) that my exam marks weren't the only thing being assessed in those mahogany-panelled rooms. And if you don't go to that sort of school it can be like doing a job interview in a different language. Brutal. And yet teachers and career advisers still urge us blithely to 'be confident'.

As Rajan writes, 'Confidence is king. I know parents, philosophers and doctors have thought about this for years, but just imagine if we could find a sure-fire way of instilling confidence in young, anxious minds, so that as soon as they get a break they're not crippled by self-doubt.'[8]

Imagine. I don't have a cure all, confidence trick that can fix all this. So what can we do about it? Firstly, we can be transparent about what code words like 'polish' really mean. I don't want to equip you to perpetuate a system that isn't fair. But I think by demystifying some of it here we can start to reduce its power – because this is not rocket science, it's more like a strange embarrassingly old-fashioned mating ritual.

So let's reveal the flimsiness of the rules and then

you can decide how much you want to play the game. Remember, lots of people don't play it and achieve great things regardless. And lots of brilliant activists, corporations and reformers are working hard to fundamentally change the game for the better anyway.

How to pretend to be polished:
- Seeming at ease in yourself (which puts everyone else at ease)
- Understatement, studied informality
- Being comfortable but sparky/enthusiastic
- Not being awkward or visibly nervous
- Not demonstrating a sense of inferiority or of overconfidence
- Poise – physically comfortable in your own skin, not fidgeting or being distracted

It's all a bit performative, isn't it? A lot of this is hard to define or describe because it's about a sense of a person vs the reality. It's about showing that you're a safe bet. A known quantity. People like us. Yawn.

While there is a relationship between corporate polish and a privileged upbringing, as Sam Friedman and Daniel Laurison point out in their book *The Class Ceiling*:

Projecting an aura of polish is not necessarily a 'given' for every privileged-origin person and often has important gendered and raced elements. Yet the key point here is that for those from working-class backgrounds, mastering the appearance of polish frequently proves especially elusive. They start from a clear disadvantage,

and are often unsettled by a lingering anxiety that they
are making 'mistakes' in their execution of dominant
behavioural codes.

If this resonates with you, please, please don't feel you are
making mistakes or getting it wrong because you have a
bad interview or a spate of rejections. Your task in an interview is to be yourself – your best, most confident self. Take
on board the practical things we cover in this book about
handshakes and eye contact and you will have a solid starting point and much less to worry about. Then listen, smile
and answer the questions really well. Employers everywhere are learning that they need to hire beyond 'type'
and look beyond their mirror image. The problem with
hiring for 'polish' is that it's possible to be highly polished
and utterly talentless. Recruitment processes must start to
prize social mobility and diversity because they are missing out on too much talent not to. And in the meantime,
while these codes still hang about, please don't be scared
of them. They do exist and you can fake it if you want to,
but I'd really rather you didn't have to.

Obviously, you have to turn it on in an interview. If
you are sullen and disengaged in the conversation you
won't get hired. If you're chipper and lively and upbeat
you will. It is not inauthentic to act differently in an
interview than at a party with your friends. You're not
betraying your inner self by trying really hard to sound
impressive in an interview. It's an entirely artificial situation and therefore your behaviour will feel artificial.
Work isn't like that, but interviews are. It's test conditions, just like every exam you've ever taken.

References

*Lucy is a class act loved equally by clients and
colleagues. She builds extremely close working
relationships with the team around her and can
always be relied upon to deliver great results. Her only
weakness is her craving for a McDonald's or Burger
King after a heavy night out. But she's only human.
I would hire her again like a shot.*

REFERENCE WRITTEN BY TOM VICK, LUCY'S BOSS AT
J. WALTER THOMPSON AND FORMER ASSISTANT AT
AN ELECTRICAL SHOP

Good references are human. They prove that you know a
person. They are a window on your personality as much
as your professionalism. And that's important when
someone is sifting through loads of references.

If an organization has all but made the decision to hire
you, they'll usually ask for a reference from your previous employer (or relevant teacher or supervisor if you've
been in education directly prior to the job) and may also
ask for a further 'character reference' from someone
who knows you well.

In its simplest form a reference is a confirmation of
your dates of employment or education to check that
what you have told them is true. Unless you've wilfully
lied about your past in your application (NB don't do
this) it seems a rather academic exercise.

*

If you are asked to provide more than this, remember to do the following:

- Consider the people you know who will be credible in the eyes of the recruiter or employer and who know enough about you to be able to make a useful comment
- Don't worry if your connection to them doesn't seem relevant to your desired new role; even if you've been operating rollercoasters all summer, your theme park manager will make an excellent reference for your new job in corporate finance
- Ask your referees' permission and prepare them for the task by saying what will be expected of them i.e. a phone call or filling out a short form
- Thank your referee(s) for their time afterwards

Some references will be open, in the form of a letter or email that the referee shares with you. Some will be closed (you're not likely to be able to dial in on a phone call). It's worth discussing with your referee what you'd like them to focus on – in particular the 'soft skills' you would like your prospective employer to know about, rather than asking your referee to restate your CV. It's powerful to have someone else talk about how reliable, trustworthy and smart you are.

Don't assume all references will be glowing. For example, while a previous employer must supply a reference that is factually correct, if your employment ended badly they could include details about why. You might never see the contents of your reference and it may lose you opportunities without you knowing why. If you think this has happened, have a conversation with your previous employer and ask for a copy. Check it is accurate and ask if they will provide a more balanced version in future, if appropriate.

Gone are the days when people wrote references that resembled eulogies. Fear of litigation means that many organizations advise their staff to confine themselves to facts alone. Your prospective employer may also be checking social media, to cross-reference your application, scan for any chatter around you, and have a good look at your LinkedIn profile, so make sure you are happy with your online presence.

Accepting an offer

Congratulations! Call your parents, call your friends – celebrate.

But before you say 'yes', remember to buy yourself some time to consider the details. If you are given the news in a phone call or by email, respond promptly, be excited and enthusiastic, but don't feel you need to accept straight away just because your body is high on endorphins and approval. On the phone a simple 'That's wonderful news. I'm delighted and I look forward to hearing more about the details/the offer . . .' will do.

Then ask for confirmation in writing and consider whether you want the job and whether or not the terms you're being offered require negotiation. It may be that you have other irons in the fire or that you have some concerns about whether this is the right role for you.

Make sure you:

- Check the terms of the offer
- Check the salary and any other benefits and do the maths to make sure you can survive
- Check the timings

Don't leave them waiting, make your decision and reply promptly.

If you decide to accept:

- Write to your new employer thanking them, confirm that you are accepting the offer and any further agreements, and suggest or agree your start date
- Write a considered, robust response to the offer and be clear about the areas you want to find out more about or want to discuss (see Section 3 for more on how to navigate these conversations)
- Progress to contract (always get a second pair of eyes on that before you sign)

What to expect in your contract

Different countries have different requirements for contracts, so this is only a general guide. If you are in any doubt about the terms of the contract (or the lack of them) you are being asked to agree to, it's worth seeking legal advice.

It's important to check your status (e.g. are you an employee, do you work for an agency or are you considered self-employed?) as each of these have different implications. It matters because your status determines whether you are able to claim certain rights, such as paid holiday. Zero hours contracts are where an employer can ask you to work at different times, but has no obligation to offer you work. And there is lots of debate about the rights of people working in the gig economy.

In the UK, when you agree to work for an employer in return for them paying you, a contract exists – even if it's not written down. In the US there is 'at will employment', which means an employer or employee can terminate employment with immediate effect (as long as the reason is not illegal, for example on the grounds of racial discrimination) and written terms can be minimal.

Contracts often have 'express' terms, such as the hours you are expected to work, and 'implied' terms, such as mutual trust, being willing to make and being prepared to deliver reasonable requests (which does not include illegal activity) and maintaining a safe working environment.

Some common features you can expect in a written contract are:

- The name of the organization you are working for
- Your name and start date (and end date for a fixed term or temporary contract)
- How much and how often you will get paid
- Your hours of work
- Where you will be working
- How much time off you're entitled to
- How much warning (notice) your employer must give you if you're dismissed

- How to make a compliant
- The procedures for sick pay and redundancy pay
- Disciplinary and dismissal procedures
- Details of pension contributions, health insurance or other benefits
- Expectations for confidentiality
- Who owns the intellectual property rights of the work

If you need more details about what to expect in a contract, sources of advice can be found in the Further Resources at the end of this section.

Not accepting an offer

For various reasons, you may find yourself in a position where you need to turn down a job offer. It's always best to deal with this quickly, honestly and in writing. Compose it properly, formally, and make it gracious. Say why you're rejecting it and thank them for the opportunity. Remember, all industries are scarily small once you're inside them – people move around and you'll inevitably meet them again some day, so it's important to handle this situation well and recognize that there may come a time where you need their help or their job offer again.

When you don't get the job

It's depressing, and sometimes even devastating, when you've put time and energy into something and it doesn't pay off. Not being offered a job can feel like a very personal rejection, which to a certain extent, it is. It hurts: the same part of our brain that feels physical pain is stimulated by rejection.[9]

I've had to reject countless candidates for jobs. It sounds like a trite response, but the letter that reads 'we had a number of strong applicants for this post, and on this occasion, we decided that another candidate was more suited to the role' is usually telling the absolute truth.

Spend some time being disappointed, there's no weakness in that. However, it's all too common to move from disappointment to self-criticism, and for that to become a negative loop, so the sooner you can turn that feeling of rejection into motivation the better. Remember, all the stars from The Beatles to J. K. Rowling experienced early rejection and turned out fine. So, don't wallow, crack on. If you hold on to this setback, you're setting yourself up to repeat it. Don't be deflated, after all, 'Failure is a feeling long before it becomes an actual result', as Michelle Obama once said.

You've been through a process that taught you tons, even if it didn't end in employment. Next time you'll be better prepared (even if you prepare in exactly the same way, you know more now simply by having been through it).

Spend a bit of time thinking about what you might have done differently:

- Describe the situation: what questions were you being asked? What did you notice about the way in which you were being interviewed?
- What were you feeling about the situation?

● How might you approach the same situation
  again?

Ask for feedback so that you can tailor your approach
next time or work on any areas you've identified.

Most importantly, don't panic. If you're in need of a
pep talk listen to the podcast that accompanies this book,
where there are loads of examples of people struggling with
this bit at the beginning of their careers – failure, rejection
and missteps – the whole works. It's also full of uplifting
examples from real people who love the jobs they do these
days and are very good at them. Use it as a palate cleanser
between rejection and gearing up to go in again.

A final word on interviews

I've been thinking a lot about charisma. If you've made
it into the room, you know it's because you're good on
paper. But the interview is when everything gets three
dimensional, it's when you stop being a name on a
résumé and start being a personality.

Raven Smith (creative director, writer and columnist at
British *Vogue*) says: 'Charisma is a funny one, I don't think
you can learn it. It's magic. It's like love, you can see what
you think it is but you can't really explain what it is.'[10]

That's true. But what's also true about charisma is that
it's ageless, classless and everyone has their own version
of it. It's pure, unpractised and enchanting. It's free and it's
available universally to all humans, daily. And you don't
need to have a name as cool as Raven to give it a whirl.
It's the difference between saying a sentence flat or saying

it one more time with feeling. It's the difference between being dead behind the eyes or sparkling. And in interview, it's the difference between 'I wouldn't mind being stuck in a lift with you' and 'Let me escort you to the door, madam'.

When I asked my very small son what charisma meant, he said (with precocious clarity), 'It's having courage inside.' The point is, it's not jazz hands or Hollywood charm – it's simply having confidence in your ability to do this thing. Not the interview. The job.

Smile, connect, feel.

Be who you are, but on a really good day. And if that sounds terrifying, or like too much pressure, just try saying the same things you wrote in the application, but with some pizzazz. That usually goes down a treat.

Further Resources

Laszlo Bock, *Work Rules! Insights from Inside Google That will Transform How You Live and Lead* (John Murray, 2015)

Robert Cialdini, *Influence: The Psychology of Persuasion*, revised edn (HarperBusiness, 2007)

How to Go to Work, the podcast

James Reed, *Why You? 101 Interview Questions You'll Never Fear Again* (Portfolio, 2015)

Simon Sinek with David Mead and Peter Docker, *Find Your Why: A Practical Guide for Discovering Purpose for You and Your Team* (Portfolio, 2017)

For advice on apprenticeships:

www.ersa.org.uk

Section 3
The Early Days

Let's start with leadership. Leadership conjures up images of lecterns, global politics and the United Nations. It's intense and high pressured and forward looking. It's shouty and intimidating. So how can it possibly be relevant to you now?

I want to begin with leadership principles because if you can adopt this thinking early on you'll be empowered throughout your career. Sure, lots of leadership is born out of experience. But the principles are applicable from your very first day at work. It's not some distant future, it starts right now.

First, let's look at what it really means . . .

What is Leadership?

There are plenty of views about what makes a good leader, but these qualities are always on the list:

- Being decisive
- Motivating those around you
- Keeping the energy up/making it enjoyable

- Seeing the bigger picture (while being all over the detail)
- Having integrity
- Knowing how to handle difficult situations

Fundamental to leadership is the ability to create followership. As Harvard professors Nitin Nohria and Michael E. Porter put it in their chapter of the weighty *Handbook of Leadership Theory and Practice*: 'The CEO can only fulfil his or her role, and do so effectively, by enjoying legitimacy in the eyes of those who must be led.'[1]

Leadership used to be about controlling people. It was *all* about leaders and followers, when one person in charge told everyone else what to do. As L. David Marquet, former nuclear submarine commander, reminisces in his book about leadership *Turn the Ship Around!* 'This model has been with us for a long time. It is pervasive. It is in the structure depicted in the *Iliad*, in *Beowulf*.'

But times have changed and, in Marquet's view, the superhero model of leadership is being replaced by a better, more distributed model. 'We can all be leaders,' he says, 'and, in fact, it's best when we are all leaders. It's not some mystical quality that some possess and others do not. As humans we all have what it takes, and we all need to use our leadership abilities in every aspect of our work life.'

So leadership is not about one person barking orders, it's open to all of us. And I'm not going to argue with a nuclear submarine commander.

How to Demonstrate Leadership When You are Not the Leader

Firstly, don't be in a rush. Early in your career there's a pressure to propel yourself forward, you move at a speed that blurs the edges and makes you miss things.

But there's an amazing moment in your professional life when you have all of the agency and none of the ultimate responsibility. Try to notice that moment and enjoy it.

Soon enough you'll be the one the buck stops with, and bucks have a horrible habit of sticking around until retirement.

Equally, when you're in a position of power, try to bring ALL your potential to that role – think of it not as the inevitable culmination of time spent on the job but as a platform; to improve things, promote change for the better and foster a future for those who follow you. Leadership is about more than a promotion and a pay rise, it's a privilege.

What has defined Oprah and Madiba as leaders is their humility. They are true to their beliefs and values.

They set a standard and keep it. And they call it out when that standard is not met. To lead, you must communicate what is acceptable, and what is not acceptable. You must own what you lead. Don't be shy to say when your values are not the same. Consider how others see you lead.

And read. Read everything.

GUGU NDEBELE, EXECUTIVE DIRECTOR, OPRAH
WINFREY LEADERSHIP ACADEMY FOR GIRLS, AND
FORMER RESOURCE CENTRE COORDINATOR

There are lots of ways you can start to think and behave like a leader even when you are not in charge. And while this might sound a bit premature or presumptuous, it's actually wise to get some practice in early – there's nothing worse than finding yourself in a position of authority and trying out leadership for the first time. Instead, practise along the way.

Some leadership theory is really powerful, and while I don't recommend trying to read it all now, here are some principles worth being familiar with. They'll help you start to think like a leader before you officially become one.

In *How to Lead*, Jo Owen recognizes that what we expect of top leaders is not the same as what we expect of emerging leaders, so he sets out a range of leadership behaviours for people at the start of their careers:

- **A focus on people**
  Taking the time to know who you are and how you affect other people, managing upwards and supporting others.

- **Being positive**
  Having drive and ambition, being self-aware, being adaptable, finding solutions not problems and being willing to volunteer.

● **Being professional**
  Learning about the business, learning about
  leadership and being loyal and reliable.

The First Three Months:
What to Do on Day 1 and
Day 2 . . . and Beyond

I vividly remember my first day in my first 'proper' job –
as a graduate trainee at J. Walter Thompson in London
in 2003. In a manner typical of the advertising industry's bravado and fondness for the inappropriate, they'd
invited us to start not on a fresh Monday morning, but
on a Thursday night at the agency summer party.

It's a scary thing walking into any new workplace for
the first time. It's an equally scary thing walking alone
into a party where you know no one. Combine those
fears and you have just about the worst social experience
imaginable. All the usual anxieties about what to wear,
how to behave and what to expect were exacerbated
by the strange circumstances and the seemingly inexplicable Rio Carnival theme that night (actually, there
was an explanation, the agency had just won a Brazilian
booze account and the Caipirinhas were free and flow-
ing). On arrival I was greeted by the head of account
management, surrounded by a troop of dancing girls in
thongs and feather headdresses and was forced to drink
shots. That's advertising, baby. My day two was a hungover write-off.

The point is, don't place too much emphasis on your

first day. It doesn't need to be a roaring success, you just kind of have to get through it. You aren't in control of all of the elements at the beginning, all you can do is stump up and try not to disgrace yourself immediately. Try also not to judge everything all at once, or to feel like you need to make the best impression in the first week. Instead:

- Learn your role
- Have a plan
- Get on with it
- Regularly check in on how you're doing/ask lots of questions
- Do what is asked of you

Before you start your new job, try to get your head in the game. It's useful to set out some questions that you might need to answer. Here are some examples:

- **What new things do I need to learn to do my new role?**
  This will differ based on where you work, so watch what others are doing and identify any new skills you'll need.

- **What do I need to know about the market, industry or profession?**
  Try and get out and about, offer to join meetings, especially external ones, and observe how other people work together. Don't be afraid to tell people that you are learning. Read the major books on the area you're working in and ask for recommendations from colleagues for other resources.

- **What do my colleagues expect of me and what impression are they forming?**
  Often you'll be taking over a job from someone else and there will be lots of assumptions about how that job gets done. Show people what you are doing, explain why you have chosen to do it that way and, if necessary, why your way is different from your predecessor.

- **What does my boss expect of me?**
  It's all too common for bosses to think that they need to let you settle in and not set clear expectations at first. Unfortunately this only leads to uncertainty about what it is you should be doing. Find out what it is they want you to do and break that down into things you can achieve in your first few months – this is going to be super helpful if you have to do a 'probation' meeting to confirm you in post after three or six months.

- **What do I want to have achieved at the end of my first few months?**
  Make your goals clear and realistic, and celebrate when you complete one.

Review these questions at the end of each month to check in on the progress you are making. Once you've got to the end of your first three months, you'll have a clear record of what you thought this new job would be like compared to the reality. Take personal notes along the way (this arms you for review or appraisal conversations later and it's always impossible to remember when and what landmark moments occurred in the everyday flurry of working life). Three months in, you will have learnt a lot and still have a bunch of questions and thoughts that you need to answer. And you'll have shown what you're capable of, at least to begin with. Which all adds up to a pretty good start.

Remember to look after yourself through these first three months too. Your brain is working double time, learning, checking in and gauging reactions. I don't want to sound like your mother, but make sure you eat well, get some sleep and some fresh air. Deep breaths. You can find out more on wellbeing in the workplace later in this section.

Expectations

Yours and your employer's and what to do about bridging the gap

Your expectations going into employment will be determined by all sorts of factors – experience to date, raw ambition, how relevant your education is to your chosen field, how much contact time you've had during the interview process and how realistic your reference points are. (If you've watched *The Wolf of Wall Street* on repeat in preparation for your first day at a provincial high-street bank you might feel a bit disappointed. Or relieved.)

If you have been fortunate enough to have encouraging teachers, until this point everything around you has pointed you towards high aspirations and broad horizons. That's one of the core purposes of education, after all. However, when you join the workplace, you're in a different set-up entirely. The people who surround you now may (if you're lucky) be inspirational leaders, but spending their time inspiring you isn't their primary concern.

The best employers will invest in you and grow your career from day one. But what most employers really need is someone who can get to work as quickly and effortlessly as possible. To see it from their perspective, hiring someone who has never been in a workplace before means that they have to put in extra commitment, give you a lot of attention and train you up, in contrast to a more experienced person who, though they may not have been a stellar employee, at least knows the basics of the workplace and the role.

There is a disconnect between the expectations of young people and their prospective employers on almost every level.[2] And employers are aware that they don't do enough to help young people get into work.[3] Young talent wants more flexibility and a greater understanding of how they contribute to the overall goal of the organization and are more likely to change jobs more often. Some employers are working hard to improve recruitment practices and address the skills gap in their industry from the outset or encourage young people to take a longer view of their careers through routes like apprenticeships. But whether it is a small business looking for energy over experience or a large company seeking qualifications, what matters to them – and to you – is whether you can do the job. Working that out depends entirely on setting the right expectations on both sides.

When you are taken on, alongside the contract you sign that sets out your basic terms and conditions (like the hours you must work or the amount you will be paid), the things you expect from each other form an unspoken contract between you. If this 'psychological contract' is not fulfilled by a new employee because they can't understand and adapt to the expectations of the role or the culture of the workplace, and if the employer doesn't deliver on the clarity of the task or investment in the employee, the relationship can quickly break down, with disappointment on both sides. For the employer this means some extra management time and potentially the cost of a new recruitment. For you it could be the difference between getting your career off to a flying start or being shown the door.

This chapter is an attempt to help you navigate that expectation gap, as much for your own benefit as for that of the places where you'll work. Most of this is just about reframing your attitude on the way in and continually assessing as you progress. Most industries don't do a great job of transparently promoting the reality of an entry-level job and what it entails.

Across the globe, children can experience hyper-real versions of potential careers at a place called KidZania. The company is one of the fastest growing education and entertainment brands in the world – they describe it as an 'action packed adventure', a massive interactive city for children to role-play more than a hundred exciting careers. Budding journalists put together a front page broadsheet and take it home to show Mummy and Daddy. Would-be surgeons operate on a baby's heart. Detectives solve the case. And of course, it's all great fun. But it also demonstrates society's tendency to imagine all industries are full of people doing the headline job and I think that's dangerous. There's a detailed, discovery element to careers that education isn't great at providing. And this has an impact on your expectations because most likely your understanding of a job is based entirely on the most famous role, not the one you'll actually be doing for ten hours a day, five days a week. You aren't going to be putting together that front-page newspaper splash for a while. And this can be a shock. One way to avoid it is to do more of the discovery earlier on. You can find out more about the wide range of roles that make up different industries in the podcast that accompanies this book.

Adjusting your expectations in these first few months and learning new skills that you didn't know you'd need is vital for a successful career.[4] You may be familiar with the technical skill required to be a lawyer or a plumber, but you may not have thought about the commercial skills that you'll need in both of these jobs to sell your work to new clients. If you're lucky enough to be part of a structured scheme like a graduate recruitment programme, pupillage or apprenticeship then you may be learning these skills, but if not, you'll need to fill those gaps yourself. If you can do this, you'll avoid the risk of a fundamentally dysfunctional relationship with your employer, the outcomes will be better in terms of your contribution to the business, and you will fulfil your role as the guardian of your own happiness. The stakes are high.

So where do you begin?

When you start out, you have to get comfortable with the fact that you are not the decision maker (yet). You are there to get stuff done. Think of it as a luxury, not a disadvantage.

One of the joys at the beginning of your career is the lack of responsibility. I don't mean that your work doesn't matter, I simply mean that you're not personally responsible for the profit and loss of the organization, for hiring and firing, or paying the electricity bill. You don't have to lie awake at night worrying about payroll. You simply have to do your bit and learn on the job. There is great freedom in that, so use it. It's really only at the very start that you can focus entirely on just doing your job – as soon as you have people to manage, a team to organize or politics to process, your energy is more thinly spread.

There's a charming, apocryphal story about US President John F. Kennedy visiting NASA and asking a janitor what he was doing. The janitor replied, 'I'm putting a man on the moon.' The reason that story resonates and is so often repeated is because it's a seductive demonstration that, however small your role, you are contributing to the grand ambition of your organization. No matter how junior you are, if you love that business, you're part of the whole. Your personal endeavours support the big picture. So at the outset, try to enjoy the clarity of simply being able to learn your job well. Become a really excellent and reliable cog, it won't last forever.

Yours and the rest of the world's

This is a time where you are making lots of decisions and forming aspirations about what you want your life to be. You'll be surrounded by references beyond your immediate circle and social media allows us to benchmark ourselves against all sorts of other lives. That isn't always desirable. There's lots of lazy journalism about social media and depression and anxiety, and you've probably been told a hundred times that Instagram imagery is contributing to a decline in your generation's mental health. It's not that simple.

Young people are the creators, consumers and distributors of digital content and interactions. This means that both the harms and benefits of the offline world are replicated and intensified on it. For example, the bullying that someone experiences in the classroom now follows them on the phone back home into their bedroom and onto their digital footprint. Even those without mental health conditions would experience a heightened sense of threat and this would impact on their relationship with others. One of the common themes among young people is how their expectations and aspirations (of work, relationships, their bodies, etc.) are mediated and augmented by online content and this has an impact on their perception of the world around them and their own sense of happiness, fulfilment and belonging.

DR MARC BUSH, CHIEF EVIDENCE & POLICY ADVISER, YOUNGMINDS, AND FORMER DJ

It's worth noting that, at a time when you are vulnerable to outside influences, social media can exacerbate negative feelings and people who have underlying mental health conditions are more likely to feel these effects. You don't need me to tell you that constant comparison to other people's expressions of success is not a useful way to spend your time. Scarlett Curtis writing in *Elle* magazine puts it perfectly:

> It's a common gripe that Instagram is a fire pit for self-comparison and jealousy.
>
> . . . But mostly these shiny, well-edited pictures leave me a little relieved that I don't actually have to eat avocados for every single meal.
>
> The place where my jealousy is really set alight is with the women and men who fall into the category I liked to call 'quite similar to me but just a little bit better'.
>
> Instagram gives us the opportunity to find people we relate to when we thought we were alone . . .
>
> It's a dark, dangerous thought pattern that turns this unprecedented opportunity for connection into a twisted way to self-loathe, and it's something I'm personally going to try and fight one double-tapped like at a time.[4]

If your social media habits are all-consuming or feel damaging to you then you might need to recalibrate your relationship with your phone. Follow and curate positive groups of inspirational people. And try to challenge your negative feelings, remembering that we all experience a wealth of highs and lows at work and in our everyday.

Work WhatsApp groups can ping all through the night and that can be really stressful, especially if you have complex relationships with your colleagues. You can lie awake worrying about the passive-aggressive inspirational quote your boss just posted (that may or may not refer to the thing you messed up this morning) or you can just give yourself a break. Turn your phone off two hours before you go to bed and start to be disciplined about the times you are and aren't contactable.

But don't buy the story that social media is the *cause* of a generational malaise. While there is lots of irresponsible social media messaging from celebrities or people we are supposed to admire (appetite suppressant lollipops anyone?), a few filtered bikini photos and a prolific gaming industry are not alone responsible for a mental health crisis. Take responsibility for the influences you allow in: only give your attention to people or brands who make you feel good about yourself vs those who stoke your inadequacy in order to sell you something. Seek out those who speak a truth you recognize. And then turn the screen off and read an improving novel for a bit. Genuinely, it helps.

You are not going to be famous overnight

In most of the conversations I've had with employers in the process of writing this book, they mention their frustration that they sense a shift in expectations that now means new hires think they can become famous overnight. Not celebrity famous, but professionally famous. An instant sensation in the workplace. It's a cruel cultural myth exacerbated by social media that you can become celebrated in your field immediately. The truth is, you have to put in the hours.

Even supposedly 'instant successes' are in fact the result of years of work, it's just that you don't see that in the jump-cut, highly edited version of their rise to fame. And if you're not prepared to start at the bottom, then you'll feel pretty gutted. Rob Fitch, a hair stylist, told me they often encounter this issue with juniors or assistants.

Rob: 'Hey, can you sweep this floor?'

Assistant: 'I've got 70,000 Instagram followers.'

Rob: 'Sure, but there's still hair all over the floor.'

Rob swept the floor for years, he still does when the floor needs sweeping. There is no shame in it. You can't expect to be exempt from the small stuff; it's where you learn your trade. Sweeping the floor is essential to the perfect-haired hero image on the magazine cover because one cannot exist without the other AND because it's a team effort (remember the NASA example?). So get your hands dirty and become famous later. And if you want to be the best session stylist in the business, get sweeping.

The Shock of the New

The first few months of any job can feel like an exhilarating rollercoaster. As Viv Albertine describes in her book *Clothes, Clothes, Clothes. Music, Music, Music. Boys, Boys,*

Boys: 'I'm ejected out of the protective environment of film school and into the world of work, at speed, like zooming down a water chute, legs in the air and landing hard on my arse on the mat of real life.'

Exciting. But the thought of turning up every day and needing to do that forever can also feel overwhelming. Suddenly your ownership of time has shifted beyond recognition. And work stretches before you until distant retirement . . .

Don't panic.

Yes, you're going to need to adapt. Your life is not infinitely flexible any more but equally, you're being paid, so that's a bonus. It's perfectly normal to find the transition into full-time work challenging in terms of how you manage your personal life, admin and leisure. I remember in my first few weeks at work having to buy emergency knickers because I hadn't done laundry since starting. Everything I owned was unwashed. That's an embarrassing thing to admit. But it's actually quite healthy to see those first few months as an immersive time; get stuck in, get your head around it and know that it won't always feel this intense. (Although it's always a good idea to have some emergency knickers.)

Definitely don't be depressed by the idea that you have to do this forever – some estimates suggest that as many as 85 per cent of the jobs your generation will be doing haven't been invented yet.[5] There's a lot to look forward to.

You have a myriad of experiences ahead; this is simply the start. Whatever your future holds, it is important to commit to it from the beginning. The more energy and enthusiasm you can muster from day one, the more goodwill you'll bank for later. At the same time, it's a good idea to start thinking now about what you need to learn in order to do one of these as yet uninvented jobs in the future. If you're interested in something, if you spot an area of growth that no one seems to be an expert in yet, pursue it alongside your day-to-day; you never know what it might turn into.

Making an Impression

In the brilliant podcast *How to Fail* by Elizabeth Day, she interviews writer and actor Phoebe Waller-Bridge who confesses that her mother told her to be perfect for the first few terms of secondary school so that she'd later get away with anything.[6] There is some truth in this at work too. Your reputation is forged from the outset and you may later come to rely on it, or regret it. In psychology, it's called 'confirmation bias' – the tendency to believe that a person will behave in a certain way in the future based on our previous experience of them in the past.

If you can use confirmation bias in the right way, you can skilfully build your reputation. Put those extra hours in to show that you have good attention to detail, are able to organize your time well, can act tenaciously and tactfully, and you'll build up a lot of scope for being given new and interesting challenges – and a lot of flexibility – later. As Mishal Husain puts it in her book *The Skills*:

> Employers and peers can make very swift decisions about the value you represent and what you bring to the role, but your aim should be to establish positive credentials, even for just one thing. If and when something goes wrong later on, you will hopefully have some credit to draw upon and cushion you.

Equally, confirmation bias can go the other way. If you're late for a couple of meetings or hand in poor-quality work a few times, even when you are legitimately late or you have been encouraged to send your work in draft, your boss will assume that this is all just a fundamental part of your character. They'll label you as flaky. And this impression sticks.

Worse than that, you can fall into the trap of 'halos and horns' i.e. no matter what you do you will be perceived as 'good' or 'bad' at your job.

Worse still, it becomes blunt discrimination when things are assumed about your character because of who you are and how you identify. In *Biased: The New Science of Race and Inequality* Jennifer Eberhardt describes how 'simply seeing a black person can bring to mind a host of associations about the portrayal of black people in society: this person is a good athlete, this person doesn't do well in school, this person is poor, this person dances well, this person lives in a black neighbourhood, this person should be feared. The process of making these connections is called bias,' says Eberhardt. 'It can happen unintentionally. It can happen unconsciously. It can happen effortlessly. And it can happen in a matter of milliseconds. These associations can take hold of us no matter our values, no matter our conscious beliefs, no matter what kind of person we wish to be in the world.'

In her book, Eberhardt gives examples of black and ethnic-minority candidates and women changing their names to make their applications more likely to be read. 'When we are forced to make quick decisions using subjective criteria, the potential for bias is great,' she says. 'Yet more often than not, these are the very conditions under which hiring managers make decisions about job candidates.' To tackle this Eberhardt recommends being concrete and specific about accomplishments and to quantify what you have achieved, so that there is no doubt about your ability. See our advice on writing your résumé in Section 2 for some practical examples of how to do this. No one should need to change their name.

We all have the right to be judged on our merits at work, regardless of who we are, where we come from, how we choose to live or how we identify. In turn, we all have a duty to demonstrate our merit from day one and to build our reputations based on what we contribute, what we believe in, on our talent, our commitment and our empathy.

A Note on Scale

At the risk of stating the obvious, the scale of the organization you're about to enter matters when it comes to your expectations.

Expectations for big organizations

You've proven your qualifications, passed the psycho-metric tests, aced the group exercises and impressed in individual interviews and now you're part of a structured programme.

If you're beginning at a big corporation, i.e. through the Milk Round or an established grad scheme, you're likely to have more visibility about what life might look like there. Those companies are good at promoting their culture and customs and you may even have met some of the previous grad intake or seen case studies about how their careers progressed. But it's worth noting that some of the language used to entice you through the doors in the first place can be a bit misleading. Terms like 'fast track to management' are often bandied about in the recruitment process and that promise can feel somewhat distant during the first few months of clinging to the bottom of the ladder. Don't despair. Watch, learn and, most importantly, LISTEN and have faith in the process. 'Fast track to management' doesn't mean 'Bossing people about from day one'. And that's a good thing for everyone. Be patient.

If you're not part of a structured recruitment scheme, working for a large organization can be daunting, especially if you aren't given a good induction. Large organizations usually have more layers of management, the offices may be spread over multiple sites, each with their own character, and while your job might well be more clearly defined than in a smaller place, decisions are less likely to be yours to make. People who work for large organizations may be more risk averse and stick to the rules, so it's important as a new 'cog in the wheel' to find out as much as you can about the systems that govern the organization. Notice the people who are well liked and respected, seem to know everyone and have access to all the latest information – without playing politics or gossiping. These people exist at various levels in the hierarchy of an organization and are very influential. They will have good advice to help you choose what to focus your energy on and can also influence others on your behalf. Later in this section we tell you how to spot these influencers.

In this sort of set-up your employer has a responsibility to train you (formally and in the role itself) and you have a responsibility to pay attention. Beyond your initial training, continuing professional development is a way of making sure you're always meeting and exceeding expectations. Even if you're not part of a recruitment programme, big organizations usually have lots of access to learning opportunities. Make sure you keep a keen eye on those opportunities throughout your career. The rule is, you should ALWAYS feel like you're learning. Either in the day-to-day, or from your colleagues and bosses. If that's not happening then you need to seek out new challenges, further training or more responsibility. Otherwise you'll become bored and stagnant.

Expectations for smaller organizations

You've demonstrated your willingness to get stuck in, given some great examples of your adaptability over an informal chat, left a good impression on the founder and they've taken you on, perhaps with a fairly broad job description.

When you start at a small company or a start-up, it's much, much harder to have realistic expectations or to anticipate anything about how your days might look or how your career might evolve. There's usually far less structure or predictability in these environments and that's a massive opportunity. But it can make it hard to navigate.

It's essential to approach this situation by regularly reflecting upon your progress; be benchmarking/assessing continually. But don't do that in isolation, make sure it's a conversation between you and your employer – check in, ask for feedback, talk about your goals, move things forward. There is more emphasis on you carving out a niche or setting the path ahead here, but there's also usually more freedom to follow your interests or develop an area to own. The rules about having realistic expectations still apply, but if you're clever and good you can create something peculiarly perfect for you as opposed to being siloed into a specific role.

Expectations in professions

You've been learning forever, you've trained and qualified and now you've started in your role.

When you join a profession there will be lots of people who need lots of things from you. You'll quickly come face to face with clients, students or patients who need you to deliver for each of them to the best of your ability, every day. Your colleagues will each have different views of the organization's priorities. There will be common standards to meet, regulations and assessments to go through. And then there are the emails piling up while you're in court, on site, on the ward or in the classroom . . .

The truth is that you won't be able to please all the people all the time. When you have a bereaved husband or a bullied teenager asking for your help, you're going to have to rely on your judgement alongside all those policies and inspections frameworks. And to do that will require having a strong sense of the part you are there to play and what matters most.

In jobs like teaching, medicine or policing it's easy to get caught up in the machinery when what you wanted to do in the first place was serve your community. All too often, people who join a profession because they care end up getting sucked into the stress and chaos of everyday life in an institution where there's a pressure to be perfect.

In the early days it's important to get a clear sense of what your priorities are and to be organized. Talk to your supervisor to find out what's essential and what good looks like. Don't forget why you love this work and note the moments where you made a difference to people's lives. And remember also, try to take care of yourself while you're meeting needs of others. In a professional role you could work every hour of the day – but that's only going to lead to a fast burnout. Find a cut-off point and stick to it.

Company Culture

*Growing up, few if any of us could have envisaged the
entirety of what Stormzy and the team have achieved
on their own terms: the success, the respect, the bridging
of cultures, the giving back, the ambition . . . It is a
family. It is a level of work, a standard to uphold, and
a way of thinking.*

JUDE YAWSON IN *RISE UP: THE #MERKY STORY SO FAR*

Company culture isn't an optional extra. Anywhere you
find people, you find culture. So every institution, however small, has a unique atmosphere, hierarchy, set of
values and traditions, punishments and rewards, foibles
and frustrations. Even if you're freelancing from your
bedroom you have a culture, albeit probably a messy one.

Culture is not made of football tables or mini-fridges
full of free snacks – that's furniture. Culture is a live,
evolving and all-pervading presence in the workplace.
And from the moment you arrive, you're part of it.

All culture is formed by personalities, not systems.
It can be found in the history of an industry, the type
of people it hires, in the plans and in the structure of
an organization. It's often entwined with the culture of a
country or region. Shaping it preoccupies its leaders,[7] and
it's so powerful that it can determine the overall success
or failure of an organization.[8]

The strongest organizations are full of happy, fulfilled people who feel valued within and central to

the collective purpose. And apathy, anxiety and disengagement are the hallmarks of the weakest. The best company cultures are inclusive, rigorous, celebratory and fair. The worst are impenetrable, discriminatory and toxic.

How you can 'fit' or adapt into the culture is one way in which your early suitability will be measured. And to do that you first need to be able to read the culture around you.

PepsiCo's Global Talent lead Allan H. Church and business-school professor Jay A. Conger speak about the perils of not reading the culture of an organization in their *Harvard Business Review* article on the topic:[9]

> We know too many talented individuals who have stumbled in their new company because they failed to read the cultural tea leaves. This happens because most organizations don't explain the cultural rules to newcomers, and new hires are so focussed on the job and the new boss that they overlook the rules' profound influence.

If you fail to take the initiative after an informal meeting with a senior member of staff in an action-focussed, non-hierarchical organization, they'll think you're slow off the mark. Turn up to a meeting without having done your homework in an organization used to making decisions from fifty-slide PowerPoint presentations and they'll think you're lightweight.

Beyond this are the behavioural codes embedded in the culture that govern who gets in and who gets on.

★

Most of the time, these behavioural codes are fairly arbitrary and usually reflect the history of occupations and the type of people who have traditionally dominated such work in the past. Over time, these codes have become embedded to the point that most people just take them for granted. Sam Friedman and Daniel Laurison's skilled analysis in their book *The Class Ceiling: Why It Pays to be Privileged* points out that there are 'fuzzy, ambiguous notions' that 'represent metaphorical "glass slippers" rendering workplaces a natural fit for some and uncomfortable for others'. Things like how you communicate, how you dress, how you think about work, knowing the in joke or the right cultural reference, are powerful signals that are hard to navigate if you're not from the same background as your colleagues. If you don't fit in, don't assume that there is something wrong with you and that you have to change or assimilate. Once you know how to look for them it's easy to see how ludicrous these codes can be.

As a box-fresh recruit, your first challenge is to observe the way things play out and to assess the nuances of how the culture works so that you can determine your own role within it. For example, if you spend your time getting to know people and demonstrating how your ideas will help them do their job better in a consensus-building organization, you're off to a strong start. It's all about making sure you present in a way that is easily understood by the people and processes around you. But never feel you need to become a different person in order to fit in.

So how do you manage all this?

Observe

- How is success rewarded (at every level)? Are people recognized for individual initiative or as a team? What is it that they are doing that gets noticed – e.g. delivering a personal service or improving sales?
- How are decisions made? By committee or by individuals? Are there lots of formal meetings or casual chats? How is information shared? Who are the ultimate decision makers?
- How do people interact? Does the office feel like a house party or a doctor's waiting room? Do people appear to be playing it safe and following the rules or are people 'dropping by' to kick around experimental ideas?
- What values are the organization and the industry built on? What are the founding principles? Are they still relevant today?
- What are the professional standards that people are working to or are there none? (A hospital is going to operate a lot differently from a small creative studio for obvious reasons.)
- Who are the clients, beneficiaries, partners and paymasters and how are they talked about? What are the tonal changes from internal to outward-facing communication?
- Where does the money come from and how is it expected to be earned and spent?

Get stuck in

The best way to benefit from culture is simply to engage with it. Volunteer for things. Attend stuff. Contribute. You'll find that once you've shown your face and your enthusiasm a bit, doing your day job becomes much easier because you've formed relationships outside your immediate team circle and you have a reputation beyond the All Staff Email announcement of your arrival (which, honestly, no one read anyway).

Decode by asking the questions

Befriend someone who seems to understand it all. Throw the organogram out of the window and find the character who likes to be at the heart of things. There's always one (just as there are always some people who naturally prefer to sit on the sidelines). You'll spot them in the positive references to their character in the conversations of your colleagues. They may have been around for a long time or just happen to know everyone. People gravitate towards them and their view is sought after, beyond their official remit. They are usually the ones who will happily tell you all about those unwritten rules or the grand or grim traditions. As long as you filter this information with a healthy awareness that nothing is unpolitical (more on politics in Section 5) then this is a good shortcut to understanding the way things operate.

To thine own self be true

Beware of compromising your personal values for the sake of the organization's culture (for more on how to negotiate this complex balance read Section 5). Fortunately, the days where deals were done outside the boardroom and in basement strip clubs are on their way out, but there's no guarantee that you won't encounter moments where you'll feel an expectation to behave in a way that feels wrong or uncomfortable. The best moments in your career will be where you find a match between your personal beliefs and the values of the workplace you're in. The worst will often be where there is a startling disconnect between the two – so be on the alert for this.

Show Me the Money

The reality of a starting salary

Curiosity is a luxury reserved for the financially secure:
my mind was absorbed with more immediate concerns,
such as the exact balance of my bank account, who
I owed how much and whether there was anything in
my room I could sell for ten or twenty dollars.

TARA WESTOVER IN *EDUCATED*

Quite often, buoyed up by the excitement of your entrance into the big wide world, raring to go and keen to make a difference, it's not until a few weeks in that you realize you can't afford toothpaste.

According to research by the Office of National Statistics in the UK, half of sixteen- to seventeen-year-olds are expecting to earn £35,000 by the age of thirty if they've achieved a degree and £25,000 if they haven't. The reality is that the average salary of a thirty-year-old in 2016 was £23,700.[10] The expectations gap is a trend also repeated in smaller surveys in the US and Asia.[11] In Malaysia, for example, 60 per cent of graduates expected to earn a monthly salary of around $850 when the average is closer to $500–600. In Singapore, similarly, where the average month salary is around $2,000, graduates are expecting $2,500. In the US expectations were closer to the reality, but 17 per cent were expecting to make twice the average salary.

For those without a financial buffer, waiting for that first payslip can be a risky time. As James Bloodworth writes in *Hired: Six Months Undercover in Low-Wage Britain*:

> By far the worst thing about a monthly salary is the initial wait from when your money from a previous job or your jobseekers' allowance dries up to when you get your first paycheck. Waiting a week is bad enough; waiting an entire month is an intolerable burden that throws people into dire straits and only encourages opportunists who prey on poverty's perpetual victims.

Everyone's personal financial circumstances are different, and where you start from, where you live and your choices up to this point will determine how decent, decadent or dire your starting salary is. In the UK it's more usual for graduates to start on a pitiful wage than it is in the US, where the cost of a college education means grad jobs tend to be better remunerated. Salaries for non-graduates are notably lower. In the UK the minimum wage for an apprentice aged under nineteen in their first year is £3.90 an hour.[12] Starting salaries across other countries differ widely with a starting salary in India sometimes a fifth of that in Singapore.[13]

But regardless of the detail, this is likely to be a time where you are under pressure to form a new life in a new place, often without the proximity or safety net of your family, with a new wardrobe and new habits, where you are required to be social and connected to the world around you – all of which costs money. Money you have only a limited amount of. Now is the time to get your head around the cost of living, prioritize your spending and begin to be curious and critical about your relationship with money. If you can form a good basis for this thinking now you will be better off, in every respect, as you progress.

In the interests of full disclosure, I am the worst person to speak on this subject. Even writing the paragraphs above, I feel like a fraud. I continually, wildly overspend on nonsense and my definition of value for money has always been bizarrely and unjustifiably distorted by delusions of grandeur. When I was seventeen and working in New York City as an intern for a fashion start-up, I spent my last dollars at a sample sale on an Alberta Ferretti bias-cut satin skirt and lived for a full two weeks on tap water and Cheetos. My skin turned orange, but that was only temporary and I still have the skirt.

I was fortunate that I had a roof over my head that gave me the security to make stupid decisions. And for me, I guess, it felt more important that I could visually pass as credible in that high-octane New York City fashion environment (despite coming from a small market town in rural England) than it was that I went to bed on a full stomach. I'm not suggesting this is a sensible approach, but I do, even today, understand it.

Anyway, seriously, here is some proper, well-researched, expert advice on how to handle your finances.

Set a budget

The first thing to do is set out how much you have coming in versus how much is going out. There are some good guides and tools online, like the Money Advice Service, to help with this.

Work out some basic categories of things like rent, household bills, travel, leisure and any fixed costs like your mobile phone contract or house insurance. Be brutally honest – aspirational budgets will make you feel better, but they are useless – this is reality. Now match this up to income – are you up or down overall?

Track your budget

Record what you spend as accurately as possible each day for a few weeks. Now check it against your budget. Inevitably and irritatingly, there will be lots of things you've forgotten to factor in like that emergency taxi or your dad's birthday present. Then take a look at your budget. What are you really spending your money on? Ask yourself: is the balance right? This approach is more effective than whether or not you think you should be spending money on particular things, because it's always easy to justify spending. It's better to look at the whole picture and make choices about how your (albeit limited) financial resources can help you live the life you want. There are a plethora of apps that can help you to get a good overview of your budget, keep track of your money and set goals to control your spending.

Money and you

If you want to delve a bit deeper, examine your relationship with money.[14] What did it mean to you growing up? How do you view things like debt – does it create opportunity or is it a burden? Is it important to you to have something kept by for a rainy day as well as making ends meet each week? Are you lavishly generous or carefully cautious in the way you spend?

The language used about money is often deeply sexist too. As Anne Boden, the CEO of Starling Bank, points out, 'the "thrifty-splurger" trope in women's magazines is in direct contrast to the "adept financier" archetype you see in the pages of men's magazines'.[15] How many times have you read 'Skip your daily latte and save $xx per year!' It plays out in reality, too, with some banks giving smaller lines of credit to women.[16] And as *Slay in Your Lane* authors Elizabeth Uviebiné and Yomi

Adegoke found, negative stereotypes about money and pay gaps affect black and ethnic minority women even more harshly.[17]

Our relationship with money strongly affects our mental health.[18] Worrying about money can become a negative spiral. We might find ourselves avoiding looking at our bank account, leaving bills unopened, or waiting until the last minute to pay off our credit card. All of this will inevitably have an impact on our levels of stress as well as financial and mental wellbeing. Managing your money can be difficult, but it's important to learn how to do the basics and bring this into your routine. This can help us to better understand how we can live within our means and how much money we need to live the life we choose. Experiencing poor mental health can make managing money even more difficult. If you are facing financial difficulties then making decisions about money will feel even more challenging. If you find yourself getting anxious or depressed about money, make sure you talk to someone you can trust about your concerns and get organized with your payments and budgeting.

And think about your future self by starting pensions early. I know it sounds so unsexy. It might be the last thing you want to think about, but that tax-free pension allowance could be worth twice as much if you start saving in your early twenties than if you wait until your late thirties. Find out what's available to you and get some professional advice at the start of your career. Sure, it's not sexy, but neither is being penniless at sixty-five.

Earning More

Long-term strategy

In the early days you may be flattered that anyone is prepared to pay you anything or offended that they aren't paying you more. You do need to start to plan ahead to secure your financial future.

Through the course of your working life, as your skills and reputation grow you'll be able to command a higher price. If you choose to build a business or start a number of different income streams you'll also become responsible for the earnings of others. If you follow a more structured career progression you'll start to exchange greater responsibility – like managing, budgeting or setting direction – in return for better pay and benefits. For now, it's important to set out some basic expectations.

Increasingly, companies are being more transparent about what they offer. There is a long tradition of misplaced secrecy around pay and benefits, which has helped mask the gender pay gap for generations. This makes it hard to benchmark your wage against your peers' (unless you live in Norway where all salaries are published[19]). When you're starting out, it's worthwhile discovering the salary range for similar roles with a quick bit of research online. It's also worth factoring in the broader company offer, for example how many days' leave can you take each year? Are there benefits or policies that can save you money, like travel loans or contributory pensions and health insurance? Is there a stake in the business that comes with the job offer?

Consider setting financial goals from the start of your career. Deciding how important money is to you alongside the other aspects of a fulfilling career will be crucial to delivering those goals. Bear in mind that these may also change over time, and that the choices you make now can shape the trajectory of your later lifestyle. Interestingly, studies have found that the optimum salary for happiness is around $75,000 to $95,000 USD or roughly £58,000 to £73,000.[20] What price is yours?

Short-term pay rise

In the short term you may find that you are asked about your salary expectations when you're offered a job or you may want to negotiate a pay rise. Yet despite most of us wanting to earn more money, it can feel like a challenging conversation to have. A survey by University College London found that people were seven times more likely to tell a stranger details about their sex lives than talk about their income.[21]

Harvard Business School Professor Deepak Malhotra offers some useful advice in his article in the *Harvard Business Review*, '15 Rules for Negotiating a Job Offer'.[22] He reminds us that if you've got as far as being offered the job, they fundamentally like you, so it's worth keeping hold of that thought when having the discussion.

Inevitably, there will be constraints that the person you are negotiating with will need to manage – no one's budget is limitless, and it's worth taking the time to build your case. As Professor Malhotra says in his article, 'Suggesting that you're especially valuable can make you sound arrogant if you haven't thought through how best to communicate the message.' Don't negotiate for the sake of it or press your case too hard – this is not the time for ultimatums. And bear in mind that what might not be possible today could be in the future.

It's also important to remember that the decision is about getting you into (or keeping you in) the organization, so link the discussion to your performance review, a wedge of work or a big win, tracking your contribution and using it as a tool for demonstrating your value to the business. Put your salary request alongside a range of suggestions such as access to training or working more flexibly, so that you can have a broader conversation about how the organization can support you to become even more valuable to them.

Bonuses and why they sound good, but cost less

Obviously, if someone offers you a bonus, say yes. (And thank you.) But be aware that the bonus culture (for entry-level employees) is often used as a tool to keep you happy without actually giving you a pay rise. A bonus may feel flashy and rewarding, but it can be a cheap way for the business to not pay you what you're worth. Direct labour costs are almost always the single biggest business overhead. Give a member of staff a pay rise and you've made a year-on-year commitment. Give them a bonus and not only have you motivated an employee, set up an expectation for gratitude and loyalty and earned your department some good internal PR, but also you've only committed to a one-off cost to your business.[23] Don't mistake it for a pay rise, it's not the same thing.

Working for Free

It's hard for young people nowadays because there is so much emphasis on 'if you do x and y for free, we'll give you credit'. The late Michael Goulding OBE told me, 'You always get more of the same. Be careful.' If you do low-grade work you will be asked to do more of that and if you aim high, you will be asked to do more of that. Because unfortunately, quite quickly, you get typecast. If you get clients who appreciate your ethos, you'll get more of them, if you compromise your style the next client will ask you to compromise too.

SHANE CONNOLLY, FOUNDER AND CREATIVE
DIRECTOR OF SHANE CONNOLLY AND CO.
(ROYAL WARRANT HOLDER TO HM THE QUEEN
AND HRH THE PRINCE OF WALES) AND FORMER
RESEARCH PSYCHOLOGIST

Beyond the financial pitfalls of internships (which we've covered already), the concept of working for free never really goes away and it's smart not to dismiss it altogether. Working for free can be a useful tool for exploring new avenues or accelerating your progress. But you MUST always be smart about working for nothing. You want to build a reputation based on your work, not on your affordability.

Sometimes you'll identify opportunities that are worth investing your time in, even if time is money and there is no money. Here are some occasions when it might be worth taking a short-term financial hit in the hope of long-term gain.

Punting work on spec

This is particularly relevant for creative industries, but I'm a firm believer in the power of a bit of speculative work. You could get all angsty about giving away your ideas for free but, honestly, what use is an idea if it remains in your head or on a notepad in your bedroom? Ideas need a life outside yourself or they shrivel up and lose all their potential. Good ideas are sociable and attention seeking. In his relentlessly brilliant book *It's Not How Good You Are, It's How Good You Want to Be* (much of which I love so much that I could happily have extracts tattooed on highly visible parts of my body) Paul Arden says, 'Do not covet your ideas: Give away everything you know and more will come back to you.' So many people are mean and furtive with their creative output. It's common even in these days of open-source and the universal scrapbook that is Instagram. I have lost count of the number of 'I've got this idea for an app . . .' conversations I've heard that don't acknowledge that the idea is one per cent and the execution is everything (and you ain't gonna execute that app unless you're prepared to share with us WHAT IT IS!).

As Arden warns, 'The problem with hoarding [ideas]

is that you end up living off your reserves and eventually you become stale. If you give away everything you have, you are left with nothing. This forces you to look, to be aware, to replenish. Somehow the more you give away the more comes back to you.' In my experience this is a solid piece of truth. And it's totally liberating.

He wasn't writing about punting work on spec but I mention it here because the spirit of his thinking is relevant. I wouldn't have had a magazine column if I hadn't written one as a test and sent it to them. Could they have stolen my idea and produced it themselves? Easily. But I had confidence in what I'd written, in the way the idea was rendered (by me), and I believe that generally people aren't sharking about waiting to nick even the very best ideas. It's far easier, when presented with something good, to give it a platform than it is to rip it off. Relax.

When you're starting out, you need that platform more than the platform needs new concepts. Recently, a young friend I've advised over the years started to do illustrations alongside her degree in historic building restoration (side project, tick). Her illustration style is cheerful, pastoral and potentially highly commercial. I suggested she paint a Christmas cover for a local London borough magazine (smart postcode, right demographic, clearly no budget and always in need of artwork) and offer its usage in exchange for a credit printed in the magazine to celebrate her work. They said yes. She got the cover and was able to take that published work to a big Hearst magazine, who featured her paintings for sale and a link to her website the following month. Everyone wins. She won't have to give her work away more than once; from now on she should be able to sustain momentum. You only need to be published for the first time once.

Often there will come a point when gifting your time must transition to paid employment. Consulting fees, day rates etc. – there are lots of ways to cut a new deal. By the time you get to that stage you are a known quantity who is making a tangible, measureable difference, but it can be hard to suddenly start charging for something you used to give away. It's a tricky transition, but it's worth remembering that you are ultimately in control of the situation – you can, after all, politely stop doing any more work if it really becomes clear that no one will pay for it.

If you do think that there is scope to convert free work into paid, it's best to start by finding out what is required, then come back with a proposal and a costing. Ask what might be a likely budget and who makes the decision on costs – don't be shy, it's a fair enough question. Be careful, though – it's fairly common for people on the client side to appear to be the person in control of the budget, the schedule and the creative direction, when in fact those decisions are made by several people. So it's worthwhile connecting to the relevant staff in the organization and asking them about how everything works. It won't happen overnight, but once you're known for reliably producing high-quality work you can become the go-to freelancer for one, or ideally several, organizations.

As a guideline, the only things that replace cold hard cash are credit (having your name publicly applied to a thing and celebrated for it), contacts (exposure to a whole host of new, interesting people you wouldn't have had access to otherwise) and credibility (building your reputation and experience beyond the normal 9–5). If you can identify these opportunities, then they will enrich the overall return.

Nurturing a sideline interest

A sideline interest is something that is separate from but informs or supports your overall ambition. Elsewhere in this book we've told you to focus and commit to things wholeheartedly, so it may seem like contradictory advice to encourage you to explore interests beyond your day job here. But side projects don't have to be distractions from the main gig – and even if they are, the psychology suggests that doing something else for a while can be very beneficial. The prolific inventor Thomas Edison famously asked himself a question every evening before he slept, to draw on his subconscious mind to help solve the problem. In a similar way, side projects can give you new perspectives and leave your mind to mull on the solutions to your challenges in the background. And don't forget that the thing in itself can be inherently worthwhile. As Josh Cohen says in his book *Not Working*, 'even a life of hard work looks and feels different if we know we can stop if we need to'.

For me, swapping energy for personal enrichment is a fair exchange, even without the potential for increased employability. This is more than having a hobby, it's about investing in your growth and learning to cultivate new skills. And there are fewer things more joyful than finding that the pursuit of something that interests you also enlightens or improves the work you're paid to do elsewhere. Even if you don't want to run a blog or start a podcast – consider doing an evening course, a museum study group, ANYTHING that complements (directly or indirectly) your professional ambitions. You'll find that by giving your brain a break from the daily grind and applying your thinking to something else, the daily grind will benefit, as if by accident.

Giving back

Beyond volunteering (which we covered in Section 1) there are other ways of giving back and gaining experience at the same time. Become a school governor, sit on the committee for a fundraising event or coordinate the social media accounts for a local charity. One day you might be chair of the trustees, but any interaction with the way charitable organizations or social enterprises operate is of benefit to them while giving you a new sense of perspective.

Supporting other people's projects

You'll have a bunch of friends who do a bunch of interesting things. They might be making a short film or building their photography portfolio. If you think your mate is super talented and under resourced, offer to help. I once styled forty actors and dancers for a low-budget zombie music video in a carpark basement; the shoot ran till 4 a.m. and I don't think the final thing ever aired but, my god, did I learn a lot that night. Mainly that I never wanted to be a stylist on a low-budget zombie music video again.

By putting yourself in entirely new situations you'll learn new things, navigate new dynamics and be repaid for the loyalty one day when it's your project you need help getting off the ground. Because it's not your actual job, you can enjoy collaborating freely without pressure. And the results of those collaborations grow into beautiful things as often as the ones that never see the light of day.

Turning Up

Time keeping

There's nothing more arrogant than bad time keeping. It's not about you being late, it's about what that signals to the person or people waiting for you – that you do not value their time. And that's no place to start.

If you want any day, or any meeting, to go well, then be on time (which generally means being five minutes early). If you aren't practised at this, if you haven't had a diary that requires you to be in a certain place at an appointed hour before, then get into the swing of it by planning and factoring in time for error. For train delays or for getting lost. You can plot your journey from the comfort of your bed, a few phone clicks will let you know estimated travel times, routes and problems along the way but do this in advance and set your alarm with a reasonable buffer, so that if you take the wrong exit or misread the map you'll have time to recover. Being lost is stressful. Being lost AND late is hell. And tearing around in raw panic, muttering like the White Rabbit, isn't the best frame of mind for a fruitful day at work.

As for stumping up on time at your official workplace every day, this is just habit. If you get into the habit of being ten minutes late, that will develop into twenty before you know it and from then on it's a slippery slope to seeming slovenly. I recently overheard a young woman say to her friends, 'I think I'm just going to talk to them about coming in at 10 a.m. I can't do 9 a.m. actually and I don't see what difference it makes, it's only an hour.' It took great restraint for me not to whisper at her, 'It makes a difference because everyone will hate you' – you simply can't swan in on your own schedule and expect to be treated fairly. You be fair. Turn up on time.

If you genuinely find this stuff difficult, I'd suggest trying the radical approach and forcing yourself to be really, really early for a bit. If you have a frenetic job or a bustling atmosphere and a tendency to be late then try experiencing the pleasure of being first in. Having a moment of total calm, a silent office, a cup of tea. A space for mindfulness, list writing and headspace is a radically different way to start the day vs arriving flustered and apologetic. And you might find that after a couple of weeks experimenting like this, your definition of punctual shifts altogether.

My great friend Miranda (we were grads together for our first job) is wonderful at many things but time is not one of them. She used to live in Wandsworth, London, and our agency was in Knightsbridge. It's not far, but at least twice a week she would phone me moments before our training session was about to begin and shout, 'Tell them I'm going to be late because there are NO FUCK-ING TAXIS!' not realizing that was not a sentence I could sympathetically repeat to our bosses because a) they didn't care WHY she was late, only that she wasn't there and b) no one gets a taxi to work every day.

If you are running late, be thoughtful about it:

- Warn the people your lateness will impact
- Don't make a massive fussy fuss about it. State the facts and avoid hysteria
- Apologize when you arrive and then get swiftly down to business. Don't waste more time by wanging on about transport strikes or lost car keys

Your time keeping is your responsibility and the details of your routine interest no one. Just turn up on time, all the time.

Working 9–5

So if being on time is super important, once you've arrived, how long should you stay?

In most careers you'll find that the hours of work detailed in your contract are there only as a guide and often bear little resemblance to the expectations about how much time you put in. You may choose to work differently to the standard form: flexibly, remotely or as part of the gig economy.

The origins of our standard working days go back to

the Industrial Revolution. Mill owners needed to keep factories open so made their workforce do long hours, six days a week. Nineteenth-century reformers like Robert Owen campaigned for an eight-hour day and a forty-hour week. Later, twentieth-century employers such as Ford adopted this structure and found that better paid workers with fewer hours were more productive. More recently, Graham Allcott, author of *How to be a Productivity Ninja*, experimented with the possibility of working 5 a.m. to 9 a.m.,[24] and while he struggled with low energy levels and the guilt of not working when others were, he reflected:

> It turns out successful 'work-life balance' is nothing to do with the hours you work at all but how you manage your own mental boundaries. When you are thinking about work, you're working. It's only when you're able to let go and be present in the moment, you're not.

Some people really care about adhering to the 9 to 5 and being seen to be physically at work and you have to be sensitive to that. Be aware that the people you work with will have pressures outside work that you cannot see but which impact their attitudes towards the working day – they might have caring responsibilities or they need to do the school run – so it matters to them that the hours devoted to work are used for that purpose and that there is discipline around it.

Different environments foster different behaviours; in some workplace cultures you'll find a strange competitiveness about being the last to leave. It's wise to avoid being sucked into situations where you find yourself staying because you feel you ought to. In others you'll find presenteeism, where people turn up even though they are streaming with a cold, as if to demonstrate their dedication, when in fact they are doing a bad day's work and making everyone else ill too.[25]

One of the biggest pitfalls you're likely to encounter is the dilemma of the lunch break. Like the eight-hour day, it's there for a reason. Each year on average we clock up the equivalent of thirty extra days of leave in lunch breaks. The evidence shows that we are more productive if we take the break, yet few people consistently do, for fear that we will be perceived badly by our peers and our bosses.[26] And it's a paradox – read a novel at your desk and you look like you're slacking, stuff a sandwich in your gob while checking your emails and you'll be mentally exhausted by 3 p.m. The best thing to do is move away from your work and take the opportunity to refresh your mind. If you're doing physically demanding work or you're on your feet, take some down time if you can. If you're at a desk, get out of the office and go for a walk.

In my experience the people who brag about being the most overworked, the most swamped, the most stressed, are also the ones who are worst at managing their time. So separate yourself from that mindset and focus instead on being productive. Rather than obsessing about being permanently physically present at your desk, focus on the work you produce being of quality and on deadline. Most employers would far rather have someone who is efficient and productive than someone just reliably sitting there all the time. But play it smart: if you're always absent or uncontactable, you'll obviously garner suspicion.

When you are present, make sure you are genuinely, fully present. If your head is half elsewhere (for example, distracted by the messages on your phone), then you'll be half as productive and it's likely to take twice as long. Do the task in front of you as best you can. Although working from home and remote working are more common than ever, don't forget that there are times when there is no substitute for being in the room. Technically, everything can be done via video call, but never underestimate the power of an actual meeting, of genuine eye contact and of doing things the old-fashioned way. Often, the digital shortcut ends up being the long way round.

There's often no official end-of-day time. If people just slope off where you work then pay attention to the patterns and leave when it's sensible or when you've finished. Don't wait for someone to tell you it's home time.

Managing your time effectively: why being organized is not the same as being efficient

Your time is your most important asset in work. But given we all have the same amount of time each day, why is it that some people look flustered while others seem much more in control? How can the CEO steer the ship when they must be inundated? As the saying on the popular coffee mug goes, 'You Have the Same Amount of Hours as Beyoncé' – so how does she do it? It comes down to three things:

- Preparation
- Planning
- Prioritizing

This is about not winging it. You'll have moments in your career where you find yourself winging it – that unique combination of thrill and fear. But those moments should always come as a surprise. Ideally, you avoid that freefall sensation by preparing.

Preparing for things doesn't have to be an arduous slog, it can be as simple as giving yourself a moment of quiet before barging into the room. Or having your to-do list written down for the day. Or thinking through the ideal sequence of events ahead before you engage with them. There are practical tips on how to do this below, but they won't be useful if you don't build in the time to apply them. Like revision, it's critical that you don't start to prepare when it's already too late.

Lists are wonderful. Try making one on a piece of A3 each day (A3 is good because you can see the whole landscape of your duties all in one glance). Write down all the big things you want to achieve and then, under each heading, what you need to do to achieve them. If you have a clear run at your day, start with the task at the top of the list, do it, then cross it off and move on to the next one. You'll rarely have that luxury, so look at your list and plan out the work on the basis of what you need to get done.

Stephen R. Covey, author of *The 7 Habits of Highly Effective People*, draws the analogy of filling a jar. He asks, if you have in front of you rocks, pebbles, sand and water, how do you most effectively fill the jar? The answer is, of course, rocks first, then pebbles, then sand, then water. Don't make life difficult for yourself by bunging in a few pebbles to make yourself feel better, put in half a rock, then add all the water, only to find you've got all the rocks still to do and no time to do it. Take on the big stuff first.

That said, in work you'll quickly find yourself snowed under. Everything will seem to be a priority and your boss and colleagues will tell you that their task is the most important. So how do you work out what the priorities are? A deceptively simple method is attributed to the 34th President of the United States, General Dwight D. Eisenhower.[27] Divide the tasks in front of you into four categories based on what you need to do about them:

- Important and urgent: do it immediately
- Important, but not urgent: decide when you will do it (before it becomes urgent)
- Urgent, but not important: delegate to someone else
- Not important, not urgent: do it later

Remember when you're making these decisions that they may have an impact on other people. Not keeping someone up to date because you have decided to de-prioritize their area of work can be frustrating to them if they don't hear from you until the last minute. Similarly, what might not feel like your priority could be theirs, and you're holding them up while they wait for you to get round to completing your part of the task. So consider the knock-on effect of your choices and make sure you keep colleagues well informed of when they can expect to hear from you. Don't prioritize selfishly – always consider the impact and communicate.

Productivity

Here are the four key habits for brilliant productivity, which Graham Allcott discusses in 'endless geeky and practical detail' (his words) in his book *How to be a Productivity Ninja*:

Capture and Collect

To operate productively and with a clear mind, you need to get everything out of your head. Our minds buzz with all those ideas, nagging thoughts, actions from meetings and corridor conversations. Our minds are also really bad at sorting and remembering it all, and before too long you'll either feel overwhelmed by it or some of those thoughts will take you off down unproductive rabbit warrens of procrastination or low-priority busyness. So get everything out of your head: onto paper, into an app, into the notes section of your phone or wherever feels easiest.

Organize

Once you've captured and collected all those ideas, actions, nags and questions, you need to organize them. I use an online to-do list tool. I call it my 'second brain'. My second brain remembers everything, and leaves my actual brain free to focus on thinking creatively, strategically and with single-minded focus on the stuff that matters. To organize all this information properly also requires you to ask good questions of yourself: 'Is it really up to ME to do this or can I delegate it?', 'What's the impact and value of this?', 'What's the biggest priority right now?', 'What does success look like when it's finished?' and – crucially – 'What's the first or next physical action I need to take to get momentum?' If there are things on your to-do list right now that are stuck, I guarantee it's because you're missing the answer to one of these questions. The more you think about your work, the easier it becomes.

Review

For your second brain to really work for you, taking over the job of memory and giving you clarity and focus, then you need to trust it, and that trust is earned. A quick review of your second brain each morning reminds you of what's on your plate, and then a much deeper dive into this about once a week will allow you the chance to think strategically about the bigger picture. Once a week I sit down for about an hour and go through each project that I'm working on in detail, just thinking about where it's all up to. Practise this regularly and you'll be amazed at how much more in control you feel, how you stop thinking about work at the weekends, and how much more productive it makes you. Clear thinking is the key.

Do

> *Of course, all that said, sometimes other stuff gets in the way of us getting the work done. Our own fears, guilt and emotions can hold us back. There's no cure for procrastination and everyone does it (even Productivity Ninjas!). The key is to spot it early so that you can break out of it, and focus on things that create momentum. Often, the simple clarity of picturing yourself physically starting the first action is enough, or sometimes making a commitment to your boss or a friend – putting a deadline in someone else's world so that you have accountability – can be a great trick. And of course, don't beat yourself up too much about it and feel guilty. A Productivity Ninja may sometimes appear like they're a superhero with all those amazing productive skills, but the truth is there's no secret sauce, we're all human and when it all goes wrong, remember there's always tomorrow.*

GRAHAM ALLCOTT, FOUNDER, THINK PRODUCTIVE, AND FORMER STUDENT VOLUNTEERING COORDINATOR

How to run your inbox before it runs you

There was a time when handwritten or laboriously typed memos were sent to physical 'In' boxes and replies placed in 'Out' boxes. It's a good example of how technology can make things easier, but not always better. We are now inundated with a huge range of poorly written emails full of unclear requests or information and constant interruptions from people on the phone or in person, all of which may or may not relate to the tasks that you need to do that day.

The first thing you must do is learn to filter that information. The difference between *our* working lives and the old factory model is that we need to collect and absorb a torrent of different types of information at speed and then decide what we need to know and what we need to do about it. When you read an email, ask yourself two questions:

- Is there an action worth doing? If no, bin the email or file it away for later.
- If there is an action, is it me next? If not, put it on a waiting list; if it is you next, work out what you need to do, whether it is part of a wider piece of work and when it is due by (and then do it).

When it's unclear, there's no harm in politely asking whether there is an action in there for you. It's surprising how often people will reply clearly whether it's for information, response or reaction and save you a lot of deciphering time.

Keeping your inbox clear doesn't mean trying to answer each email in turn. Try setting up folders to categorize your mail: action, waiting, read, and so on. Then plan in time to fire through each action, chase up the ones you're waiting for someone else to do something about or take the time to read them through in detail.

And it's worth encouraging clarity in others by demonstrating it yourself. Section 4 on how to write an email or focus a meeting will help you do that.

Being good value

Being good value is not the same as being the perfect employee. It's not the same as being an expert in your field or a CEO by the time you're thirty. It's not about doing the most work or putting in monstrously long hours. It's about being an all-rounder, one of the good guys. It's making people feel that a room is better, simply because you are in it with them. This doesn't mean you always come up with the most thrilling suggestions or crack constant jokes (please don't). It could be because you gave everyone a much-needed glass of water or you're taking excellent, perfectly rendered notes they'll all come to rely on later. It could be that when you're asked to do something you simply say, 'Sure, no problem,' and it really isn't any problem.

Being good value is particularly important in client-facing roles. There is nothing more painful for a fee-paying client than to leave a meeting thinking 'What were all those extra silent people there for?' You know you're being billed for their time, but you cannot see what purpose they serve. When you are junior in a role, take care to make small but significant contributions.

Your colleagues aren't expecting you to be perfect but they do want you to demonstrate that you care and that you have a work ethic. Be straightforward, be kind, be efficient. If you can do that, while showing some personality, the chances are you'll be embraced by everyone and forgiven the occasional fuck-up.

An ode to enthusiasm

Enthusiasm is really unfashionable these days. It seems as though everyone wants to look like they aren't trying too hard. But enthusiasm is my all-time favourite human trait. It's the unsung hero of every brilliant work personality. It signifies energy and interest and excitement.

I would hire enthusiasm over expertise every single time. And yet it's something that people often feel embarrassed about demonstrating. If you lack all skills, have had zero training and generally feel clueless in the workplace then make sure you show that you are KEEN.

Keenness is about volunteering for things, expressing interest, being engaged in the work of those around you, asking questions and giving stuff your best shot. You don't always have to get it right, but you do have to try. And don't confuse enthusiasm with boundless energy or constant chat, that's just annoying.

As a young person in the workplace, if you are nothing else, be enthusiastic. As Samuel Taylor Coleridge wrote, 'Nothing is as contagious as enthusiasm' – try it and watch everyone around you benefit. It's magic.

Presentation

It's completely weird that, in a world more visual than ever, people still churn out utter crap with their name on it. Emails addressed to the wrong person? Documents littered with spelling errors? Paragraphs entirely devoid of grammar? Everything is attached to your name, so remember that when you're feeling slapdash about spellcheck. It might help to imagine everything you send written on one of those smug calligraphy notecards 'From the desk of . . .'

And the same principle is true whether you are baking loaves of bread or laying bricks. Check it's all been done well. Put the final finish on.

Whatever job you do, please, please take time to check your work before you present it. Be proud of what you produce.

Deciding Who You Need to Know

If you do a quick mental scan through all the people you've ever met, you'll be able to identify them as either a radiator or a drain. It's brutal, but true. Obviously we all oscillate a little bit between the two to a certain extent. I'm a relentless radiator until I get a bit tired and then I can bleed a room dry with a single withering look. But generally, people fall into one type or the other.

Drains only see the problems, discuss the pitfalls or bemoan the process. They get their energy from forensically taking things apart, they are divisive within teams. Their favourite thing is a crisis because that's when they get loads of material to whinge about. Otherwise they have to create their own dramas, but that's OK because they're good at that too. You know that friend who you always feel exhausted after seeing? Them.

Drains are not just a nuisance; they will affect your performance. Research on the psychological impact at work suggests that being surrounded by negative views can decrease work performance while being surrounded by positive views can help to create a buffer around negativity.[28] There will always be a mix of positive and negative people in any given situation, so try to keep a balance. Negativity often stems from fear of the unknown or a lack of confidence, so see it as a style, not a truth.

Most importantly, don't get drawn into the negativity – you will only feed it. Instead, try to surround yourself with people who radiate warmth, energy and – yes, you've guessed it – enthusiasm. People who will find a way round things, who have lateral ideas and don't waste hours bitching about . . . well, about anyone actually.

The best thing you can do as a young professional is to try to get close to talent and kindness. You will always learn so much more from people who are generous and encouraging (from radiators) than you will from drains. You'll pick up great habits from radiators and bad ones from drains. There are, of course, some very talented drains, but talent alone isn't enough.

How to start building a network

'Network' is a massive, intimidating word. I actively avoided networking throughout my twenties because it just sounded so fucking awful. I didn't want to be a networker. I wanted to be a friend. And while I know that makes me sound like a cuddly animated woodland animal, it turns out to be simple, uncomplicated friendship that creates the strongest networks. I just didn't know that then.

There is a version of networking that's about forming ruthless, transactional acquaintances and that's useful for some people in some circumstances. But I've never been able to stomach that relentless exchange of introductions and favours, each made with the expectation of some sort of return. If every connection you make is based on what you might gain from it, then you'll find, when tested that those connections are pretty flimsy. And joyless. Instead, get out there, be interested, follow up and BE FRIENDLY. Over time you'll have the makings of an amazing party AND a group of voices you trust and rely upon in a crisis or a celebration. That's a network worth having.

Don't concern yourself with how relevant or connected the new people you encounter are to your career. If you do that you'll find there comes a point where you know each individual in an entire industry and that's the end of that. This is not an exercise in total coverage. It's far better to build a diverse and disparate group of characters you admire professionally, regardless of their profession. The writing of this book has been an interesting test of the concept of a network – we couldn't have done it without a pool of contributors who hail from all sorts of backgrounds. And the variety of voices we have included here demonstrates the breadth of interests and friendships accidentally created and then nurtured over time.

One of the treats about starting anything new (like writing a book) is the moment when you ask a bunch of people to help you and they universally, enthusiastically say YES. They don't do that because you've doggedly followed them about at every award ceremony or conference hall. They say yes because they like and respect you. Well over half my personal collaborators come from industries that have little or no connection to my own. The people I call when I want to sound out a new venture or test a theory don't have an identical perspective to mine – what would be the point in that? Don't make the mistake of thinking that your network should be made up of people who look or sound or think like you. Your network is not an echo chamber, it is an amphitheatre.

Finding a mentor

'Mentor' is similarly a very big word. It sounds so formal and patrician, but all it really means is someone who can point you in the right direction, chuck you a piece of advice, listen to your ideas and improve upon them by talking it through. It's someone you respect, who's prepared to talk to you. You don't need to find a guru or a life coach (blurgh) or a patron saint – again, this is about a kind of friendship. And friendship comes in many forms; usually a mentor has more or different experience than you, but that doesn't necessarily mean they are older or wiser. Be open to the idea that mentorship can come in many guises because you'll sometimes find it in the most unlikely places.

When sussing out a potential mentor, the most important thing is establishing TRUST. Do you value their take on the world; do you think they are clear sighted and honest? Will they honour your privacy or blab about your problems? Are they experienced enough to help you anticipate and prepare for the challenges ahead?

The second most important thing is GENEROSITY. It's no good having the flashiest, most dazzling mentor in the world if they can't or won't find the time to talk to you.

Rather than looking for a mentor, it's best to ask yourself if you might already be connected to someone who has experience in addressing the questions you need answers to. Often you'll meet a person through work, form a rapport and eventually feel comfortable enough to approach them when you find yourself in a sticky situation or at a crossroads with no obvious direction. Your organization may run an in-house mentoring scheme. Most industries, professions or interest groups have networks of mentors you can tap into.

In my experience mentors are most useful for the really small stuff (how do I handle this bit of murky office politics/how can I overcome my fear of public speaking etc.) and the really big stuff (how should I approach being appointed to the board/moving to the New York office) but not the day-to-day bits in between.

A mentor isn't responsible for your success and they can't be blamed for your failures. They are there to guide and to inspire and sometimes recalibrate your thinking.

Over the course of your working life, you'll have all sorts of advisers; changing mentors for changing times. You don't have to be devoted to one person forever. And as you become more established in your career, you'll find you don't need a mentor so much as a committee of characters you turn to as a sounding board. Mine are nearly all women who are my good friends but who also have peculiar and brilliant talents way beyond my own ability.

Having people you can call upon to balance out your weaknesses is immensely useful and saves everyone a ton of time. Alongside mentors you may also gain sponsors, who can not only guide your thinking, but actively help open doors for you. Surround yourself with people who challenge you, make you better and create opportunities and in turn offer yourself up to help them – when it works, it feels like cheating but it's just one of those delightful human realities. Rejoice in reciprocity.

Further Resources

Graham Allcott, *How to be a Productivity Ninja: Worry Less, Achieve More and Love What You Do* (Icon Books, 2014) and www.grahamallcott.com

Paul Arden, *It's Not How Good You Are, It's How Good You Want to Be* (Phaidon Press, 2003)

James Bloodworth, *Hired: Six Months Undercover in Low-Wage Britain* (Atlantic, 2018)

Josh Cohen, *Not Working: Why We Have to Stop* (Granta, 2019)

Stephen R. Covey, *The 7 Habits of Highly Effective People* (Simon & Schuster, 1989)

Jennifer Eberhardt, *Biased: The New Science of Race and Inequality* (William Heinemann, 2019)

Sam Friedman and Daniel Laurison, *The Class Ceiling: Why It Pays to be Privileged* (Policy Press, 2019)

Mishal Husain, *The Skills: From First Job to Dream Job – What Every Woman Needs to Know* (Fourth Estate, 2018)

THE EARLY DAYS

M. Krogerus and R. Tschäppeler, *The Decision Book: Fifty Models for Strategic Thinking* (Profile, 2011)

L. David Marquet, *Turn the Ship Around!* (Penguin, 2015)

Jo Owen, *How to Lead: What You Actually Need to Do to Manage, Lead and Succeed* (Prentice Hall, 2011)

Elizabeth Uviebinené and Yomi Adegoke, *Slay in Your Lane: The Black Girl Bible* (Fourth Estate, 2018)

Tara Westover, *Educated: A Memoir* (Random House, 2018)

Laura Whateley, *Money: A User's Guide* (Fourth Estate, 2018)

Section 4
The Every Day

In this section we'll explore the basics of how to do a decent turn every day. How to present yourself, how to behave (which is not the same as being on your best behaviour) and how to adapt to this new life in the world of work. Most of the advice here is about decoding the things that no one ever tells you and giving you a crib sheet for skills that used to be taught but have somehow dropped off the agenda (leaving you struggling to perform well with no guidance). If you read this, then you'll feel a bit more prepared as you encounter things for the first time.

Presenting Yourself

The way you present yourself is about more than what you wear and whether it's been ironed recently. Presentation is posture, tone of voice, attitude and eye contact. But it is also worth owning an iron.

Like it or not your clothes say a great deal about you.
Are you meticulous, mindful, respectful, law abiding,

153

*clean? Or are you slovenly, disorganized, a loose
cannon? Dress codes should be enjoyed as forces for
the common good, to subvert is not an act of grand
rebellion – it might be an act of career self-harm.
Wear clothes that are appropriate to the job and the
environment, that make your colleagues, customers
and constituents feel at ease, clothes that represent
you as you would wish to be represented. In the
words of Edward VIII, 'Be always well and correctly
dressed.'*

PATRICK GRANT, DESIGNER AND CREATIVE
DIRECTOR, NORTON & SONS, E. TAUTZ AND
COMMUNITY CLOTHING, AND FORMER LABOURER,
DONALDSON TIMBER

Dress Codes and How to Crack Them

A dress code might seem like an old-fashioned concept
but they still exist almost everywhere, even if they are
not written down or referred to. And, unlike school uniforms with rigid rules and identikit jerseys, a dress code
is simply there to guide you. It serves the same purpose
at work as it does on an event invitation, and if you've ever
turned up unprepared for a pool party, you'll appreciate
how important it is to know what to expect.

In some ways, the stricter the code, the easier it is to
follow. Here are some thoughts about how to navigate
the most common themes.

Power dressing

If you work in a super-formal environment, then it's head-to-toe tailoring and regular dry cleaning, but not much angst about how to style it out or express your individuality. Do resist the temptation to go wild with natty socks or comedy cufflinks, there's nothing worse than someone using the very edges of their body as a place to cram all their creative expression. Save it for the weekend and do it wholeheartedly then.

Tailoring is expensive; everything you buy will be an investment. As a rule, try to buy less and buy better. Good quality pieces will last longer, hold their shape and see you through season after season if you look after them.

In some cases there are very specific rules or customs – if you're in a court of law or an orchestra you'll be buying lots of black, for example. Don't be shy about asking questions of your colleagues and making sure you understand any codes of this nature.

Casual dressing

I take issue with the term 'business casual' – it doesn't really exist any more. I once interviewed sixth-formers at a college outside London who were expected to wear 'business casual' rather than uniform. In practice this meant boys were in simple suits (sans ties) while the girls were under pressure to wear a different, consistently fashionable and expensive thing every day. It was depressing. And unsustainable.

I suppose what 'business casual' is trying to convey is 'not loungewear but not pinstripe perfection either'; it's a middle-of-the-road, high-street-smart version of what you wear to a BBQ with your grandparents as opposed to a night at the opera or weekend at Burning Man. In reality, it tends to translate into chinos, shirts and jackets, smart shoes (no trainers) and day dresses.

Here, you'll have to assess what seems acceptable and take your cues from those around you. You'll have a sense of that already from the interviews, but you can hone that further now you're through the door. Generally speaking, if you pay attention and take the lead from the team around you, you can't go wrong.

At the risk of sounding terribly dull, start by building a collection of versatile staples, knowing that those garments can form the basis of your working wardrobe for a long time to come. If you create a strong foundation then you can rely on it to support all sorts of trends and seasons over the years.

Underdressing

Some places have an 'anything goes' approach. Depending on your relationship with fashion, this is either the hardest code or the most interesting. When no rules apply, how do you get dressed in the morning?

In creative industries there's a pressure to perform, and going to work can feel like a fashion show. Don't be intimidated, you have plenty of time to evolve your personal style and adapt it to the workplace.

Even if it's a jeans-and-trainers kind of vibe, always

be clean and tidy. Avoid offensive slogan T-shirts (obviously) and try to enjoy the freedom (and the comfort) of more relaxed rules.

You'll find that even the most casual places effectively still have uniforms – think of the ubiquitous grey T-shirt, jeans and white trainers of tech entrepreneurs everywhere. Often the clothes become so boring they're almost invisible and, actually, that's the point.

Don't ever confuse a relaxed atmosphere with slovenly standards; sloppy or skimpy is never a very good idea.

Undressing

When working from home, it might be tempting to slob in pyjamas all day, but consider how the clothes you wear make you feel. You might be your very best self in an old dressing gown, but personally, I can see a direct decline in my performance if I don't bother getting dressed. Sure, stay comfy, but make sure your clothes reflect your working attitude.

Dressing up

I'm a believer in dressing for an occasion. Whether it's a high-profile presentation, an appraisal, a pay review or an awards ceremony, take some time to plan what you're going to wear. Visualizing yourself in the outfit, in the moment, can help you feel confident in advance and on the day itself. And, importantly when the stakes are high, make sure that you're wearing something reliable. If you're tempted to fidget with your waistband, worry about your neckline or perspire through the fabric, it's probably not a wise choice for a big day.

Dressings down

Being told off for the way you dress is a pretty unpleasant experience but I've seen it happen a lot over the years. In the best cases, it's a polite word in your ear about smartening up. In the worst, it's body shaming and power play.

The report by the UK Government Petitions Committee and Women and Equalities Committee, 'High Heels and Workplace Dress Codes', revealed the troubling experiences of workers affected by discriminatory dress codes.[1] The report gives a wide range of examples of employees being humiliated, sexualized and discriminated against because of what they wore; many of these were young women in insecure jobs who already felt vulnerable in the workplace. In Japan the Minister of Health, Labour and Welfare responded to a petition to ban workplaces from requiring female job seekers and employees to wear high heels by saying, 'It is socially accepted as something that falls within the realm of being occupationally necessary and appropriate.'[2] What occupation really requires a four-inch cigarette heel?

Employers have traditionally stipulated dress codes that set expectations for their employees about what they should wear. These go beyond the necessities of health and safety and into the realms of corporate ethos and standards about how an organization wants to be represented by its employees. In practice this may mean that you'll be asked to cover up tattoos or remove jewellery from piercings if you have them.

Employers are expected to consider the risk of discriminating against people in their dress codes. Guidance may set out different expectations for men and women, but they shouldn't discriminate, by being stricter for men than for women. In most countries anti-discrimination legislation protects employees against unfair dress codes, but in practice the distinction can be murky and the law is still unclear on many of these points.

Safety gear and specialist stuff

From aprons to safety goggles, hairnets to high-visibility vests, there are multiple subgenres of workwear specific to individual industries. Similarly, reasonable ideas like not wearing a tie when operating heavy machinery or keeping jewellery to a minimum in hospitals are about protecting everyone's health. Get familiar with whatever you need and be prepared in advance if you're expected to supply these items. Mostly this stuff is simple and standard issue and all you have to do is look after it.

Uniform

If you work somewhere that provides a uniform, consider yourself lucky and save all your money for party dresses and Hawaiian shirts.

All the gear, no idea

Wherever you work, whatever you like to wear, the watch-word is 'appropriateness'.

It's such a mean word but it is relevant – if you're an early years teacher you need to dress to be eye-catching, approachable and in footwear that allows you to break into a run at short notice. If you're a flight attendant you need an outfit that's physically capable of doing anything at forty thousand feet with seams strong enough for more squats and stretches than I've done in a lifetime of gym membership. And if you're a doctor in a sequinned jump-suit you're going to struggle to gain your patients' trust.

Some tips:

- Consider who you're dressing for. How you dress is not only about fitting in, but also about showing respect. A good rule of thumb is that the more senior or traditional the person you're interacting with, the more formal you'll need to be.
- As you grow in confidence and build your reputation you can afford to be bolder in your choices. Personal taste, idiosyncrasies and style signifiers are powerful tools for 'building your brand', so don't be afraid to use them. Think Steve Jobs in his turtlenecks or Anna Wintour and her bulletproof blow dry. Or not.
- It's better to be slightly overdressed at work than the opposite. In the beginning you want to at least look like your career could go anywhere. Don't be the person who isn't

invited to sit in on the big meeting or come to the important event because you looked too scruffy to represent.

- Never dress like your client. I was given this piece of advice early on in a client-facing industry. It's tempting to try to match the person who pays the bills. But don't do that – they work in an office full of people meeting that dress code. They're paying your fee to get something else. Visually demonstrating that distinction can be really useful; it reminds everyone that you're from a different corporate culture, with a different set of skills and perspectives. And it guards against being treated like an employee vs a collaborator.

- If you have a hangover, dress up into it. It helps lift your spirits and it hides you a bit. I once worked with a complete reprobate called Christopher; he had a special hangover hoodie that he only ever wore when things got really bad. It may have felt like a comfort blanket to him but for the rest of us it was a klaxon that he'd been out late, got drunk and wasn't on top form. We teased him relentlessly.

- Your relationship with makeup is entirely personal. As a rule, try to keep it simple, low maintenance and professional for work.

- EMERGENCY KIT: always have in your desk safety pins, a hotel sewing kit, stain-removal wipes, deodorant and anything else that might save embarrassment or a trip to the shops.

Beyond Getting Dressed

We spend a load of time trying to improve our brains, but we don't train our body language or give it nearly enough attention. Here, you're at an advantage if you're an athlete or a dancer or one of those irritating naturally graceful people. But for most of us, body language is something we need to be conscious of and maybe even work on a bit. Because we are complex, awkward human beings. And we can't divorce our minds from their natural habitat – so if you are nervous you sweat, if you are stressed your heart races, if you're angry you might actually cry. But I don't want to alarm you – let's start somewhere simple . . . with a handshake.

It's a tradition at many private, privileged schools that morning and afternoon handshakes are compulsory for even the smallest children. It's a good example of culturally engrained privilege because even if you're naturally shy, by the time you are five or six you'll be so used to a grown-up handshake that you'll never worry about it. Whereas if you haven't had those years of practice you might not even encounter this bizarre ritualistic and intimate greeting until your first job interview or, worse, your driving test.

Importantly, those little kids are not allowed to let go of their teacher's hand until they've made eye contact – so you see a child straining at arm's length while the teacher eyeballs them hard, waiting to meet their gaze. The point is, a handshake is only half about your hands. The rest is in the eyes.

This might seem like a small detail but here's the context: a US study found that a firm handshake has a significant effect on success at interview.[3] Another found that a handshake has a cognitive effect that increases the likelihood of a positive interaction.[4] Small, but significant.

If you find handshaking difficult (and there's no shame in that), then just practise loads – with your friends, your parents, shopkeepers etc. Soon it will become second nature. As familiar as hello and goodbye.

And if you're wondering what the optimal handshake is, luckily for you a British professor of psychology, Geoffrey Beattie, has developed a formula for the specific attributes of the perfect handshake:[5]

- Use the right hand
- A complete grip and a firm squeeze (but not too strong)
- A cool and dry palm
- Approximately three shakes, with a medium level of vigour, held for no longer than two to three seconds
- Executed with eye contact kept throughout and a good natural smile with an appropriate verbal statement

Be aware that the way you occupy your body will be seen by those around you as an indicator of your attitude. Fold your arms and you're sulky. Slump at your desk and you're slovenly. Roll your eyes and you're rude.

Obviously, it's more complicated than that. Our identities are often expressed though our body language, our cultural heritage is encoded in many of our behaviours, and physical or communication disabilities may affect our body language.

But what I'm talking about here is when I've observed interns churn out top-quality work while undermining themselves simply by *appearing* not to give a shit. Their output demonstrates that they are diligent and engaged but their body language sends the opposite message. It's somehow become fashionable to look like you don't care, even if you really do. Don't let your posture let you down.

Here are some things to consider:

- **Leaky face**
  Where your emotions play out, unfiltered across your face. Try to master the art of impassive facial expressions, even if you are bored, exasperated or amused. That's not the same as 'resting bitch face', which has no place here (or, in my opinion, anywhere else).

- **How to sit in a chair**
  This one's easy. Straight, alert and upright. Anything other than that looks disengaged. And men, please refrain from manspreading.

- **Power poses**
  There's a school of thought that suggests that striking certain poses can build our confidence.[6] Whether it runs deeper than this and actually makes us more powerful is disputed. But

paying attention to your stance – plugging your feet into the ground rather than tying your legs into a knot or placing your palms facing upwards in an open gesture rather than looking like you're stopping traffic – will make a difference to how you feel and how you are perceived. Try it before a big meeting, it takes a few minutes standing in a comedy star shape in the loos and it might just make a difference to how you perform.

● **Active listening**
This is not the same as hearing. It's about paying attention to what is being said and communicating back to the individual speaking that you are taking on board what they are saying.[7] This might mean making eye contact, leaning forward, encouraging the speaker with an occasional nod. As the person speaks, asking the odd clarifying question or – when a key point has been made – mirroring what has just been said to confirm understanding shows that you won't be coming back to them in half an hour with a query. Try not to fake it or occupy your brain trying to come up with a response – genuinely clearing your mind and listening is a beautiful skill.

● **Taking an interest**
In his classic book *How to Win Friends and Influence People*, Dale Carnegie runs through a series of ways to be well liked and develop

intimacy, including smiling, listening and being genuinely interested in people. One very practical way of showing that you are engaged is using a person's name politely and respectfully, whatever their role or status. Do this and you will create an instant rapport. Why? Because it personalizes the connection by appealing directly to them, or, as Carnegie poetically puts it, 'A person's name is to him or her the sweetest and most important sound in any language.'

● **Curse of the millennial shrug**
The worst offenders in the body language category are the dismissive shrug and the eye roll. If you're in the habit of using either as part of your corporeal grammar, please, just stop it. These gestures belong in the playground and you're not there any more.

Tone

Just as your body is a vehicle for self-expression, so your voice is a powerful tool for communication. And you don't have to be on a stage public speaking for it to matter. Like handshakes, people form quick judgements about you from your tone of voice.[8] Don't ever get hung up on your accent, but do always consider your tone.

In his excellent guide *TED Talks: The Official TED Guide to Public Speaking* (which is as useful for anyone who ever pipes up in a room of other humans as it is for anyone actually giving a TED talk) Chris Anderson describes the power of tone to motivate and enchant an audience:

> Start thinking of your tone of voice as giving you a whole new set of tools to get inside your listeners' heads. You want them to understand you, yes, but you also want them to feel your passion. And the way you do that is not by *telling* them to be passionate about this topic, it's by showing them your own passion. It spreads automatically, as will every other emotion you authentically feel.

And it works the other way round too. If you're not passionate about a topic, if you're bored stiff and sulky in a meeting – we can *hear* it in your voice. And it's not pretty. Think about the way you use emphasis, the emotions you are conveying or concealing and the impact these things have on your listeners. How they hear you can have a big impact on how they *see* you too.

- **Vocal fry**
  This is a phenomenon where people drop their voice to its lowest natural register, creating a creaky quality. There are many popular theories behind why this trend is spreading. Whatever the reason, it's widely felt to be intensely annoying. A US study found that young women in particular who speak in the lowest register are considered less competent, less trustworthy and less hireable.[9] It's important to note that men use vocal fry

too, but most of the critical commentary around it is directed at women.

- **Uptalk/upspeak**
  This is where people are making statements with a rising intonation at the end, as if they were asking a question. If this is something you do, consider for a moment the effect it has on the listener. Phrasing everything as a question is a pretty stressful experience for anyone in the conversation. It's a style that suggests you require constant reassurance and that's exhausting for those around you. And you can't expect to have authority when everything you say is a question?

There's a generational divide at play here that's worth being aware of – in the case of these vocal patterns, young people do it and older people are irritated by it. So just be smart and make sure that your delivery isn't getting in the way of what you're trying to say.

We all have idiosyncrasies of speech and they can be a powerful way of making a point, but in the case of trends or habits that make you sound unconfident or disinterested, more often than not they're a distraction from what you want to communicate and you're better off without them.

Privilege

'Check your privilege' has become a kind of short-hand. Although it started as a way of pointing out the unrecognized behaviours of discrimination, it's lost its currency. The conversation itself appears to have become the preserve of the privileged – as Phoebe Maltz Bovy points out in her article for *The Atlantic*, 'the *vocabulary* of "privilege" is learnt at liberal-arts colleges or in high-brow publications'.[10] The sentiment comes from the right place though – unchecked privilege can be the invisible, binding, systemic source of lazy discrimination.

It's not enough simply to recognize your privilege or to hashtag first world problems, this isn't about acknowledging an issue exists, it's about pledging to actively help overcome it. Please resist using this expression as an apologist's disclaimer and instead be a champion for real change. Promise to call out inequality, even if (especially if) this doesn't benefit you directly. This sort of awareness has to be about more than good manners; it's a commitment to social justice. More on calling it out in Section 5.

Entitlement

The cousin of privilege is, of course, entitlement: the sense that young people entering the workplace consider lowly tasks are beneath them or that success is owed to them. This attitude is the bête noire of many bosses. As Joel Stein says in his *Time* magazine article 'Millennials: The Me Me Me Generation': 'If you want to sell seminars to middle managers, make them about how to deal with young employees who email the CEO directly and beg off projects they find boring.'

Jean M. Twenge's study of young people born since

1995, *iGen*, contrasts the 'hungry' new generation, more aware of what they need to do to succeed in work and who 'lack outsized bravado of the Millennials'. But she notes that this generation still have some of that sense of entitlement, combined with a new feeling of exhaustion about what it takes to get through education and into well-paid work.

Young people have been accused of showing 'entitlement' for generations. So try not to take it personally if you are. Be aware that this characterization exists, but don't feel demonized by it. If anything, it can work in your favour; if you demonstrate a generational self-awareness and behave in a way that debunks these preconceptions, you'll be embraced by your bosses, who probably feel quite paranoid about this issue and are desperate to solve it.

Respect

Being respectful is the simplest counter to accusations of entitlement. It's as easy as just acknowledging that some people have been doing this job for a lot longer than you and they have the benefit of years of wisdom that you have yet to acquire. Sure, you have new and fresh ideas, but value the perspective of those who have gone before you, even if you disagree or want to challenge it.

Talent, determination and sheer hard work are the way to rise – become indispensable to your team and success will come naturally. Be ambitious and forthright absolutely, but handle this ambition with a humility that respects the experience of others and an understanding of the need to prove your value. Don't walk into a role with expectations of what is owed to you; earn them. There will be occasions in your career when you are ready to take on a new challenge or need to stand firm about the recognition you deserve, but doing so with the respect of your colleagues puts you in a far stronger position. And, by extension, this will lead to greater opportunities when you're looking to move on.

KATIE KEITH, FIRST LADY AT PRODUCTION COMPANY RATTLING STICK AND FORMER SHOP ASSISTANT, GAP

Flakiness

I'll confess – this is my least favourite human trait. I'd take sarcastic, hysterical and drunk over flakiness. Maybe some people can tolerate it, maybe I'm overreacting, but to me flakiness suggests such a fundamental disregard for people's time, energy and effort AND it has an added layer of deceitfulness too.

If you've made a commitment, keep it. If you've said you'll be there, turn up.

Of course, there will be times when things don't go as planned, when you unavoidably let people down. But if you're in the habit of cancelling at the last minute, trying to be in two places at once or worming out of responsibilities in your personal life, DO NOT allow that to characterize your work persona too. It makes you unreliable, a horrible team member and really frustrating to be around.

Nothing is beneath you

Regardless of your expectations, it's worth remembering that when you start out, nothing is beneath you. You will be happier and more successful in the long run if you adopt an attitude that no task is too small. There is real honour in being good at the small stuff, and even if it feels mildly demeaning in the moment, it's worth it later. It's more fulfilling knowing that you started at the bottom. Whether it's ordering the sandwiches or sweeping the street, manning the printer till your fingers bleed or colouring in dents on coat hangers till dawn (these may or may not be actual examples from my own illustrious career), do it with good grace and enthusiasm.

In his book *The Case for Working with Your Hands: Or Why Office Work is Bad for Us and Fixing Things Feels Good*, Matthew Crawford makes a compelling case for completing tangible work, the deep satisfaction and sense of pride in making and fixing things. If your job exists mostly in what Crawford refers to as the 'bewildering psychic landscape' of 'vague imperatives', now more than later you can take the opportunity to enjoy the straightforward, practical tasks.

No one who is any good at anything started at the top. The myth of instant fame in any field is damaging not just because it's untrue, but because it diminishes the honest dignity of doing shitty tasks really well. In nearly all professions you have to put the hours in. Start lowly, grow daily.

Being Yourself

There's a lot of talk about bringing your 'whole self' to work. But before we look into what this means, we have to be clear what it's not: creating a detached work persona that is so distinct from who we are, that we burn out trying to meet our own unachievable standards or being so set in our views that we are unadaptable to new environments and people in the workplace.

Being your true self at work can, in some instances, require your colleagues to challenge their bias in order to simply respect who you are. It takes personal strength to overcome prejudice but the demonstration of that strength is in turn of huge value to the organization. Antonia Belcher, Founding Partner of MHBC, a leading independent building and cost consultancy, talks about her experience of transitioning in a very male-dominated working environment, where there was no history or visible LGBTQ influences to draw on:

> As a trans woman who started her transition as the millennium began, I found myself having to convince my business partners at a very well respected West End consultancy that they should not ask me to leave because of the journey I was starting. Battling with the trauma I was causing within my family and social circles, the

last thing I needed was to be 'out of work'. Obviously, the omens were not good, especially with no LGBTQ influences evident at my place of work, and an all-male equity partnership, who had already made me sense that female involvement was not really wanted/expected at equity level, and probably not via the way I was intending. As it turned out, I was not told to leave, but it was more a decision given out of commercial necessity rather than willing nurtured support, which has surprised me no end, given I have gone on to use my authenticity for so much good, both commercially and socially, and if you closely look at the changes now taking shape in the business world to be diverse in outlook and inclusive in approach. If only my old partners had realized that they were in effect groundbreaking, and could have made this decision with positive joy and encouragement rather than the 'he/she' makes too much money to ask them to go.

Being yourself at work isn't always easy, but it is the most powerful way to operate.

Knowing Yourself

Values are really important, but how do you establish what they are? Well, there are a wide range of methods to help you determine your principles, what motivates you and what you're good at.

In her book *Pivot*, Jenny Blake recommends some exercises to work out the answers to these questions, which she calls 'calibrating your compass':

- Free write some examples of what shapes your values, like a description of your ideal day, three people you admire and what you admire about them, the compliment you hear most often about yourself, what you want more of or less of in your life
- Group these into clusters on the basis of the values they express, like creativity, freedom, helping others, risk taking
- Write out what makes these values real, like freedom, financial security or the opportunity to travel
- Rank these values, focus down on your top five and write out a paragraph on what they mean to you
- Stick the descriptions up where you can see them and refer to them each time you need to make a decision
- Pay attention to what makes you happy too – do you need regular exercise, time alone, meeting friends?
- List out your experience of work and your skills. Review any results you can point to and the reputation you have. Are you known as a creative thinker? A safe pair of hands? A person who gets the job done?

It's also worth looking at the type of person you are – introverted or extroverted, detail focussed or 'big picture'. You're likely to come across personality assessment tools such as the Myers–Briggs Type Indicator or the Belbin Team Inventory at some point, and you may have already been asked to complete similar exercises in recruitment stages. They're by no means fixed views, but they can assist you with a bit of healthy self-reflection. They're also good at helping you recognize that other people may not think or value the same things or work in the same way as you, which is useful when interacting with a variety of personality types.

What to do if you're shy or socially anxious

Most of us have moments when we wobble. But if you're shy or if overcoming social anxiety is a daily struggle for you, there's no doubt that a lot of advice in this book is going to be harder to execute. The newness of work with all its unknowns can seem overwhelming. The workplace will bring you into contact with many different types of people too. As Liz Fosslien and Mollie West Duffy say in their book about emotions at work *No Hard Feelings*, 'it's not immediately obvious whether someone is an introvert or an extrovert, especially when you're just getting to know each other. In the workplace, introverts often try to mask their introverted qualities to fit in.'

Each person will approach anxiety differently, but in most cases the advice is:

- Seek to understand your anxiety: things like cognitive behavioural therapy techniques can help you work through the causes of anxiety and the responses you feel to them

- Challenge your feelings of anxiety to understand whether they are based on fact
- Don't think too much about how others see you – try to pay attention to them instead and understand their perspectives and motivations
- Divide large or complex tasks into smaller ones, taking one step at a time

It's a really good idea to have a trusted person at work. Just knowing you can talk honestly and openly about any issues takes the pressure off and helps you feel supported. There are lots of great sources of support to help you manage your anxiety. See the Further Resources at the end of this section for some suggestions.

Not taking yourself too seriously

Perhaps the most important thing to remember is not to take yourself too seriously. If you do, you risk micromanaging, closing yourself off to differing opinions or believing that professional achievement is the only route to happiness. That's why Liz Fosslien and Mollie West Duffy's first rule of emotion at work is 'Be less passionate about your job'. If you're frustrated to tears or panicking about the big meeting, you're not helping yourself and you're alienating your team. Passion is super important and you shouldn't go to work without it – but it has to be proportionate to the context. For lots of people, work is work, not a grand, all-consuming romance. And that's OK.

Authenticity

It's all about authenticity. Everything else we can train. But if I get a disingenuous person that's going to work with me on cancer patients I don't want that at all. And I would caution everybody, you may think you're clever when you're twenty-five but when you're being interviewed by someone who's sixty and who's taken care of 20,000 humans? They get people. So be authentic; if you overpresent yourself it reeks of something undesirable. Just be your best.

DR RAHUL JANDIAL, NEUROSURGEON AND
SCIENTIST AT CITY OF HOPE, LOS ANGELES,
AND FORMER SHOP ASSISTANT

While it's often talked about as essential, being authentic is mostly ill defined. And overused. In an article on the topic, a group of Dutch academics assert that authenticity in work is based on three things:

- The extent to which a person feels in touch with their core self at work
- Whether they are true to their selves at work and act in accordance with their personal values and beliefs
- The extent to which they believe that they meet the expectations of others[11]

When these are misaligned, a person becomes inauthentic. They feel a difference between who they are and what they hope to be. They are delivering work in a way that they do not believe in. And they find that others, rather than themselves, are determining whether or not the work they are doing and the way in which they are doing it is of value. The outcome is often burnout, boredom, disengagement or dissatisfaction.

However, authenticity isn't a licence to behave in exactly the same way in all scenarios. You have to adapt. You're not being inauthentic if you behave differently with your line manager from when you're with your oldest school friend. Rather than encouraging people to let it all hang out, authenticity is about finding alignment between who you are and what you do.

Vulnerability

My first job after I left university involved making telephone calls to book rooms for conferences and training seminars for the HR department of a large freezer-food company. As a young deaf person who had successfully navigated mainstream education largely as a result of intelligent guesswork, who depended on lip-reading and needed to see the person I was talking to, finding myself in this sort of job proved to be a total nightmare. When I finally confessed that I was making it up as I went along, my employer suggested that I might be better suited to a different type of role. This fairly brutal experience taught me a valuable lesson about authenticity and vulnerability – be true to yourself and play to your strengths.

SUSAN DANIELS, CEO, NATIONAL DEAF CHILDREN'S SOCIETY AND FORMER HR ASSISTANT

Like authenticity, being vulnerable in work is about having the courage to know and be who you are, complete with your assets and imperfections. In her book *Daring Greatly*, Brené Brown makes the case that you will never really love your job if you also numb yourself to the bits where you feel shame or discomfort. At the start of a new job, being vulnerable means asking questions. It means asking for honest feedback, giving it a whirl and admitting if something didn't work but you learnt from it. It doesn't mean never needing to front up or work outside your comfort zone.

Brown points out that workplaces often create cultures of blame, covering up mistakes rather than learning from them. 'I've never been to a shame-free organization,' Brown admits, but she points to 'shame being used as a management tool (again, that means bullying, criticism in front of colleagues, public reprimands or reward systems that intentionally belittle people)', with the effect that 'if employees are constantly having to navigate shame, you can bet that they're passing it on to their customers, students and families'.

There's nothing as stifling to a work culture as shame. It suppresses ideas, frightens optimism and rewards pedestrian decision making. I've worked in that environment and it's soul destroying and financially inefficient (because people are paid to do less than they are capable of).

A word of caution

The space and support to be your whole self at work is an important and welcome development in culture generally but it's worth noting that it offers both reward and risk. In the rush to embrace vulnerability, authenticity and your personal idiosyncrasies do not forget that there's nothing wrong with having slightly different personas at work and at home. In fact, you might find that some separation can be useful. It helps you protect your privacy, keep your priorities defined and stay professional. You're not doing it wrong if you don't feel like sharing your whole self, your innermost thoughts, your most personal passions with your work colleagues. Discover what feels right for you. Being yourself is a spectrum, not a job spec.

Sex, Drugs and Rock and Roll in the Workplace

When I was in my early twenties, I found myself in tears at the Playboy Mansion. This was not how I'd imagined my career turning out.

We're midway through a week-long, million-dollar production schedule and the guy who pays the bills has taken his tie off and is downing cocktails and telling me to relax. It's 10 a.m. and I am not relaxed. A retired Playboy Bunny is waiting to give me a guided tour of the infamous 'Grotto' and I'm crying because Hugh Hefner's menagerie of exotic zoo animals just turned on me. I'm very scared of animals. I vaguely remember I have a first-class honours degree somewhere, but it seems very far away.

Everything about the situation was surreal and

compromised. Which wasn't unusual in advertising, an industry renowned for its permissive approach to bad or, euphemistically, 'eccentric' behaviour. So I feel over-qualified to write this section of the book.

You don't have to be at the Playboy Mansion to encounter sex and drugs and rock and roll in the workplace. Depending on where you work you will have different levels of exposure to all three, but at some point you are likely to have to handle one of these sticky situations.

Comedian Tina Fey describes her attitude to drugs in an interview on Netflix's *My Next Guest Needs No Introduction* with David Letterman. She recalls her reaction to First Lady Nancy Reagan's 'Just Say No' campaign (1988): 'I'm real, real square. When I was a kid Nancy Reagan said "Say no to drugs" and I was like "Copy that. Got it!"'

Well, same here.

I am cringingly naïve and inexperienced on this topic. I spent a decade in an industry riddled with substance-abuse issues and became addicted only to saturated fat and bar snacks. Like Tina and Nancy, drugs are not my thing. So I once worked for a woman for a whole six months before I realized that her erratic behaviour, tendency to talk at uncomfortably high speed and fondness for working through the night after super-long-haul flights weren't hallmarks of a tricksy personality type but the result of a stonking great coke habit. In fact, I didn't 'realize' – someone had to tell me (because everyone else knew and my cluelessness was getting embarrassing). Suddenly, I felt a lot better about things. I'd been worrying for ages that I simply wasn't keeping up. That I had no stamina and not enough drive. I thought her eyes were dilated because they saw my chronic inadequacy. Turns out, she was off her face.

It's hard if you have colleagues who are in a chemically altered state. Things don't make sense. The ground doesn't feel stable. It's difficult to do well because the rules keep changing. It's inappropriate, often frightening, and you may find yourself with conflicted feelings about how to behave yourself. What if you're lured into a drug-fuelled downward spiral? (Ahhhhhhhh!)

The truth is that as a new colleague you're playing a tiny bit-part in someone else's story here and your agency is very limited. You have little power and nearly no influence. This isn't the time to start staging interventions. But if the problem is presenting at work and that's affecting you, you could raise it with a trusted member of your circle of support.

Take a note of the occasions where things are obviously not 100 per cent straight up and flying right. Find and follow your organization's policy and procedures, especially those on conduct, safeguarding and whistle-blowing. Try to always have other people around you; avoid one-on-one meetings. And if you ever feel unsafe then confidentially talk to your manager or HR department or seek help from a professional body like ACAS.[12] You must be aware of the ramifications of elevating a dispute and how it might affect someone's career. You don't have to tolerate behaviour that makes you feel unsafe, but you do have to be careful about the way you navigate any potentially damaging revelations.

There's a distinction between problems directly relating to conduct at work (e.g. driving drunk, being high in client meetings) and the wider portrait an addict is facing in their life as a whole. You are only related to one side of that equation. Don't try to be a hero, just protect yourself and stay sensible. If you need help yourself, contact an organization such as FRANK, Addaction or Alcoholics Anonymous for support in healing addiction.

Let's talk about sex

From the inconvenience of falling in love with your boss to the unwanted attentions of a co-worker – there's a range of dynamics you might encounter beyond the strictly professional. It would be easier if there was never any crossover between work and sex but that's unrealistic. Humans are messy, they misjudge things, they desire each other, pulses race, hands wander and hearts get broken. Some behaviour is understandable and some never, ever excusable. There's a spectrum from healthy, happy, respectful, intimate relationships through to sinister, predatory and criminal . . . so let's deal with these separately . . .

Relationships at work

The truth is that nasty, exploitative, abusive sexual misconduct cases exist in the same universe as quite a few long and joyful partnerships between people who happened to meet at work. I don't want loving, brilliant relationships to stop flourishing because of a hostile climate created by the *opposite* of loving and brilliant relationships. Love always wins. My child's teacher had a baby with the Head of Maths and when they brought it in for show & tell the children all cheered. Let's have more cheering.

Romantic relationships in most workplaces are possible and prevalent but they require caution, care and delicacy. Especially at the outset.

If you are considering a fledgling work romance, here are some thoughts (caveat: these do not apply to every profession; if you are a Catholic priest, or a prison officer, sorry but you'll need to look for guidance elsewhere):

- Check any guidelines in your organization about this topic
- Be aware that if you date someone you work with, proximity might be convenient at first and catastrophic in the aftermath of your break-up
- Don't use work resources to facilitate your love life (email, expense account, the bed in the medical room)
- Always behave professionally even if you have a *beyond* professional relationship with someone; remain respectful of your colleagues who might be reluctant to become voyeurs to your escapades (which is fair enough)
- Protect your privacy; don't discuss the details of your relationship with colleagues
- Always use a condom

Sexual harassment

The total opposite of gorgeous, reciprocated, respectful mutual attraction is, of course, sexual harassment. Recent research by the TUC and the Everyday Sexism Project found that one in five women in the UK had experienced unwanted sexual advances at work.[13] But as Caroline Criado-Perez points out in her essential and electrifying book *Invisible Women*, a lot of the data on this subject is patchy and unreliable. The data gap on sexual harassment exists worldwide. 'The UN estimates (estimates are all we have) that up to 50 per cent of women in EU countries have been sexually harassed at work. The figure in China is thought to be as high as 80 per cent.'

Sex discrimination and sexual harassment legislation has been part of most equality law for several decades. In the UK, the Equality Act 2010 defines harassment as 'unwanted conduct related to a relevant protected characteristic, which has the purpose or effect of violating an individual's dignity or creating an intimidating, hostile, degrading, humiliating or offensive environment for that individual'.

This includes things such as:

- Indecent remarks or inappropriate comments about your body or your clothes
- Intrusive questions or comments about your sex life
- Sexual demands or requests for sexual favours
- Promises or threats concerning your employment conditions in return for sexual activity

- Looking or staring at a person's body
- Display of sexually explicit material
- Physically touching, pinching, hugging, caressing, kissing
- Sexual assault
- Rape

In the US, sexual harassment is classified as a form of sex discrimination that violates Title VII of the Civil Rights Act 1964. Guidance on when sexual harassment can occur under the Act, includes, but is not limited to:

- The victim as well as the harasser may be a woman or a man; the victim does not have to be of the opposite sex
- The harasser can be the victim's supervisor, an agent of the employer, a supervisor in another area, a co-worker or a non-employee
- The victim does not have to be the person harassed but could be anyone affected by the offensive conduct
- Unlawful sexual harassment may occur without economic injury to or discharge of the victim
- The harasser's conduct must be unwelcome[14]

Rape and sexual assault are criminal offences. Safe and confidential advice, sources of information and emotional support are available from the police, who often have specially trained officers, or independent organizations such as rape crisis centres.

Perpetrators at the less extreme end of the spectrum

can try to dismiss their behaviour as 'just banter', but sexually charged aggression is the same as bullying – it's about power. It's serious and it needs to be taken seriously. And it's not just about old-school chauvinist behaviour from a few relics either, as Caroline Criado-Perez observes:

> One survey of senior-level women working in Silicon Valley found that 90 per cent of women had witnessed sexist behaviour; 87 per cent had been on the receiving end of demeaning comments by male colleagues; and 60 per cent had received unwanted sexual advances. Of that 60 per cent, more than half had been propositioned more than once and 65 per cent had been propositioned by a superior. One in three women surveyed had felt afraid for her personal safety.

If you find yourself in an uncomfortable scenario, or if you receive inappropriate advances, then, as with other issues of misconduct, keep a note of the incident, find out your organization's policy and seek help from HR or an external source like ACAS to help you resolve the situation.[15]

That's the form, but the truth is you might need to be more reactive than that. In the moment, confronting your harasser isn't easy. But it is a good idea if you feel safe enough to muster or yell a firm retort. It may be that their perception of harassment is not the same as yours and they didn't realize you found their behaviour offensive (it's still offensive and that's why it needs saying out loud). Or it may be that they're used to 'getting away with it' and need a fierce reality check.

- Speak clearly, loudly and as confidently as you can (frankly, the louder you are the better)
- Describe the behaviour and say that you want it to stop
- Ignore any attempts to trivialize or undermine what you say
- Don't apologize or dilute your complaint with social niceties like smiling – clarity is key

If you don't feel able to confront the situation as it is happening then you should talk to a close friend, a colleague or union representative. Note if anyone was witness to the incident. Keep a record including dates, times and location when any improper behaviour takes place (you may need this information if you make an official complaint). Sometimes it can be hard when you're at the centre of a situation to determine whether something is wrong or not. Talking it through gives you instant context and perspective. Perhaps you thought you were being oversensitive until you told your flatmate, whose horrified reaction made you reconsider? Or the opposite.

Some instances can be dealt with yourself with a few firm sentences, but if someone persists after you've confronted them, you need to tell your employer. The burden shouldn't rest on the employee and employers have obligations to prevent and reduce sexual harassment.[16] Most employers have a formal procedure for this. Your employers have a responsibility to provide a workspace free from harassment, so they should investigate your complaint and deal with it properly. Take someone you trust with you to any meetings (it's useful to have another pair of ears) and take notes so you can refer to them later. If the situation can't be resolved internally, many countries have systems to make a legal claim against the employer, which would be dealt with through the relevant legal route, such as an employment tribunal or civil lawsuit.

There is a whole other book to be written about how to navigate all this (I say that not as a dismissal; these issues deserve space that I cannot give them here), but know that everyone has the right to work without fear or manipulation, in an environment free from sexual predators or a power balance born out of gender or *any* inequality. We are not there yet, but you will work in a world where calling out behaviours that have too long gone unchallenged is normal, not scandalous. And that is something to celebrate. See Section 5 for more on making challenges and complaints. There are several organizations that provide support, including ACAS and the Equality Advisory and Support Service in the UK and the Equal Employment Opportunity Commission in the US.

The opposite of sex, drugs and rock and roll in the workplace

Regardless of your personal attitudes towards drink and drugs, you'll inevitably be surrounded by contrary or alternative perspectives. The adage 'work hard, play hard' is still bandied around as a genuine motto about balance, but we all know that it's possible to work hard without playing hard, or indeed that you might just prefer to play hard with people who aren't colleagues. Depending on the type of work you do, you'll have different degrees of separation between work socializing and leisure socializing. I've always worked in spaces where there is a wafer-thin, barely discernible line between the two (about the thickness of a wine glass), and that's fine if your job is about selling ideas and being on photoshoots. It's less fine if you're a surgeon or a social worker.

How you navigate the crossover between work and play depends on where you're working and your personal preferences and beliefs. In some organizations a glass of warm Prosecco at the leaving do might technically be gross misconduct but everyone is drinking it because it's Barry's birthday and no one is going to fire you unless you down fifteen glasses and start stripping on the photocopier.

These days there is generally less pressure to conform to party-hard cultures or to take part in organized fun. Even industries that have historically cultivated ladsy, heavy-drinking atmospheres are wising up to the fact that not every employee wants to live like that. I imagine one day we'll look back at the way we integrate alcohol and work and it will seem as shocking as the idea that people once smoked at their desks.

However, don't underestimate the importance of being able to socialize, even if you reject ALL the recreational substances on offer. Research across generations in the US found that younger people are less likely to seek out friendships at work and socialize with work colleagues,[17] and while I respect the distinction between work and life, it's worth pointing out what you might miss if you don't ever do the post-work pub shift or join the company football team. I don't know a single ful-filled, well-adjusted adult human who doesn't count in the list of their very best friends several people they met at work. My work friends have become godparents, accom-plices, inspirations and lifelong loves. One of them even married my sister. And they would not have graduated an inch beyond vague work associates if we hadn't spent time together away from the office. It's that simple. I don't want you to skip it.

I could give you lots of strategically scheming reasons why you should cultivate close relationships with the people you work with, and how socially snazzy situations are a shortcut to that, but this isn't a book about the rabid pursuit of 'success' at work, it's about being decent and happy there. So I urge you to form a connection with work that allows you to enjoy it outside office hours, even if you do not engage in alcoholic or chemical accessories to fun. Go along anyway and have a good time with a tonic water. No one will notice what you're not drinking, but they will notice if you're not there at all. They'll miss you.

Tech

Let's clear something up. Proclaiming you're a 'digital native' is stating the obvious and it makes everyone cringe. If you're born after 1980 you're a digital native. I'm one. Your boss is probably one. The gang's all here.

And because of that, it's not an indication that you're any more digitally talented than the next guy. It's not a badge of honour, it's a fluke of fate that you were born at the right time (perhaps). What does matter is demonstrating your skills in that space – which means showing you're capable, connected and innovative. Gone are the days when all you needed was a rudimentary understanding of a spreadsheet program. Now toddlers know how to text and kids come out of school coding.

Regardless of the date on your birth certificate, as a young person entering the workplace you are likely to be more conscious of new trends in tech, more confident applying them and better at tracking results. Embrace this; it's an easy way to make sure you quickly gain a reputation for being useful and (depending on the industry) occupying a niche.

Working with digital dinosaurs

Sometimes age is relevant. Before I disappeared off to do an internship in New York, I quickly showed my dad how to use email. It would be nice for us to correspond, I thought. But it quickly became apparent that he believed he had to press 'Send' after every single word, so I had to piece together his sentences from a thousand emails made up of one-word missives. It was painful.

If you find yourself working with people who find technology scary, be gentle. There's sometimes a real role reversal where your boss needs you to teach them – that's a massive opportunity so take it seriously and help them master new skills or overcome a fear of something unknown. If you can swallow your disdain, you'll prove yourself invaluable. And it's heroic, supporting your colleagues in new discoveries. It can be frustrating, though, and if you do a bad job (as I did with my father) it's actually you who will suffer the consequences.

Why your phone is not your friend (at work)

Many of us have phone dependency issues. A study found that we touch our phones on average a staggering 2,617 times a day.[18] We're used to having access to data, social lives and news 24/7 on demand and in our pockets. But when you start working full time that relationship has to change. Suddenly, you are not always available on that magical device. And it might take some getting used to.

Some people get a kind of physical anxiety when separated from their phones, proving how central they've become to modern lifestyles.[19] Instead of worrying about it, think of this as a useful moment to reframe your phone usage and redefine the boundaries. There are loads of benefits beyond a bit of separation anxiety:

- You'll sleep better: overexposure to the blue light from your phone disturbs your circadian rhythms, meaning you sleep less well[20]
- Your memory will work better: being able to access information instantly is rewiring our brains to be less good at memory and recall[21]
- You'll make closer human connections: even the presence of nearby phones negatively affects our intimacy with others[22]

Generally speaking, you should get into the habit of working in work time and doing everything else before and after. Yet a UK study found that 64 per cent of people say that their personal smartphone distracts them at work.[23] Sure, check your messages over lunch. Make and receive emergency calls. And, depending on the culture you're in, it may be possible to have a relaxed approach to your personal life encroaching on work time. But the bottom line is, if your boss thinks that you're prancing about on social media when you should be working then you have a big problem. Try to avoid that – once that opinion has been seeded it's very hard to turn it round.

Practical tips:

- Use the screen time monitoring on your device so that you can track your usage; realistically, if you're browsing other people's holiday pictures for two of your contracted eight daily working hours, you're probably not doing a great job
- Put your phone somewhere physically apart from you (especially if you need to concentrate hard – e.g. while writing or researching)
- Have a work phone and a non-work phone so you can separate and prioritize
- If you're worried about being contactable in an emergency, make sure important people (your parents, your partner etc.) have your work contact number and an emergency email address
- Turn off all but the most essential notifications, so you're not constantly distracted

But, as Cal Newport notes in his book *Digital Minimalism*, we need to move beyond quick fixes. The behaviours are ingrained within our culture. 'To re-establish our control,' he says, 'we need to move beyond tweaks and instead rebuild our relationship with technology from scratch.' We are deeply reliant on, and psychologically manipulated by, our phones. His philosophy of digital minimalism is a good guide, 'to focus your time on a small number of carefully selected and optimized activities that strongly support things you value, and then happily miss out on everything else'. If all this freaks you out and you think having less time with your phone is about denial, consider that the world's super rich are increasingly using their position to turn away from technology and re-engage in the real world.[24] For them, less screen time is itself an aspirational luxury.

AI and the future of work

At DeepMind we think of artificial intelligence as a powerful tool that can help us meet some of the world's greatest challenges such as climate change, access to water and curing disease. Similarly, AI will help people across all kinds of jobs to achieve greater things, to use their time more efficiently and to focus on those aspects of work that truly require the human touch.

THORE GRAEPEL, PRINCIPAL RESEARCH
SCIENTIST AT GOOGLE DEEPMIND AND FORMER
TEACHING ASSISTANT IN STATISTICS AT TECHNICAL
UNIVERSITY OF BERLIN

Just as communications technology changed the way we work a generation ago, so AI will transform the way *you* work. Thirty years ago, offices still held libraries of books and the best way of contacting a colleague was via their desk phone or by physically walking up to them and talking out loud.

It's not clear the pace at which AI will develop, but the potential of rapid learning by machines is already playing out in more personalization, greater productivity and significant advances in solving complex challenges. In the next few years some of your colleagues may well be machines.

We can estimate that between 10 and 30 per cent of (mostly unskilled or low skilled) jobs will be done by machines.[25] There are plenty of doom-laden predictions about robots replacing humans, but AI will create many new and different jobs too. In practice this means that the need for shelf stackers and accountants will decrease, while the need for engineers to build and maintain technology, coders or ethical supply-chain analysts will increase.

Economists think of innovations such as AI as either being a 'substitute' or a 'complement' to an existing job. A substitute does what it says, it takes over the job or makes it unnecessary, such as a long-haul lorry driver made redundant by the invention of self-driving vehicles. A complement helps the job holder do things more efficiently or better, and thus potentially increase the value of the job, such as a self-employed haulier who, as a result of the same technology, now has more time to do paperwork, planning, loading and unloading.

To get ahead of these changes, we need to invest in advanced technology and social and emotional skills, such as creativity and critical thinking.[26] And we will need to work in new, collaborative ways with machines. As H. James Wilson and Paul R. Daugherty put it in their *Harvard Business Review* article 'Collaborative Intelligence: Humans and AI are Joining Forces', 'the human-machine interface requires people to *do new and different things* (such as train a chatbot) and to *do things differently* (use that chatbot to provide better customer service)'.[27]

Far from a dystopian future, the transformational potential of AI could lead to dramatic shifts in delivering better lives for people, but our success in harnessing this opportunity will be based on learning how to work together well.

Social responsibility in tech

Technology undoubtedly plays a large part in our working lives these days, sometimes for good reasons, and sometimes less good. With over 2 billion people regularly using social media, many many people occasionally do daft things online. While companies are worried about someone from the press calling and saying 'That person who works for you, did you know they've got a second life as a porn star?' their responses for discoveries from your digital past should be proportionate. In other words, they shouldn't sack you for a swear word on Instagram five years ago.

Obviously, there are some unforgivable things that people have done online where they thoroughly deserve to be dismissed.

I spoke to someone who, while working for a major supermarket, decided to rearrange a pile of sugar bags into the shape of a big chair, which he sat upon and proclaimed he was the 'King of Sugar' on Instagram. As a result of this he was issued with a written warning by the company, who then withdrew it after he was encouraged to challenge their response as unfair. Just because you've done something silly online doesn't mean you accept potentially career-damaging criticism as a result. Just don't do anything too daft, or offensive; manage your privacy properly, and bear in mind that if you do let people at work follow you, your privacy settings won't help!

Technology at work can become invasive, and you need to remember you do have a right to privacy, and also rights to how data about you is collected, who has access to it and for how long it is stored. What you tend not to be told at school is that you have rights – basic freedoms that anyone is entitled to in law. You have a right to freedom of expression (as long as what you express isn't hateful) and a right to a life away from work. Employers can sometimes make use of technology to infringe on these rights and you are entitled to challenge this. You don't have to just accept it because 'that's how things are'. It might be that this is as simple as an employer expecting you to reply to emails and take calls twenty-four hours a day (which they cannot do unless you agree to it); however, it might also be something scarier, such as monitoring your computer screen while you work or even tracking your movements.

I was in a large chain café a while ago and noticed a surveillance camera behind the counter, pointing at the staff. So I asked why it was there, and no one knew, they had just been told it's there to 'monitor performance'. I asked if they'd given permission to be filmed at work, they didn't think they had.

While an employer is entitled to do this as long as you consent, they have to tell you precisely who has access to this information and where it is stored. You might also think about whether you would like to work for someone who thinks it is OK to track your movements all day. Before you agree to these sorts of things, ask them why they are doing it, ask them who has access to the data, and do not accept anything you haven't agreed to. You have rights – it's just that sometimes, when it comes to digital technology, employers forget that.

ANDY PHIPPEN, PROFESSOR OF SOCIAL RESPONSIBILITY IN IT, UNIVERSITY OF PLYMOUTH, AND FORMER SYSTEM ADMINISTRATOR

Meetings

Why do we have them?

In an age when nearly everything can be done remotely, why do we still have meetings? Priya Parker explains it in her book *The Art of Gathering*: 'We gather to solve problems we can't solve on our own. We gather to celebrate, to mourn and to mark transitions. We gather to make decisions. We gather because we need one another.'

There are some things that are just better face to face. You can't beat good old-fashioned human interaction. Even with travel and inconvenience – meetings are still often the most efficient way to get complicated things done, to prioritize, to reach consensus or a conclusion or to overcome a stalemate.

And yet you'll be surprised to find that the overarching view in work about meetings is eye-rolling, ennui and disdain. As Aaron Dignan points out in his book *Brave New Work*:

Organizations aren't just overloaded; they're addicted. No daylight exists on their calendars, just back to back meetings as far as the eye can see. Their every need – for information, for decisions, for feedback – seems to call for a meeting. They hate them, but they can't quit, because there's no other way to get things done.

What's going wrong here? In short, as Priya Parker notes, organizations are so used to holding a meeting as the default way of getting anything done, they choose to have a meeting rather than pausing and thinking about what would be the best way to communicate. As a result, you can find yourself not knowing what the bloody hell you're all sitting there for.

So, what's a good meeting?

In his book *The 7 Habits of Highly Effective People*, Stephen R. Covey effusively describes a perfect meeting:

> The release of creative energy was incredible. Excitement replaced boredom. People became very open to each other's influence and generated new insights and options. By the end of the meeting an entirely new understanding of the nature of the central company challenge evolved . . . Differences were valued and transcended. A new common vision began to form.

To get there, Covey refers to three levels of communication:

- Defensive: where there are winners and losers
- Respectful: where compromises are reached
- Synergistic: where new ideas are found for both sides to win – and even if it's not possible, there is a wish to find it

To get this right, teams need to work together well. So what does that look like?

MEETINGS

A good meeting:

- Starts on time
- Is attended by the fewest number of people needed, who pay attention, are invested in the outcome and empowered to make decisions
- Has a clearly defined purpose and an agenda (which ideally everyone has seen in advance)
- Isn't a free-for-all (i.e. people are well prepared, materials are ready and no one is just winging it)
- Is led by a person or people who know what they're talking about and are prepared to make some decisions
- Ends with clear, achievable outcomes and next steps
- Has plentiful snacks

A bad meeting:

- Is scrappy from the start
- Could probably have been done as a conference call or an email
- Includes lots of people who have no obvious reason for being there and who don't say anything
- Follows a messy, unstructured pattern and might involve shouting
- Finishes late
- Ends with an all-pervading sense of disappointment and no collective idea of what happens next
- Everyone is irritable because of low blood sugar (no snacks)

Reading the room

The art of 'reading the room' is something that you'll develop with experience. It's about intuition, interpreting the unsaid, assessing atmosphere and instinctively understanding the psychological temperature around you. Having the natural superpower of empathy helps but you can learn to read a room too. The most important thing is to watch and listen. Observe body language; a forced smile vs a generous one. Notice the pitch of the conversation: tense or trusting?

Being witness to lots of interactions or meetings helps; another reason why it's important to sit in on as many as possible early on. Eventually, you'll be able to recognize the exact moment when someone buys into an idea, or the second they disengage from whatever narrative is playing out around you. And if you can identify this stuff, you can counterbalance or try to redirect the conversation accordingly.

There are some extraordinarily powerful people who don't have the ability to read a room and it's amazing to watch them flounder, in spite of their status. President Trump springs to mind – watch him with international Heads of State, misjudging the mood and standing in the wrong place. He remains the same, entirely himself and often at odds with the environment. It's agonizing.

Conversely, people who are good at reading the room put everyone at ease, effortlessly manipulate the people around them through diplomacy, energy and charm, and in doing so create spaces that are ripe for cooperation.

There is something perversely enjoyable about watching someone who's really bad at all this – someone who continues to bulldoze through without noticing the wincing around them. But if you find yourself in the presence of a person who's brilliant at it, really watch and learn – when it's good, it's almost balletic.

Host, host, host

Q: Why have a meeting when a phone call would do?
A: Refreshments.

Honestly, it's one of the only reasons people actually turn up. Whether you're the youngest in the room or the CEO, pour the tea. Waft the biscuits about. Settle everyone in just as you would if you were at home hosting a party. A party, with a tight agenda.

Speak, then enjoy the silence

You're at your most powerful when you speak with clarity and then shut up. It's tempting in a public forum (particularly if you're nervous) to continue speaking to fill the silence. But just as in interviews, even if that first sentence is stunningly impressive, it can be undermined by a rambling, incoherent second half. Practise articulate sentences with firm full stops. And don't panic if the silence is deafening – it often means that people are taking in what you've said and are processing it. It's more often a compliment than a judgement.

Get your pen out (how to take notes)

Someone very important once told me (in a tone that suggested he was doing me an honour, dishing out Grade A wisdom), 'I never write things down in meetings. It looks weak.'

Obviously, this is complete nonsense.

Why use up all your brain remembering things when you could simply write a note, freeing your mind for more inventive or exciting activities? For me, writing notes is essential; part to-do list, part aide-memoire, part for the record.

Because this is the way *my* brain works, I'm always deeply worried by people who don't write stuff down. Just as, when I order in a restaurant and the server simply stares at me, it makes me nervous. Are they paying attention? How are they going to recall all this? What about my side order of fries?

You might not need to faithfully record every meeting, but it is useful, especially at the beginning, to get into the habit of making notes. Why rely on the accuracy of your memory when a pen and paper can be your insurance? When you start in a job you're taking on so much information, a daily sensory overload of newness – so do yourself a favour and write things down. Taking notes is also a sign of respect and professionalism – your boss will feel a lot more confident if you're jotting down key points and actions from your conversations. If you're being briefed on a task, it's particularly important to look like you're listening and taking instruction seriously. Believe in the reassuring presence of stationery.

In some professions, the recording of conversations is an essential skill or a legally binding document. In those cases you'll most likely be taught how to 'minute' meetings, or at least be made aware of the house style. For the rest of us, here's a simple guide to taking notes:

- Get organized: write down the date, title and objective of the meeting and the names of the people attending it (I draw a table and write the names around it in the order they are seated to help me remember who said what)
- Don't write down everything verbatim; write down the actions – the tasks that have been given to a person or a group of people – and then enough information about each point being made
- Create a symbol for your actions (that way you can flick through your notebook later and tick everything off); put relevant initials against other people's actions
- Don't be afraid to clarify and ask key questions of the meeting: when the action is needed by or who specifically needs to do what
- Go back over your notes regularly – things that don't make sense initially will become clearer and you'll form new connections between conversations; it's pointless taking notes if you never read them

If you are suddenly asked to take notes in a meeting with no forewarning (this happens a lot when you are the new recruit), do your best and write down more than you need, you'll have a chance to edit them later. Minute-taking is not a time to demonstrate your creative literary style. Instead ask to see a previous set of notes before you start transcribing your scribbles into something shareable – there will usually be a set style or format that you are expected to present the minutes in.

How (and when) to be the most junior person in the room and still pipe up

It's all too often the case that people are desperate to get into meetings because they think lots of important decisions are being made there. Then, when they are given the chance to attend, they are desperate to get out, having found that the rambling forum is not the power-house they expected.

So how do you get what you want from meetings? Firstly, ask yourself some questions:

- Do the people round the table direct or gatekeep resources that I need?
- Will I or my team be affected by the outcome of this meeting?
- Do I have specific knowledge or a unique perspective that will be relevant to the discussions?

If the answer to the above is yes, then you might want to get an invite or at least a chance to comment beforehand and learn the outcome after. If you're in the room, think ahead about the things you want to raise and write them down to refer to in the meeting.

There are a hundred ways a meeting can play out. But if you want to get what you want as the most junior in the room:

- Speak through the chairperson – a muted low hand up or a nod to the person chairing the meeting while another person is speaking should do the trick; the chairperson will usually respond and come to you in due course (NB in meetings with no official 'chair' there will still usually be someone in charge; often it's not the most senior person but the one who most 'owns' the project or the team, so treat them as if they were the chairperson)
- Make your comment a 'build', i.e. refer to a comment that has already been made and add another point to it or mention a challenge to it

Learn to chair, fast

Chairing a meeting requires a different set of skills from participating. Depending on how formal the meeting is you'll need to adapt your approach. The seminal 1896 work *Robert's Rules of Order* set out the parliamentary protocols of the United States, and while your meeting may not need all this detail, the principles are broadly applicable:

- The meeting needs to have enough of the right people attending
- There is a chairperson to host the meeting and make sure it runs well
- Someone takes a note of the meeting
- People speak one at a time
- The actions need to be agreed to by the majority

Your job as chairperson is to make sure everyone can play their part as well as possible:

- Check everyone knows everyone else and, if they don't, ask for a brief round of introductions: name, role, organization
- Set out the purpose and the ideal outcome of the meeting
- Set out the agenda, if there is one, or if not, agree one quickly and then work through it
- Take comments one by one
- Make sure everyone gets their say – some people will naturally talk a lot and others will stay quiet but may well speak if asked (if they have nothing to say, reassure them and quickly move on)
- Hold everyone to time
- Keep everyone focussed on making useful and relevant comments
- Clarify the agreed actions and the next steps

Remember – when you are asked to chair, everyone has tacitly agreed to accept that you will set the standards for the meeting. Don't be relaxed or silent, take responsibility for the outcome – you've been asked to help the group reach a solution to a specific problem and they want you to make sure they get there. Practise chairing small meetings with close peers and you'll soon be ready when it's your turn to step up.

Conference Calls

When people are joining remotely, there is a whole extra level of etiquette, frustrations and benefits. People are likely to dial in from other offices or from home, so you could have dogs barking in the background and participants not paying attention and catching up on emails or painting their toenails because they know you can't see them.

If you're chairing, you'll need to regularly check in with people so they can have their say or adjudicate if people are talking over each other. If you are participating in the meeting, then help the chair by indicating in good time when you want to come in with a comment – it will make it all run smoother.

Make sure you have the phones set up and your dial-in details in advance – it's exasperating trying to join a call by tapping in a random succession of numbers to no avail, forgetting that you needed to dial '9' for an outside line. Once you're in, you're more than likely to find the first ten minutes of each call will be echoes on the line, automated voices announcing people's arrival (and dropping out again) and roll calls. It's painful.

I once worked with someone fresh out of management

school who consistently said to me, and to me alone, 'Let's do a conference call.' Don't say that. It's a phone call; two people talking on the phone is just called a phone call.

Video Calls

Like conference calls, the main thing you'll need is preparation and patience. These calls are even more likely to suffer from disruption as connections drop or slow down. And remember, we can see you, so be dressed and point your camera at something neutral. If you're freelancing or working from home, choose a spot where there's no drying laundry in the frame. We don't need to see your damp underpants.

Language and Jargon

Beyond the hateful and unacceptable (racist, sexist, anything -phobic) there are also other styles of speech that are to be avoided. These fall into a few distinct categories; all are equally infuriating. Here's a short guide to what not to say (and why):

- **Things that are not words (e.g. ideation, diarize, solutionize)**
  We don't need made-up words, the world is full of real ones. Loads of them available, for every occasion.

- **Things that are words but whose usage is twisted to the point where they may as well not be (e.g. cross-functioning synergies/ multi-stakeholder-value-chain-partnerships)**
Does 'synergy' mean 'cooperate'? Why 'reach out' when you mean 'Hello?' Are 'optics' just 'what it looks like'? – scrambled language like this means no one knows what the hell you are talking about. As columnist Marina Hyde says, 'What is this fucking word salad?'

- **Things that someone once said and everyone thought it sounded snazzy but no one actually understands (e.g. Open the kimono/Eating our own dog food/Let's create a strawman/When we unpeeled the onion/Getting to Yes)**
I imagine the first time someone unpeeled the onion, their colleagues thought it was pretty cool. But these sayings sound worse with every repetition. And, just like my excessive use of hair straighteners in the early 2000's, we will look back on these moments and cringe. In fact, we already do.

- **Things that are just wrong**
Man Up – As author Matt Haig says (on Twitter), 'Man up? No thanks. Manning up isn't a call to strength. It's a demand of weakness. It's saying if you express your vulnerability it will make me feel uncomfortable . . . It's not stoicism, it's conformity. Never man up.'

Dear Sirs – For all the obvious reasons (otherwise known as women).

My Bad – This is an admission of messing up without taking responsibility for it. And it's always heard as a non-apology. Admit fault, apologize and suggest a solution instead.

Can I just say? – Don't ask permission to speak – earn it by making valuable contributions.

Oversharing – Please don't tell me about your allergies in forensic detail. Thank you.

- **Things that were once fashionable but are very unhelpful (e.g. killing it/destroying the competition/epic fail)**
  By the time you've dragged your sorry carcass into work on public transport during rush hour, everything feels like a battle. So let's not use the language of war all day too. It's so tiring. It doesn't benefit anyone, and it normalizes aggression. It also implies that if you're not 'killing it' then you're not doing a good job and that's bollocks. Plenty of people have brilliant careers and deeply fulfilled lives without ever once 'crushing' anything.

In summary, language is the most powerful tool you have to communicate and to make yourself understood. Every time you open your mouth to speak, make it meaningful (or at least funny). It can be difficult, if you're in an environment where jargon is the dominant mode, not to catch the habit but try to resist falling into the trap of talking lots while saying nothing.

And what do you do if your boss operates like this (endless, complicated, urgent and demanding sentences that are impossible to decode)? Respond with clarity, cut through with total simplicity. A straightforward 'what would you like me to do?' can usually help strip things down to the essentials. Be aware that sometimes people use this style of speech to hide behind (perhaps it's insecurity, perhaps there's a lack of genuine understanding); what might present as total confidence can in fact be a symptom of the opposite.

No one enjoys a conversation made up entirely of industry-speak or business bullshit, it's an exhausting and empty register. Instead, make your sentences buzz without the buzz words – it's far more powerful to speak plainly.

Emails

We're swamped by emails. The constant ping, the endless admin of reading and responding – it can sometimes seem like a relentless stream of consciousness from your colleagues.

Whether you like it or not you're going to send and receive a lot of emails in your working life. So here are some basic rules on how to write them well . . .

Learn how to write

Before emails, there were memos. Shaun Usher's brilliant book *Lists of Note* includes an all-staff internal memo written by the father of modern advertising, David Ogilvy, which sums up best practice neatly. This list was written in a different era, but its principles are as fresh and true as ever:

The better you write, the higher you go in Ogilvy & Mather. People who *think* well, *write* well.

Woolly minded people write woolly memos, woolly letters and woolly speeches.

Good writing is not a natural gift. You have to *learn* to write well. Here are ten hints:

1. Read the Roman-Raphaelson book on writing.* Read it three times.
2. Write the way you talk. Naturally.
3. Use short words, short sentences and short paragraphs.
4. Never use jargon words like *reconceptualize*, *demassification*, *attitudinally*, *judgementally*. They are hallmarks of a pretentious ass.
5. Never write more than two pages on any subject.
6. Check your quotations.
7. Never send a letter or a memo on the day you write it. Read it aloud the next morning – and then edit it.**

* *Writing That Works: How to Improve Your Memos, Letters, Reports, Speeches . . .*, by J. Raphaelson and Kenneth Roman.
** This one might not stand the test of time, everything is too fast now for it to apply. UNLESS you're angry or emotional, in which case force yourself to wait. Never send these emails in haste.

8. If it is something important, get a colleague to improve it.

9. Before you send your letter or your memo, make sure it is crystal clear what you want the recipient to do.

10. If you want ACTION, *don't write*. Go and *tell* the guy what you want.[28]

If you really must write an email

Most people will thank you for not sending them an email. But sometimes getting a job done, following up from a discussion, showing progress or just remaining visible will require it.

How to structure your email

An email should be as easy to read as possible. Barbara Minto from the management consultancy firm McKinsey & Company spent a lot of time analysing the hallmarks of a perfect email. She distilled her analysis into a book, *The Minto Pyramid Principle*, and it works.

For the most part, when we communicate we set the scene, tell the story and finish with the punchline. The pyramid principle turns this on its head. So, put simply, an email should run like this:

- The situation, the complication, the question, the answer
- The supporting arguments

- The things that support your arguments
- The conclusion

Apply this to our subject matter and what you get is:

- Young people aren't getting the insight they need to go to work, because no one is telling them about the things they need to know, so we're going to write a book that has all this useful stuff in it
- We can get lots of amazing people to give advice; we can find a great publisher; we reckon we can write it
- There's a gap in the market for this book; we plan to write well and we want to put the time in
- Let's pitch this book

Add to this what you're going to do and what you need the recipient to do:

- If you think this is a good idea, I can pull together a summary of ideas
- Then it would be great if you could review it and feed in your ideas
- Then we can submit it to the publishers we think would be interested
- Maybe we could do a podcast too?

And what not to do
(courtesy of the Productivity Ninja)[29]

- Forget to put in a clear subject line
- Copy in lots of unnecessary people
- Use txt spk or abbrevs (obvs)
- Leave out your other contact details
- Mark it as urgent when it isn't
- Not start with a salutation
- Forward sensitive messages or data
- Email and then phone to see if they've got it

Some of the best people I've worked with expertly take control of email chains. They'll update subject lines, summarize conversations, take people out of the cc list when they no longer need to be there. Tread carefully with this, but don't just be a passive recipient.

Treat email with respect. If you need something done quickly or sensitively, or it's particularly complex, it's probably not the best medium. Pick up the phone.

To kiss or not to kiss?

I'm a really keen kisser. I'll 'x' my colleagues, my neighbours, the plumber and all invoices. I'm aware that this isn't normal and that, in most places, an overfamiliar sign-off is frowned upon. I can 'Lucy x' away because I work for myself and most of my working correspondence is intimate enough to cope with a bit of affection. But generally speaking, it's probably safer to resist adding your love to the end of every email. At best it's unprofessional, at worst you can give entirely the wrong impression to Simon in the accounts department.

Email signatures

At the bottom of your email you need a signature. This usually includes:

- Your name and job role
- Your contact information, including your work phone number
- Work-related social accounts and your organization's website
- A legal note including any disclaimers, confidentiality notices and data-processing requirements

Most organizations have a set format for these that you will use. If you are working for yourself, make sure you know the legal requirements for email footers.

Beyond email

Many organizations are abandoning email and turning to shorter, faster and more collaborative ways of communicating.

Tools like Slack allow you to have less formal conversations at greater speed. The tool creates 'channels', smaller subchats on specific topics that people can move in and out of. Rather than having to bring people up to speed when they join, participants can scroll back and find out what's happened so far.

The popularity of these tools is spreading as people seek to drop the quasi-formality of email and want to work smarter and with greater flexibility. Open channels cut across hierarchies, giving everyone the opportunity to interact, whether they are full-time employees or remote workers on a specific project. As Anna Pickard, creative director at Slack, explains: 'People spend their whole evening messaging outside of work. And when they do they sound like themselves. We are helping create a bridge between how we communicate with friends and family and work.'[30]

The transparency of the format means that there's nowhere to hide, which is a great thing for anyone who has wasted time politely nudging the office shirker to do something – if it's posted on an open channel it will be obvious if they don't take action. And don't get carried away with too informal a tone or hog the limelight, the same rules of appropriateness and courtesy still apply.

Tools like Slack or Zoom (for group calls) save time and encourage flexibility. So for people who work outside standard office hours or who want to manage their time more creatively, they're a game changer.

Speaking and Public Speaking

According to some studies, fear of public speaking ranks higher than fear of death.[31] So if you feel nervous about the prospect, you are not alone.

Here's some thinking that might help:

Overcoming nerves

Nerves can be a good thing. A little bit of adrenalin never hurt anyone. But if you find yourself debilitatingly nervous, try some of these tricks:

Yoga-esque, considered breathing – Focussing on the exhale – breathing out fully, until you feel empty and then allowing a long natural breath in.

Identify your tension points and release them – So relax your jaw, release your shoulders back and down, roll your neck. Do this regularly not just before the presentation but the day before, the night before, the morning of . . .

Grounding and alignment – Stand with your feet hip-width apart, weight going down through your spine, spread through pelvis, down through legs, and out through the firm base of your feet.

Power pose – Watch Amy Cuddy's TED talk on how this works and adapt it for your own purposes; practise quietly somewhere public and don't think about how silly you sound or feel.

Old-school tongue-twisters – Saying 'red leather, yellow leather' several times or repeating consonants going through the alphabet ('bbbbbbbb, cccccccc, dddddddd') will help to prepare your mouth for speaking out loud and guard against tripping over words.

Never present on an empty stomach – Few things make nerves worse than caffeine and no carbs.

Getting your message across

If you're making a speech or a presentation, the key is CLARITY. Minimum number of words for maximum impact.

There's usually a terrible first draft of a speech and a brilliant third one. Write it early, test it on your colleagues, practise out loud in front of a mirror. You'll get used to what works, your cadence and emphasis. You'll trip up and tweak it and trip up and tweak it again. Reading out loud forces you to edit what you don't need and refine what you do.

The pauses are important – they give your audience time to digest, to catch up, to consider. So practise them too.

The more nervous you are, the more you have to rehearse. It's that simple.

Death by slides

Visual aids need as much thought as the words in your mouth. Less experienced speakers tend to cling to their presentations like life rafts, using too many slides and placing too much importance on the screen itself. Instead, use slides carefully and only where you need them.

Avoid recreating your talk in slide form by dumping your words into the presentations – your audience will spend their time reading the screen and not listening to you. Instead, use slides only to genuinely support your argument with images, graphs or illustrations. You are the presenter, the screen is your support.

Be as familiar with the slides as with the script so that you don't have to turn your back to the room to talk it through. And consider some of the alternatives like Prezi that take a different approach to presentation.

Remember that death by PowerPoint is a very real risk; around about slide twelve people start to lose the will to live.

Further Resources

Chris Anderson, *TED Talks: The Official TED Guide to Public Speaking* (Houghton Mifflin, 2016)

Jenny Blake, *Pivot: The Only Move That Matters is Your Next One* (Portfolio Penguin, 2016)

Brené Brown, *Daring Greatly: How the Courage to be Vulnerable Transforms the Way We Live, Love, Parent, and Lead* (Penguin, 2012)

David A. Carbonell, *The Worry Trick: How Your Brain Tricks You into Expecting the Worst and What You Can Do About It* (Little Brown, 2016)

Dale Carnegie, *How to Win Friends and Influence People*, new edn (Vermilion, 2006)

Stephen R. Covey, *The 7 Habits of Highly Effective People: Powerful Lessons in Personal Change* (Simon & Schuster, 2005)

Matthew Crawford, *The Case for Working with Your Hands: Or Why Office Work is Bad for Us and Fixing Things Feels Good* (Penguin, 2010)

Caroline Criado-Perez, *Invisible Women: Exposing Data Bias in a World Designed for Men* (Chatto & Windus, 2019)

Amy Cuddy, *Presence: Bringing Your Boldest Self to Your Biggest Challenges* (Little, Brown, 2015)

Aaron Dignan, *Brave New Work: Are You Ready to Reinvent Your Organization?* (Portfolio Penguin, 2019)

FURTHER RESOURCES

Liz Fosslien and Mollie West Duffy, *No Hard Feelings: Emotions at Work and How They Help Us Succeed* (Portfolio Penguin, 2019)

Barbara Minto, *The Minto Pyramid Principle: Logic in Writing, Thinking and Problem Solving* (Minto, 1978)

Cal Newport, *Digital Minimalism: On Living Better with Less Technology* (Portfolio Penguin, 2019)

Priya Parker, *The Art of Gathering: How We Meet and Why It Matters* (Portfolio Penguin, 2018)

Jean M. Twenge, *iGen: Why Today's Super-Connected Kids are Growing Up Less Rebellious, More Tolerant, Less Happy – and Completely Unprepared for Adulthood – and What That Means for the Rest of Us* (Atria Books, 2017)

Shaun Usher, *Lists of Note* (Canongate, 2014)

For national and international advice on drugs and alcohol misuse:

Addaction: www.addaction.org.uk
Alcoholics Anonymous: www.aa.org/
Drinkline: 0300 123 1110 (UK)
FRANK: www.talktofrank.com

For advice on mental health:

mentalhealth.gov
mind.org.uk
samaritans.org
stonewall.org.uk

Support for victims of rape and sexual assault:

rainn.org
rapecrisis.org.uk

Section 5
The Bad
Days

U p until now your focus has been on making yourself desirable and hireable. You've run the gauntlet of rounds of recruitment and then you've been outstanding and keen in your shiny new role. So far, so good. And then you hit a bad day. It's not an endless upward trajectory – sometimes stuff goes wrong. This section is about getting good at the bad days.

Even if you love your job, you'll have bad days. If you don't love your job, you'll also have them. And not necessarily more of them, but you might find you have fewer nice days in between to balance things out. And that's a slog.

But whatever the ratio, you can't expect a trouble-free existence. Plans go awry, personalities clash, mistakes and misery are part of the human condition – so naturally you'll find them in plentiful supply in the workplace. Do not despair.

There are lots of strategies that can ease the pain – dodging bullets, rolling with the occasional punch and picking yourself up again are all essential skills, and in this section we'll share suggestions and coping strategies.

Importantly, please try to remember that even if

you are having a horrible time, you can still be learning something – building resilience, understanding and grace. These are hard-core, impressive characteristics and you get to take them with you when you move on – so even the worst experiences have a silver-lined second life. That might sound like poor compensation when you're struggling, but believe me, it's so true and so useful in the long run. What you learn about yourself in times of trouble is yours forever, even when the trouble has passed or been left behind and forgotten. Try to keep track of the times you thought you couldn't keep going and look back on them once the dust has settled. Just knowing that you are capable of carrying on when you've been challenged beyond what is comfortable will embolden you the next time and for all the times after that. And there is no purer pride than the feeling of 'triumph in adversity' – it's so special it should be available in pill form.

But until then, here's how to get it . . .

When It All Goes Wrong

When you really fuck up

When you first begin any job, it's very hard to distinguish between little mistakes and giant, reputation-ruining fuck-ups. It all feels the same because you don't yet have enough context or nuance to know for sure what's important. So any error, of any scale, seems disastrous.

My first proper boss, a managing partner at the

advertising company J. Walter Thompson, taught me the importance of this very early on in my career and I've been grateful to him ever since.

I was a junior, baby grad working on the Kellogg's account. I was happy because we'd finished our formal graduate training (a scheme so famous it's often credited with the comedy title The University of Advertising) and were now real live worker bees on proper pieces of business. And I was especially happy because I was working on a massive FMCG brand that was a household name. It was nice knowing that when you talked about your job at parties, everyone had heard of Kellogg's. I hadn't yet had a meeting with Tony the Tiger but I felt sure I'd run into him soon and no doubt we'd have a jolly good laugh. I had very little responsibility, my tasks were all supportive or administrative – lots of couriers, lots of note taking, endless walking about the building. And I had layers of account managers, account directors, board directors, business directors and managing partners above me. It was great.

And then everyone left.

There's an inevitable moment in your career where you will be thrown in at the deep end. This was it for me. For some inexplicable reason in an otherwise ordered and organized world, everyone was off at the same time. 'Leave' had been double booked, someone was sick, there was a shoot on and suddenly it was just me and the managing partner, Enda McCarthy – a man so senior that I'd only been in a room with him once when he gave us kids a motivational lecture with the punchy title, 'How to Make the Board Before You're Thirty'. He is a bouncy, bold and brilliant man and I was terrified of him.

Important people are often busy people. And so it transpired that on the day I got something spectacularly wrong and didn't know what to do about it, the day that every member of my team was AWOL, the day during which the clock kept ticking and my heart kept pounding and I paced the corridors trying to find a solution or a someone to confess to . . . was the same day that Enda McCarthy was entirely unavailable in a very important meeting, for five whole hours.

So I waited. I waited at my desk, emailing my grad friends about the crisis I was the chief protagonist in (they didn't know what to do either, we were all novices). I waited through lunchtime, when I made a desperate call home (they didn't know what to do, what with never having worked in an ad agency). I waited outside the meeting room, ear to the door, hearing snippets of very important meeting (I considered bursting in and throwing myself to the floor and begging for mercy, but pulled back at the last minute). I waited outside his office, repeating the story again and again to his PA until she got bored and let me sit inside his office. I waited there while the enormity of the situation swelled further in my mind as I gazed at the selection of Hockneys on the wall and remembered how important this man was. I had a very serious think about making a run for it and going back to waitressing. And still I waited.

By the time he appeared I was so strung out and weak from exhaustion that I was actually sitting on his desk in what I think was an attempt to be as close as possible to the source of my salvation or my doom but which must have looked pretty weird when he finally entered the room and found me there. 'It's Lucy isn't it? Did you want to see me?'

'HOW COULD HE BE SO CASUAL?' my brain screamed as I tried to calmly convey the severity of the situation, my voice quavering in panic. I know I told him that a tragedy of almighty proportion had befallen us and that it was all my fault. I apologized for ruining the company. He tried his best not to smile and then said the following words which I will never forget: 'Lucy, one day you will fuck something up and it will cost this corporation tons of money to bail you out. But today is not that day.'

And I cried with relief.

It's testament to his kindness that, now, I cannot remember what it was I'd actually done wrong. It was, it turned out, completely insignificant. He made a phone call, then and there and things pretty much carried on as usual. Except that for the next week he kept an eye on me and made himself available daily, in case I needed to check anything.

And I made the board before I was thirty (twenty-eight to be precise, but I don't want to show off).

The point is, every career has moments like these. At the start it's hard to know how to make a judgement about the severity of the situation or how to read the reaction to it. The most important thing when you make a mistake is to admit it early. Take responsibility and seek advice at exactly the same time. Fuck-ups in their infancy are a lot easier to deal with than those that have been left to grow to a monstrous size. And it's much harder to confess to something that you've allowed to become truly catastrophic.

When we are under pressure or panicking it's sometimes tempting to hide behind sharky language or to fudge things. A straight-up 'sorry' is more powerful than any variation. And it's far more elegant than those non-apology statements you sometimes read from politicians or love rats in the newspapers. You'll be forgiven sooner if you say it simply. And once you've apologized fully and clearly, you can stop – it gets very irritating very quickly.

It's tempting to try to exonerate yourself by shifting the blame (to the actions of another person, a system or a failure elsewhere that you weren't responsible for). And you might be vulnerable to falling into the trap of being given the blame by others, including perhaps your boss. Be clear about what you did (or didn't do) and then take the opportunity to genuinely learn from your mistakes.

When the shit hits the fan, take the following steps:

- **Tell someone, as soon as you realize your error**
  NEVER try to cover it up, you're creating a nightmare for yourself; if you've accidentally killed someone, don't make it worse by trying to ineptly bury the body

- **Seek advice and act quickly to rectify and recover**
  Uncomfortable though it may be, make sure you actually say 'I'm sorry' – those *exact* words

- **Don't try to shift the blame**
  It's better to take responsibility for your actions even if there are mitigating circumstances or other colleagues are implicated

- **Take a note of what happened in the fallout**
  Write it down in case you need to recall this information or the sequence of events in detail if things kick off, if there is an investigation or the story changes

- **Discuss what you learnt with your boss**
  Not only will they appreciate your self-awareness, they'll like that you want to get better next time

The April 2011 issue of the *Harvard Business Review* dedicated a whole issue to failure, which gives us some useful pointers.[1]

In Amy C. Edmondson's article 'Strategies for Learning from Failure' she identifies a spectrum of reasons for failure, from those deserving of blame (deviance from a prescribed practice, inattention, lack of ability) through to praiseworthy (taking actions in uncertainty, testing and exploring). Edmondson's article shows that it's important to distinguish where the failure lies and to understand that there are usually multiple reasons behind it. In my example, was it me making the rookie error or the error of whoever was responsible for scheduling everyone's leave that left me in that situation? Once you accept that the conditions for failure are complex, and the cause wasn't deliberate, a different conversation can open up.

Similarly, in my case, how Enda reacted to the situation reflected a lot about how he saw failure. In the same issue, Ben Dattner and Robert Hogan's article 'Managing Yourself: Can You Handle Failure?' diagnoses eleven personality types for dealing with blame, from the person who overreacts to every minor mistake to the blame avoider, blame denier and the blissfully unaware, to the self-criticizer and the person who accepts more blame than they deserve. It's impossible to predict how those around you will react, but it's important to remember that there is no one correct perspective. We all mess things up (and not just at the beginning of our careers), so it's worth taking time to consider how you react to failure to help you understand how to deal with it.

Office Politics

Avoiding ending up on the wrong side of office politics

Just as every workplace has a culture, so every culture has its own internal politics. And it's wise in the beginning to observe as much as you can before you get involved. Every environment has different rules, plots and subplots, old feuds, scores unsettled and complex characters. So don't just steam in.

Some people are instinctively good at playing politics. They seem to effortlessly negotiate hierarchy, ego and jeopardy, and they're not stressed by the snakes-and-laddersness of that kind of career. They use their

emotional intelligence to cajole and coerce, and influence an organization by making sure their carefully
crafted image is maintained. It's a dark art.

I am not one of those people. I prefer a policy of
being close to talent as opposed to close to power and
that's always worked out in my line of business. I'm also
uncomfortable with the ruthless nature of office politics;
it seems to reward characteristics I don't possess myself
and don't prize in other people. But even if I don't enjoy
it, I do understand the draw of power and why people
choose to pursue proximity to it.

And in some industries, you don't have a choice.
Politicians, journalists, estate agents, lawyers and bank-
ers consistently rank as the lowest trusted professions.[2]
There are many considerate, clever, altruistic individuals
in all of these jobs, but the structures of competitiveness
and incentives to be economical with the truth can lead
to nefarious behaviours.

Equally, office politics can be the outcome of a toxic
culture:

- If trust is low or information is not shared,
  people will search for the truth through gossip
- If hitting targets is so highly valued that the
  means of hitting them is irrelevant, people
  will tread on others to achieve them
- If low performance is not visibly tackled,
  disengagement will set in and negative
  sentiments will spread

- If bullying and blame shifting is rife among the leadership, those who report to them will copy their behaviour

So here are some things to think about before you get yourself immersed:

- Office politics should come with a risk warning. Even if you are flavour of the month one minute, you can be unfashionable the next – especially if you've built your reputation on politics rather than actual output. Make sure your relationships are built on real, credible things (shared effort, collaboration, trust etc.), not just on appearances.
- Beware of aligning yourself too closely or exclusively with one person, particularly if they're very senior. Sure, they might be your ticket to promotion, but what if they leave (or are fired) tomorrow and you only had that one friend in a high place? That's a lonely position to find yourself in. Don't neglect your peer group or your close colleagues – even if they seem insignificant in comparison to the shiny attentions of some big boss. Collaboration is a far better use of your energy than sycophancy.
- Don't be seduced by playing the game or proximity to power and forget to learn the basics. In any work you have to nurture your craft, and having the right connection is never a substitute for that.
- Avoid gossip. Like sexually transmitted diseases, gossip is something you want neither

to give nor to receive. It might be a temporary thrill in the moment, but afterwards it leaves a nasty legacy. It doesn't benefit anyone and it has a corrosive quality that can do you real damage. Because if you get into the habit of occupying that conversational register, you so easily spring to mind when other people start gossiping, and then the gossip is about you.

- It's not always the case that being good and working hard will result in happiness and hard cash. I once decided to resign when I learnt that a man I knew to be a talentless, duplicitous, slimy little weasel had been promoted to MD. Not because I hated him (although I did), but because I knew that if that behaviour was considered suitable for management material, I didn't want to be management material. Again, we come back to values – I had a moment of clarity then when I realized that I could only succeed there if I compromised myself, and I chose not to. Sometimes you need to compromise, but if that unsettles something important to you, or makes you feel dishonest or unsafe, do something else.

What does it look like?
The hallmarks of workplace politics

All right, so how do you recognize politics and how should you respond?

Ultimately, workplace politics boils down to people.

And the chief protagonists are, as Bob Sutton, professor of management science at Stanford, an expert who has written widely on the topic, calls them: assholes.

Thankfully Sutton has written an excellent guide to handling them, called *The Asshole Survival Guide*. But before I reveal his advice on how to deal with them here are some of my favourite nasty behaviours observed over the years:

Game playing

The hallmark of the narcissist, this tactic keeps control centralized around one person. You're subject to a draconian application of the rules in some cases but then not in others. A laid-back attitude to deadlines unexpectedly becomes oppressive micro-management. Things that were high priority yesterday are insignificant today (and vice versa). Goalposts are moved as a way of creating and disrupting control. Deeply personal feedback praises and criticizes at random, chipping away at your confidence. And you're left with a constant feeling of instability (which is the opposite of growth).

The best thing to do here is to clarify the rules (repeatedly if you have to) then document them diligently and build a wider network of trust to gain some perspective.

Passive aggression

This behaviour is usually masking a hidden anger or jealousy, so see it for what it is. They make mistakes while claiming to be the victim. Huge drama is created from minor challenges. You're pointedly ignored or left out of an event. You'll know very little about them, while they plug you for information. They're your best friend in person, while sniping through the rumour mill and complaining to your boss about you in secret.

Keep calm, don't get drawn into their world and keep conversation open with others. Don't spend too much time analysing or worrying – it might in the moment feel aimed at you, but this is often a behaviour that defines a person-ality type and is therefore more about the aggressor than the target.

Being screwed over

The curve ball that's a bid for one-upmanship or a desperate attempt to cover up personal failure. Your resources are pulled away at the last minute. You're buttered up before the meeting to make a radical sug-gestion with the assurance that they'll have your back, and then, when the moment comes – silence. You're given impossible tasks by a person who then delights in watching you flounder. They're all signs that you are being manipulated.

Keep your distance – emotionally and physically. If you have to work with them, be cautious, politely offering to give them the chance to pipe up in the meeting or agree shared responsibility.

Problematizing your projects

Your work is met with reductive, negative comments. You're told that something you've produced is irrele-vant. That what you thought was a new idea has been tried before and didn't work – or that it sounds good, but will fail in practice. You're left feeling stupid and embarrassed. Often this response has nothing to do with you, they're just drowning in work and can't take anything else on (and aren't any good at saying no), they could be burning out, bereft of ideas, or perhaps unwilling to relinquish control.

If you need this person to engage, arrange to meet, reframe their comments as useful critique and find out their reasons for caution – the truth often comes out quickly in a private conversation and there might be some changes you'll need to make. Or, if it's pernicious, bring in other people to help think through the problem, building a coalition of support for your ideas.

Achieving their goals at your expense

The classic asshole move. They've held a private meeting with your boss and taken the work and resources you want. They bullishly plough on, ignoring your helpful comments. You're barged out of the way and they take the glory. And you're left with the 'what have I done to deserve that?' feeling.

Don't get drawn down to their level, find a way to move on – it's more likely than not that this behaviour is visible to others who will help support you. Channel Michelle Obama – 'When they go low, we go high' – and go really stratospherically high.

Limiting information

Simply not telling you the stuff you need to know. Creating an environment where you can make a fool of yourself, or are not privy to the essentials of the situation. This risks you being caught out or tripped up.

And it's ultimately to the detriment of the work, wasting everyone's time.

Find new routes for information and ask your boss for advice rather than complain. Openly ask for understanding of areas that are shadowy. 'I'd love to understand more about X' is a frank but non-confrontational conversation starter and hard to ignore without sounding like a shit.

Project fear

This is the full-scale, emotionally draining onslaught. It's worst-case scenario-ing everything. Creating a sense of impending doom or the expectation of your own personal humiliation. It's energy-sapping and eventually becomes a self-fulfilling prophecy.

Honestly, the best thing I can suggest here is to laugh (I know, that's not very helpful). Harbingers of doom talk in hyperbole and invite tragedy – they're not grounded in the real word. The more ridiculous a statement, the funnier you should try to find it.

Manipulation

The attention-seeking one, the one who cherry-picks the best jobs, the one who cosies up to the client and keeps you in the backroom. They're obstructive and demeaning, but everyone seems to love them. They're what Bob Sutton calls 'strategic jerks' and they're the worst kind.

It's important here to check if you're encouraging the behaviour or whether everyone feels the same. Have some choice, careful conversations to see how thick the veneer of adoration from others really is. And take the long view – think ahead to where you'd like to be in three months or three years – it's unlikely you'll have a career ahead that means you 100 per cent have to work with this person.

You'll probably realize, as you come to the end of this list, that workplace politics is utterly exhausting. I'm exhausted writing it. It stirs trouble and fosters anxiety. It's worth saying that often the people who thrive on this are people for whom work is everything – they may be creating drama at work because of the absence of it elsewhere in their lives or because they're feeling out of their depth or threatened by you. It might look like a demonstration of power but it's often born out of feelings of insecurity or inadequacy. Or their private life may have its own challenges and it's playing out at work. Maybe they believe that success will be the outcome of these behaviours.

Or maybe they just like being an asshole? Sometimes remembering that can make you feel a bit better about being a victim of someone else's crisis or scheming. Remember, also, that if you see this behaviour, your colleagues see it too. And they probably don't like it much either.

Broadly, Bob Sutton's advice is as follows:

- Don't be fooled into thinking things are better than they seem or that it will get better with time. Often, the best thing to do is to get yourself out of the situation
- If you can't quit, keep your distance; Bob recommends a minimum of about 25 feet

- Keep your emotional distance too; reduce your time with assholes as far as possible
- In the short term, lay low if you have to; there's always a lot to be achieved, so do it elsewhere, without them
- Keep focussed on the future and the happy days ahead when you don't have to deal with them
- Be charming and positive – 'petty tyrants' crave your negativity to reinforce theirs
- Tackle them in a private conversation – but only if you think you have enough support and other options to fall back on if it doesn't turn out well
- Be patient, document and build allies; over time, the problem person may be sidelined or moved on[3]

Perhaps most importantly, check *you're* not the asshole. Are you interrupting people because you think your comments are more important? Are you jumping in and taking the credit? Do your jokes belittle others? Are you ignoring the feedback you're getting because you are convinced your way is the only one that works?

If you're doing any of these things, stop it.

Beyond the asshole

Kevin Dutton, from the Department of Experimental Psychology at Oxford University, has studied people whose cold detachment plays out in the workplace – for better or for worse (depending on where you stand in relation to them). You may meet more of these people in work than you think. Dutton's 2011 'Great British Psychopath Survey' found that this personality type was closely associated with professions that required a level of detachment: lawyers, journalists and surgeons. For a compelling analysis of this, read Jon Ronson's *The Psychopath Test*, although be warned it may make you suspicious of your colleagues.

How to play the game without playing the game

If you have a distaste for politics or just aren't very good at it, simply being aware of the strategies and principles will help guide you even if you don't fancy joining in.

There are, however, a few basic things that are worth trying, even if you want to avoid a full *Game of Thrones* backstabbing situation.

- **Try to impress influential people**
  This is obvious: perform at your best when your boss or their boss is watching.

- **Take credit for your successes and promote that story**
  Self-promotion isn't easy but don't be shy of claiming results and rewards. Celebrate others too – publicly thank people and put them forward for accolades. When you have a team success, make it count and be grateful to the key players (not just in your head, say it out loud).

- **Talk about 'We' not 'I'**
  Be a credit to your team and share in the highs
  and lows. The management guru Jim Collins
  puts this beautifully when talking about good
  leaders, who 'look out of the window at success,
  and look in the mirror at failure'. Get that
  embroidered on a scatter cushion, pronto.

And if you want to protect yourself from the ebb
and flow of political complexity, make sure you have
one solid primary relationship. Ideally that's with your
boss, but if your boss is a nightmare or you find it hard
to connect with them (more on that later in this section)
then find someone else. Another line report? A head of
department you can legitimately approach for mentorship or advice? Someone you trust and who can help you
when you get caught up in something that isn't about
your performance. Someone who can help you neutral-
ize a situation or swerve it completely. Allegiances can
be useful and protective, so align yourself with people
you admire on principle as much as anything else.

IMPORTANT: Do not confuse complaints with office
politics, it's not always the same thing. If someone com-
plains about you or criticizes your performance, you
really might have done something plain wrong or need
to improve in an area. Don't immediately assume it's part
of a grand plot to destabilize you and derail your entire
career. Usually a criticism is pretty straightforward –
but when we are feeling defensive, a conspiracy theory
can be a more comforting interpretation than the truth
that we could just do better. Resist that.

Complaints
(External, Internal)

In the workplace a complaint is often called a grievance. Which somehow sounds worse. It could be a concern raised about something you, a colleague, a client or a representative of an external organization has done – or the way in which it was done. It could be that a request wasn't actioned or a procedure wasn't followed.

A lot of jobs attract complaints: telesales or customer service, for example. Most of these complaints are dealt with through a standard procedure and resolved quickly. If they escalate and you are involved, make sure you know the policy and seek the proper representation.

Internal complaints can be complex and emotive. If things have gone so far that someone is demanding action be taken against you, then dialogue is essential. As hard as it may feel, be open rather than defensive, state your case clearly and rationally, work with your boss and the relevant internal teams to resolve the situation as quickly as possible. A bit of hurt pride is definitely preferable to disciplinary action.

Never be afraid to ask for an advocate or a chaperone in any 'hearing' kind of meeting. If you're stressed or worried, it's good to have a supporter and don't hesitate to ask for that even if it's not procedurally part of the process. Seek advice and document the proceedings carefully and make sure the record is clear and understood.

Crying in the Loos and Other Hideous Realities

I'm passionate about the topic of crying at work. The conventional wisdom is that if you cry at work it's the end of your career. It needs to be contained. And that especially if you're female you're going to be an emotional wreck. The biology is that women have shallower tear ducts, so their tears are going to come out faster than if a man is feeling the same amount of emotion. Also biologically, women tend to cry when they are angry or when they care. Men only tend to cry when they are sad or upset, so they are going to look at a woman who is crying and think: she's upset, this needs to be contained. But women express the anger through tears when a man would yell. So understand the impetus, maybe she's really angry or she cares a lot.

MOLLIE WEST DUFFY, ORGANIZATIONAL DESIGNER AT IDEO AND FORMER BAKERY SHOP ASSISTANT

The truth about bad days is, sometimes they're just REALLY bad. If you find yourself crying in the loos, sobbing into a wedge of soggy tissue so your co-workers can't hear your pain, then remember: *you have not failed at this work lark, you're just having a really bad day.*

There's a school of thought that says you should never ever cry at work because it is widely associated with being weak, unstable or out of control – the opposite of the qualities often valued in the workplace.[4] This is unhelpful, largely because if you do cry at work, it's probably not an active decision. We don't tend to think, 'I'll just have a small cathartic wail to take the edge off before I get back to chasing those Q3 invoices.' No. Tears tend to spring out, unwanted, at the most inconvenient moments. When you're angry. When you're bone tired. When you're asking for a pay rise. When you feel beaten. You can't schedule them in like a committee meeting.

People who think crying at work is a display of constitutional weakness are probably the same people who think business isn't personal (see more about this in Section 6). It is. It's personal because we are all people and there's no way of taking personality out of any encounter with other personalities. And why would we want to? And because it's personal, it can, at times, be emotional. That means the full works – from euphoria to despair. It's not a weakness to feel these things, it's human.

So although you shouldn't feel guilty about succumbing to tears, crying at work is honestly one of the worst experiences of adult life and I do not recommend it. It's likely to happen if you feel shitty about something and it's guaranteed to make you feel worse. And snotty.

It might sound terribly British but my instincts are always to cry in private (loos are good but also consider empty meeting rooms, back stairways and the stationery cupboard) and to do so for the minimum time with maximum effort to get a grip, hide the damage and get back out there. That's only because if something is bad enough to bring you to tears, it probably needs more examination and therefore more time than you can feasibly get away with in the course of a working day (locked in the loos/alternative room of your choice). Take it home, give it space, consideration, vent a bit and if you have to, cry some more. Think about why you feel like this and what can be done to change things for the better. And don't imagine that because a situation feels acute, it needs to be resolved quickly. If you are crying, you're processing lots of emotion and it's therefore not the best time to act. Often it's a sign you are temporarily overwhelmed. So wait until tomorrow (at least), sleep on it and see how it looks in the morning (the actual morning, after coffee – not the 3 a.m. version where everything is worse). Some days are just bad days; others are warning signs that we need to take stock and make changes, but it's impossible to know the difference when you're all snotty.

Imposter Syndrome

As women of colour, we often place unrealistic expectations on ourselves; if we aren't killing ourselves for the job, imposter syndrome kicks in and we are left questioning how we've gained a seat at the table which we've worked hard to acquire.

LIV LITTLE AND CHARLIE
BRINKHURST-CUFF IN 'RUSH'
FROM *RIFE: 21 STORIES FROM BRITAIN'S YOUTH*

Imposter syndrome sounds like a super-serious, critical condition when in fact it's more like a nasty cold – really common and always a struggle. Sheryl Sandberg famously described the feeling in her book *Lean In*:

> Every time I was called on in class, I was sure that I was
> about to embarrass myself. Every time I took a test, I was
> sure that it had gone bad. And every time I didn't embar-
> rass myself – or even excelled – I believed that I had fooled
> everyone yet again. One day soon, the jig would be up . . .
> This phenomenon of capable people being plagued by
> self-doubt has a name – the impostor syndrome.

It doesn't matter how successful you are, imposter syndrome can affect anyone. In fact, the more successful you are the more likely it is to strike. Fear of being exposed or being found out can threaten your confidence and your ability to perform. 'Far from being a realistic self-assessment, the imposter syndrome mind-trap prevents people from believing in themselves, to the detriment of us all,' writes Fiona Buckland in the *Guardian*.[5]

Both men and women experience imposter syndrome but how it feels can often be governed by gender. For men, fearing a negative societal response to showing weakness can mean they are less likely to talk about how they feel. For women, constantly undermining attitudes around them can exacerbate these feelings of inadequacy or, as Michelle Obama put it, 'that haunts us, because the messages that are sent from the time we are little is: maybe you are not, don't reach too high, don't talk too loud'.[6]

But even just knowing that those gnawing, self-critical feelings are a recognized phenomenon (identified in 1978 by psychologists Pauline Clance and Suzanne Imes) helps.

Buckland suggests:

Next time you fear being exposed as a fraud, name it for what it is – impostor syndrome. Notice the cascade of bodily sensations and automatic thoughts. Perhaps your stomach flips or heart pounds. What are the scripts that your mind starts running? They will be the same ones again and again, which makes them easier to spot: 'I'm useless and people will know,' for instance. Remind yourself that this is not reality, just your perception of it. To name impostor syndrome is to start to sense control over it and recognise that it is a complex condition that you can – with practice – overcome.

You may not be able to stop those corrosive thoughts from appearing, but you don't have to believe your own anti-hype. Talk back to it, tell it to pipe down. Marie Forleo has some powerful advice for overcoming the 'fraud factor' in her book *Everything is Figureoutable*, including the idea of starting a 'Hype File', where you 'stockpile compliments, thankyous and any comments from people who've said you have positively impacted them'. Use it to combat the destabilizing demons of imposter syndrome. And, yes, cheerleading texts from your best friends count.

Bad Bosses and What You Can Learn from Them

The only person who ever reduced me to tears was my first bad boss. I'm aware that the expression 'reduced me to tears' contains an implied judgement that under-mines what I just told you about not being ashamed of crying. But in this example, I WAS reduced – not only in that moment, but every day. Because this person's man-agement style was all about making people feel 'less'.

Less capable. Less confident. Less liked. Less them-selves. It was contrary and confrontational and careless and I really, really hated working for her. So did every-one else. As a team, we were united in that dislike but that didn't help much, because she also did a nice line in making everyone feel as though we were in competition with one another, so trust was in very short supply.

It was a micro culture, a subgroup within the wider organization with its own expectations and behaviours, defined by razor-sharp blame and low-level fear. And although it was creatively stagnant, emotionally exhaust-ing and absolutely no bloody fun, it wasn't that that made me cry. It's often not the big stuff that sets you off. It was when she asked me, in front of everyone, in a tone that suggested I was the lowest of the low and with the added flourish of a few finger clicks and a sweeping gesture towards the entire office, to 'TIDY UP, MISS CLAYTON [pause . . .] NOW!' as she stamped out of the room towards a posh lunch engagement.

Lots of things were my job. And lots of them were unglamorous. But I was not there to tidy. And I was not her child or her husband. I wasn't even the most junior person in the room (not that her tone would have been forgivable even if I had been any of those things).

I was so humiliated and mad angry at being spoken to like that, at being made to feel small in front of all my colleagues, that I walked briskly to the bathrooms and cried. And then I tidied up.

Bad bosses are really useful people. I have thought about that woman frequently over the last decade. Her daily micro-abuse of power, her fragile ego and her ever-visible jealousy are things that I vowed always to eschew. I have throughout my career actively strived to avoid being anything like her. She gave me a blueprint for everything I didn't want to be, and I am really grateful for that.

If you find yourself stuck with a bad boss, treat it as a training exercise. You can learn so much from sticking close to talent, you really can, but nothing teaches you more about who you want to be, at your core, than working for someone awful. It's not much fun, but it's a valuable lesson.

So how do you identify them? And more importantly, how do you know what to look for in a good boss? The Stanford professor Bob Sutton (who wrote the *Asshole* book) turned his attention to bosses in another book: *Good Boss, Bad Boss*.[7]

Characteristics of a bad boss

- Controlling, micro-managing, insisting on being copied into every email and attending every meeting and offering advice on areas they know nothing about
- Blaming others rather than taking responsibility
- Not listening
- Lacking the courage to act, fight for and defend you

- Having favourites
- Presenting the work of the team as their own
- Sticking to their vision and their plan even in the face of evidence they are wrong
- Sucking energy rather than inspiring with optimism and opportunity
- Kicking you for mistakes rather than helping you grow

When you meet a bad boss, you might think 'Why is this person so highly regarded when they're so horrible?' In companies where this is the norm, over-delegating, credit-stealing bosses can make themselves look good upwards or outwards for a short time. These bosses don't coach, defend, support or share success with their teams, they constantly instruct, stripping individuals of their autonomy, and usually slowly they lose their staff and reduce those left into numb, compliant underperformance.

Characteristics of a good boss

- Protect you from bad meetings, bad processes and toxic people
- Teach teams to have constructive ideas, healthy arguments and get on with implementation
- Are aware that they are in the spotlight and behave well
- Set a direction and then get out of the way, trusting their teams to do the work
- Get rid of troublesome characters and promote according to merit

Whether or not you like your boss as a person, a good

boss will get the best out of you. While there's temporary comfort in being told what to do, a good boss will give you the freedom to get on with it. They're people too, so don't expect them to be faultless all the time. They'll know that they have to be selectively unreasonable at times, dish out some of the boring but necessary work, and they will make some bad calls. But fundamentally, a good boss is trying to be a great boss.

In Sutton's view, after studying thousands of bad bosses, if you want to find out whether you have a good boss or a bad boss it's as simple as answering the question of whether you leave the meeting with your boss feeling energized or exhausted.

If you have a bad boss then hang around for a while and see the contrast, but not too long otherwise you'll get tainted and lose perspective. And before taking the next job, check out who your boss is, and size up their reputation as best you can.

Impossible Situations and What to Do About Them

The toxic workplace

Not all problems can be solved, not all relationships are worth working at, and it's important to identify situations that are beyond your power to fix. Sometimes we can think circumstances will improve, after a while, by doing things differently, through a change of personnel or by taking a new direction. At the start of your career workplace politics may seem a lot worse than they really are, and after a while you start to see that there are some things that are common to lots of workplaces that you'll just have to learn to put up with. But your time, integrity and enthusiasm are important and you mustn't waste them hoping the situation will get better, to no avail. If you find yourself in a truly toxic working environment you're better off out of there.

Nowhere is perfect, but if you see the hallmarks of shrill voices in meeting rooms, careless employees or lightweight recruitment processes, alarm bells should be ringing. You can stick with it and be part of making it better or cut your losses and exit (look later in this section for how to resign) – ultimately it's up to you. But there's not much to be gained from sticking around too long in a truly toxic environment.

The poisoned chalice project

Alongside cultures, colleagues and bosses, are projects. There are great projects with critical paths and milestones and innovation and learning and marvellous shared results. And then there are overly hyped, unclear, wandering, unaccountable messes. The latter can get hierarchies and resources and consultants thrown at them, and still not achieve much.

A poisoned chalice is easy to spot – as the name suggests, it's the thing everyone dreads, the project that's stalled a few times, the job that's fraught with difficulty or the one that involves working with the bloke whose breath stinks of mothballs.

Sometimes these projects have an aura of institutionalized teeth-gritting about them, jobs so grim that everyone takes their turn working on them and you just have to do your time. That said, it's still worth interrogating what's really going on at the beginning, when it's handed to you. Maybe the team has just run out of steam; maybe its reputation is worse than the reality. You might be fresh eyes on an old problem.

It's tempting to indulge in fantasies about turning things round and covering yourself in glory. But be realistic, if this is a crap gig, and a perennially crap gig, it may be better to adjust your expectations and take one for the team by getting it done with no fuss or bother. If you can take something from dreaded disaster to OK outcome, you'll still be considered a kind of hero because not all transformations need to be enormous.

Protecting Your Values

I am just doing this because I want to do this myself and I am one of the very, very few people in the world who actually can . . . then I think I should take that chance. There are always going to be people who don't understand or don't accept the united science and I will just ignore them because I'm only acting and communicating on the science, and if they don't like that then, what have I got to do with that?

GRETA THUNBERG, CLIMATE CHANGE
ACTIVIST ON BBC NEWS

We've talked a lot about values. They're easy to nurture when the conditions are perfect and are much harder to protect when the going gets tough. Many senior staff hours have been thrown at workshops to create company values, and in a way they provide a useful benchmark. It's good to know that as a Greenpeace employee you will be expected to retain your independence by not taking money from governments, corporations or political parties, and that your actions will be non-violent.[8] Values like these are a guidebook for your decision making and a check against your own personal morals. At the other end of the spectrum, Coca-Cola's value, 'Integrity: be real',[9] is much fluffier and God only knows what it means in a Tuesday status meeting.

Sadly, when budgets get tight and the pressure is on, or when a true set of values is revealed by actions rather than words, you can find yourself facing an unexpected ethical dilemma. Companies in trouble peel away from their values. After a damning report which concluded that Uber's corporate values had been used to justify bad behaviour, the company rewrote them (because presumably the original 'Always be huslin'' had led them to develop a covert system of identifying and circumventing local law enforcement?[10]). For example.

There is pressure on all of us to have values and to demonstrate them. Even if you find yourself in an organization where there is complete synergy with your own beliefs, where they are emblazoned on the walls in neon and written up in policies, you might still find yourself tested when what's happening doesn't *feel* right. These times are often unpredictable and it might only be after the event that a feeling of unease creeps in. Often the conflict of values plays out not in a heroic moment, but in the day-to-day, when you choose to back a call or not, to object or let something slide. Sometimes it's part of your job to protect certain values. Your team or role may have a mandate to champion a value, perhaps against the prevailing culture.

Some professions face daily ethical dilemmas. Codes of conduct, decision guides and principles, alongside training and peer support, give practical advice about navigating these challenges. The pressure can feel acute in the early days, so it is important that you are prepared for tough decisions and supported by your institution to make them.

The true test of how much you believe in something is if you're willing to fight for it even if it makes you unpopular, disruptive or unemployed. The Institute for Business Ethics surveyed people across eight European countries and found that 30 per cent of employees had been aware of misconduct at work, 16 per cent had felt pressure to compromise their organization's ethical standards and 27 per cent agreed with the statement 'My line manager rewards employees who get good results, even if they use practices that are ethically questionable.' Of those who were aware of misconduct, only half of them spoke up, with the main reasons for not doing so being because they felt action would not be taken, it might jeopardize their job, it was none of their business or that they might be seen as a troublemaker.[11]

If you do choose to speak up, it's best to be really straightforward, particularly if you are passionate or emotional and the atmosphere is heightened. That's a recipe for saying things you regret or struggling to articulate your opinion. Instead just be really honest. People are unlikely to challenge the stark simplicity of statements like 'that feels wrong to me' or 'I am uncomfortable with the ethics of this decision' – you've made your feelings known without being inflammatory or obstructive. What happens next is beyond your control.

When you feel you need to draw the line, first weigh up the pros and cons and try to understand why this uncomfortable thing is happening. If you feel you can, ask questions, rather than make accusations – you may find there are other factors at play. If you need to take it further, then build support with others and use the processes available to escalate your concern.[12]

Calling It Out

We've covered complaints and how to make them but what about the smaller AND the bigger problems? The daily injustices that aren't worthy of official procedure but which deserve to be flagged? Or the massive responsibility of whistleblowing? Here are some thoughts on how to approach these occasions . . .

Everyday discrimination and bias pervade workplaces, from the deliberate mansplaining and deprecatory comments about women catalogued in Laura Bates's Everyday Sexism Project,[13] excluding a deaf or hard-of-hearing employee from participating in a meeting, homophobic jokes and speculation about a colleague's sexuality, to assumptions about an employee based on racial stereotypes. It is often both subtle and deeply pernicious, and it's an area that the hard edge of anti-discrimination legislation can fail to reach.[14] In these cases, the individual suffers directly, the work suffers as staff become demotivated and disengaged, and the outcomes are worse for everyone. And experiencing this can have a significant, negative effect on mental health.

The team environment matters enormously when it comes to how confident you feel about speaking up. The good guys raise the standard of the whole one comment at a time, building on points rather than shouting them down. Google's Project Aristotle (a tribute to Aristotle's quote, 'the whole is greater than the sum of its parts'),[15] which set about identifying the essential traits of an effective team, found that in good teams, each member spoke roughly the same amount on every topic in meetings and the team members could tell how their colleagues felt based on their tone of voice, their expressions and other non-verbal cues.[16] A greater diversity in background and viewpoint contributes significantly to this. Diverse teams foster a supportive atmosphere and positive attitudes and behaviours in the workplace. As a result, employees feel more secure and positive about their work and their employers than those in a less diverse environment.[17] The outcomes are better for everyone.

There's a huge amount employers can and should be doing to consciously tackle everyday discrimination in their recruitment policies and workplace culture.[18] But calling it out often falls to individuals. To avoid being caught in the trap of inviting more shaming and being asked to lighten up or be told that it was all only office banter (NB more controlling behaviour there) it's best to, over time, build your case, saving emails, taking notes and building allies for support.

The antidote each one of us can take, every day, is showing civility in the face of unacceptable, disrespectful behaviour – basic, dignified habits such as saying please and thank you, being on time, being kind, showing empathy and offering to help.[19] Encouraging civility avoids the bystander effect of allowing poor behaviour to happen while others look on passively. The civil workplace challenges the tacit acceptance of disrespect, disregard and rudeness like arriving late without apology, talking over people, belittling others, spreading rumours, throwing tantrums and a whole bunch of other ways people think it's acceptable to behave towards each other in work that they wouldn't think of doing elsewhere. Each of us has the opportunity to tackle such everyday incivility.

Research by Plan International found that among girls aged fourteen to twenty-one, 66 per cent have experienced unwanted sexual attention or harassment in a public place. But each one of us can make girls feel less threatened by taking actions like standing in the eye line of the intimidating lecherous individual on the train. This sort of subtle move can make a big difference to the overall tone of society and begin to change its culture.

Whistleblowing goes beyond individual grievances and into public interest. In many countries whistleblowing is protected by law and tends to cover areas where an employee passes on information because they reasonably believe that they have seen evidence of criminal activity such as fraud or bribery, failure to meet legal obligations, endangering people's health and safety or damage to the environment.[20] Organizations should have whistleblowing policies which set out how a concern can be raised and there are often legal protections in place for the person making the complaint. If you whistleblow, it's important to consider how you can make sure that there is sufficient protection for you if the complaint takes time, is inconclusive or is not well received. As elsewhere, it is important to read the guidance available and discuss the situation with a relevant body such as ACAS in the UK, the Department of Labor in the United States or your union.

Not working

> *People often tell me that everyone on benefits is lazy and doesn't want to work, when the reality is so different*

SHONA COBB IN 'EXCLUSION',
FROM *RIFE: 21 STORIES FROM BRITAIN'S YOUTH*

Throughout this book we make reference to the reasonable adjustments or accommodations that can and should be made to make work accessible for disabled people and people with long-term health conditions, including mental-health conditions. In many countries these are legal requirements through legislation such as the Equality Act in the UK and the Americans with Disabilities Act in the US. As well as this, in the UK the government funds an Access to Work scheme which can pay for some adjustments that might otherwise have to be covered by an employer.

The social model of disability states that barriers are created by society, not because of an individual's impairments. For many people, working – at least in its 9–5 office- or site-based format – is not always possible for periods of time or at all. Not being able to work is not the same as not wanting to. There are many ways to play a part in society and the sooner we drop the stigma against those who can't work, the better.

Allyship

Listening to and understanding people of different backgrounds and identities is the essence of good leadership

DAVID RUEBAIN, CHIEF EXECUTIVE OF THE
CONSERVATOIRE FOR DANCE AND DRAMA, VISITING
PROFESSOR OF LAW AT BIRKBECK, UNIVERSITY OF
LONDON, AND FORMER TELEPHONIST

I'm white, British and privileged. I grew up in a culture where history was something taught to me as a narrative of ownership. My ownership. And the stories I read as a child were full of people who looked like me. Often they were locked in turrets and their power was limited to their unspoken sexuality – they certainly weren't perfect role models, but they were *visible*.

So my lived experience doesn't include discrimination

of the kind many people experience every single day. I can't claim to know how that feels, but I can do my best to be a robust and reliable ally.

Each of us constructs our identity from the multiple ways we intersect with the world. Our identity is never all one thing or only one thing. And each of us brings our identity to work.

As we've covered, bias (unconscious or deliberate) pervades workplaces, creating hierarchies of power and structures of exclusion, and sets up some identities to prosper and others to fail. And while almost all organizations will say in principle, and often publicly, that they value and promote equality and diversity, lots of the workplace policies, processes and mandatory training offered in the pursuit of these goals can make very little difference.[21]

What does work, however, is a continual process of engagement and development to remove the barriers that exclude people from marginalized groups and promote their opportunities. But this shouldn't just be the work of the HR department. We all have a part to play. We are all allies.

Allyship is a continuous process of developing trusted relationships with people from marginalized groups by learning about their lived experience and intentionally seeking understanding. It means challenging norms and using any power, platform or privilege to support those who are marginalized to be heard.

In work, we can all be allies by:

- Seeking to understand the power that your identity affords you

- Finding out how the systems in your organization exclude some identities and seeking to understand why and how this happens
- Listening and creating deep, thoughtful connections with people who do not share your identity, being respectfully curious about their identity and their lived experience
- Being accountable to others, open to explaining your decisions and the way in which you have sought to address bias
- Using inclusive language
- Using your power to call out discriminatory behaviours and champion equal rights for all

As Chelsea Kwakye and Ọrẹ Ogunbiyi say in the brilliant *Taking Up Space*:

Allyship requires you to have difficult conversations and call out racism in the communities we can't reach – in your own households, for example. It means educating people in your everyday life and finding ways to relieve our burden. It also requires understanding that sometimes we invite you into our spaces to listen, not to speak over us.

And don't try to take the lead, this is about freeing up space for all voices and being willing to help change the space you occupy.

Importantly, using comforting buzzwords is not enough. It's no use saying 'I celebrate diversity' in a room where only white middle-aged men's voices are heard (for example). So listen – who is being represented or underrepresented? Educate yourself to help make meaningful progress. Notice micro-aggressions that reinforce 'otherness' or 'difference' and challenge them. You can be a passive bystander, or you can be an active ally.

In his book *Everyone Leads*, Paul Schmitz quotes Michelle Obama reflecting on her work with Public Allies:

> We can't do well serving communities if we believe we, the givers, are the only ones who are half full and that everybody we're serving is half empty. Our job as good servants and good leaders is not just being humble, it's having the ability to recognize those gifts in others and help them to put those gifts into action.

Rising Above It

Not everything you disagree with is a threat to your values or the core of your being. Some things are just irritating or boring or not to your taste and they are therefore not things worth making a fuss about. Even people of strong moral fibre make compromises and suck stuff up sometimes, just never on the occasions where it really matters to them. You cannot consistently object to every little frustration or imperfection, because doing that totally ruins your credibility and it's a gruelling register to adopt for yourself (or to work alongside).

Work out what matters to you, and protect that. If you're a feminist (and if you're not, why not?) then you'll not tolerate behaviour that talks down or infantilizes

your female colleagues. If you're passionate about reducing single-use plastic, you'll be reviewing the practices
in the catering team. Or if you care about the Living
Wage you'll make sure the cleaners in your building
are paid properly. These topics matter, they are worth
fighting for. If you want to be heard when you're fighting, don't confuse the issue by spending the afternoon
putting Post-it notes on every putrid item in the shared
fridge. Sure, it's gross, but in the scheme of things, is it
that important? Save your energy for the battles worthy
of your time.

Time Off

Calling in sick (the rules)

Sometimes you will be sick. Anywhere on the spectrum
from a twisted ankle to a stint in hospital. We are all
sick sooner or later and it's always inconvenient. And
now you have the added problem of having to tell work
you're not coming in. The main thing is, don't ever be
tempted to put on a croaky voice or ask your mum to
do it. Beyond that it's about being honest and realistic –
your boss needs to know how to staff your absence, so
the more sense you can give them of how long you'll be
absent the easier it is for them to manage.

The culture of an organization often dictates attitudes
to sick days. If you feel a bit rough, you can probably
soldier on. If you're infectious, don't be tempted to
haul yourself into the office and make everyone else

sick – they won't thank you for your dedication to work; they'll wish your bacteria had stayed at home.

Most countries have some legal entitlement to sick leave and pay (but not always; for example it isn't federally mandated in the US), so check what you're entitled to, how much and for how long, and bear in mind that this may be pro rata depending on the number of hours you work. You'll often be expected to get confirmation from your doctor of your illness if you're away for more than a specified period. When you return to work you might have a 'back to work interview' where your boss can assess whether you are well enough to return and put in place any measures to help reduce future illnesses. Where work absence is related to a disability, this will need to be taken into account by an employer with reference to relevant equality legislation to ensure they are not discriminating against you.

Pulling a sickie

Are you faced with the prospect of relinquishing a precious day of annual leave when all your friends want you to be on that early Friday-afternoon flight? Is your heart sinking at the prospect of facing another gruelling desk day? Or are you just ruined from a late, late night? You may be tempted to phone in feigning food poisoning and just take the day off. But before you do, take some time to think why. Does it link back to broader issues around how you feel about the role? If you're skipping off on that flight, you may well be doubling the work of one of your colleagues that day. How does that make you feel? Will you spend the day wracked with guilt instead of swanning around celebrating? If you can't face the day ahead, is there anything about your stress levels or workload that needs a conversation? And beware the repercussions of getting caught out – the obvious sickies like the day after the Christmas Party are reputation wreckers at best, disciplinary proceedings at worst.

Duvet days

A duvet-day policy recognizes that there are some mornings when you just don't want to get out of bed. You don't need an excuse, or a doctor's note; you just play your duvet-day card.

As architect William Smalley says of his practice in London:

> I decided that everyone should have a duvet day every year. One day when they can just call up or text and say 'duvet day' and have the day off. You don't have to give any excuse. I don't mind what you're doing that day. You can have the worst hangover, you can have fallen in love, you can have eloped. I just think everyone has that day once a year and how awful that on that day you have to either lie and say you're ill or drag your sad bones into the office. And the unintended consequence of that is that every day you haven't deployed your duvet day you are making a conscious choice to go to work.

Remember, though, this is also about trust – if you take your duvet day on the day of your appraisal, before a massive deadline or at the pinnacle of a project you're leading – you won't be very popular.

Maternity, paternity and parental leave

Legislation on maternity and related leave, such as adoption, varies significantly internationally.[22] The provisions may include leave before and after birth or adoption, and may also be shared or allocated to both parents and carers. There are often legal deadlines you'll need to meet as well as duties for employers during the process, like keeping in touch during the leave period and legal entitlements to return to work.

Even if employers have robust policies, public attitudes to gender roles and work still cloud this discussion.[23] Nike reversed its policy of reducing performance-related pay for female athletes 'who decide to have a baby' after several complaints from female athletes who had their pay cut due to their pregnancy.[24] For many women, telling your employer that you are pregnant can cause anxiety about the future. As the six-time Olympic gold medallist Allyson Felix said, 'If I, one of Nike's most widely marketed athletes, couldn't secure these protections, who could?'

Agree a plan with your employer about how the arrangements will take place and have an open conversation with them to get the time you are entitled to, while making sure that the work you are responsible for can be well managed. Again, expectations differ about when you need to have this conversation and it's important to check the requirements relevant to your country and the policies of your employer. And remember, being pregnant isn't an illness, or a fireable offence.

Other absences

In many cases employers will allow you to take paid or unpaid compassionate leave, depending on their policy, for example, if a family member is sick or you need to attend a funeral. You may also be entitled to time off for things like jury duty. There may be opportunities to take leave for education or training too.

Don't necessarily expect your employer to know all the details, there are restrictions, entitlements and variations across all these areas depending on the size of company, local or national legislation and your job role, so if you are considering using these provisions, empower your-self by finding out what you're eligible for before you start the conversation.

Overwork, Stress and Sleep

There will be times when you're overstretched: some-times they'll be the best, most vivid moments of your working life; on other occasions, you'll be frazzled.

The importance of good mental health in the work-place is becoming more recognized, but continuing realities of poor working conditions, low pay, long hours, time pressures and unhelpful attitudes to mental health persist.[25] At the same time, the changing nature of work, with concerns about job insecurity, technology disrupting how we work (for better or worse) and emerging patterns such as the gig economy,[26] means that taking care of our mental health in work is ever more critical. Let's examine the spectrum of stress and what you can do to manage it.

Stress

We live in a world where competitive stressing out is a common (though baffling) habit. It's a perverse badge of honour to be SO STRESSED ALL THE TIME. It's almost as if you're not doing your job properly if you don't feel suitably strung out.

But let's keep things in perspective. You might be freaking out about an impending deadline but it really isn't life or death (assuming you aren't a heart surgeon or something similar). Being stressed is not always *all* bad. In fact, some stress can be a good thing; there are benefits to being under pressure, including a particularly delicious sense of fulfilment that comes only from having achieved something you imagined was almost impossible. As individuals we need to distinguish between the perversely pleasurable feelings of being addicted to toxic stress (which releases an opioid response in your brain) and manageable and positive stress (where we learn new things and gain a sense of achievement).

So let's start with an important distinction between the enriching experience of pressure, challenge and striving, and the negative effects of stress, which can be detrimental to physical or mental health when it is badly managed or prolonged.[27] Your brain is a muscle. We all know that if we keep running and running, it'll get harder and harder, and you'll get a stitch. Same with the brain. In Ruby Wax's book *How to be Human*, neuroscientist Ash Ranpura describes how techniques like mindfulness rest and relax our thinking network of muscles that make up the brain, giving it a chance to recover. But even if you've rested, remember that if you are in a stressful situation you essentially aren't able to use your prefrontal cortex, the bit of your brain that enables you to do higher executive functioning like problem solving. The harder you try, the less likely it is that you will be able to think straight. Which is why so many people end up shouting at themselves to work harder or concentrate and paradoxically make themselves less able to do so.

Sometimes we experience stress when we are promoted, when there's an important project on the horizon, or if we've been given a role we really yearned for. If you're never out of your comfort zone you may as well be a house cat. Out of your comfort zone you achieve greater things than, say, on your holidays.

So you'll see a lot of exhortations to 'get out of your comfort zone' or 'do something that scares you'. You may have had this feedback before at school or college. And for the most part it's a helpful nudge to remember your ambition and re-engage with what makes you feel happy and proud of the work you do. A change of scenery, a new challenge or an opportunity to learn may be what you need. If that's the case, it's time to have that conversation constructively with your boss.

If they agree, you can begin to explore a new area of work.

However, as Melody Wilding notes in her article for *Anxy Magazine*, your comfort zone is not something to dispense with before you're ready – it can also be an important space to manage your mental health.[28] In her article, Wilding questions the assumption that the stress of pushing yourself out of your comfort zone increases your performance. Instead, she suggests, we should follow the advice of the early twentieth-century developmental psychologist Lev Vygotsky and find the 'zone of proximal development'. 'This conceptual space, which is near the comfort zone,' says Wilding, 'allows for healthy and gradual growth, the way children naturally learn new skills'. So if you do want to get out of your comfort zone, be sure to make it a thoughtful process, and feel free to move back into it when you need to protect yourself and consolidate your learning. People who experience anxiety often tend to be perfectionists. If this sounds like you, you may find it harder to try something new or stretch yourself. Try to give yourself permission to not be perfect the first time you venture into new territory.

Holidays are important. So is rest, exercise and taking decent care of yourself. That's not all about vitamins and chia seeds – sometimes it's about reading a novel, or binge-watching *Ru Paul's Drag Race*, or cuddling a puppy. Learning ways to self-regulate, self-care and self-soothe affords you the strength to move beyond your window of tolerance.

It's important to learn to identify where stress comes

from and to recognize how it is affecting you. Some careers have greater risk of prolonged pressure leading to the build-up of stress. But in all jobs there may be long periods when workload increases or there are changes to the pace.

When you're new in work or in a new role, the additional pressure of lack of experience can heighten stress too. While you'll learn a lot from being thrown in at the deep end, you also need to build your confidence in the role. As we learn, we experience a range of positive emotions – enthusiasm, excitement, challenge and reward. But equally our risk-averse and negative emotions emerge, like low self-esteem, fear of failure, anxiety about failing in front of your peers or bosses, and plain old fatigue.

To help manage this, Dave Alred's book *The Pressure Principle* suggests converting some of these negatives into positive actions, like being realistic about the amount of time it takes to master new skills, concentrating on learning through the process rather than whether you will deliver the outcome, focussing on what you want to do rather than what you feel you can't do, and challenging your universal statements ('I always mess this up') with reflections on the times you improved. Practise little and often and reward your successes.

We can't all be stressed all the time and everyone's experience of stress is unique to them. Equally, if there are many sources of stress in your life outside work, they may play a part in how you cope with stress *at* work. You might manage for a few weeks, you might be able to get through a stint and come out on the other side a bit depleted and in need of some calmer weeks to compensate. If the pace is unrelenting or there is a negative attitude to managing stress where you work, or if you have a condition that makes dealing with pressure more challenging for you personally and you want to keep working through, here are some useful tactics for managing the situation:[29]

- During your working day, take time to pause and reflect, detaching yourself from the situation
- Try a quick mindfulness session – recounting and noticing your thoughts, but not judging or reacting to them; take a moment to abandon the internal dialogue about how your work will be received or the doubt about how you should spend your time with conflicting priorities
  This doesn't have to be long or indulgent, it's a recalibration, not a retreat
- Pace your day, moving between small, achievable activities and 'deep work' where you need to get into the detail and concentrate hard
- Form some habits like making a 'to-do' list at the end of the day, which will release you from today's work and give you a basis to start from tomorrow
- Identify the sources of stress (people, environment, role in the organization) and

    the sources of balance and organize your
    time to account for these; if there are personal
    stressors outside of work you should account
    for those too

It's not incumbent on you to manage these feelings away. Sometimes they're a red flag for a reason e.g. when someone at work is harassing you or doing something illegal or dangerous. And sometimes it's just a phase and it will resolve or recede in time.

The significance of sleep

In the early days, and when the pressure is on, eating well and getting a good night's sleep is essential. The rest of your life matters too, and if you're burning the candle at both ends that feeling of total exhaustion and despair at four in the afternoon probably has more to do with last night's booze and the post-carb crash of your lunch pasta than how robust your career trajectory is looking.

In a new job, you're being bombarded with fresh information each day and you'll need sleep both to rest and to consolidate your learning. In his book *Why We Sleep*, Matthew Walker points out that sleep is not only good for helping your brain recover, but for committing new learning to memory through a process of consolidation. He also shows how when we sleep our brains perform a kind of 'overnight therapy' where 'REM-sleep dreaming takes the painful sting out of difficult, even traumatic, emotional episodes you have experienced during the day, offering emotional resolution when you awake the next morning'. So as we sleep we decode waking experiences, adding greater understanding to the emotional response of others.

And when we sleep we open new opportunities for creativity. In his book, Walker recounts the story of Keith Richards of The Rolling Stones, who kept a guitar and tape recorder next to his bed in case inspiration struck him in the night, waking one morning to find that he had composed the opening verse to '(I Can't Get No) Satisfaction' in his sleep.

For work, the benefit of sleep is invaluable. As Walker puts it, 'The return on the sleep investment in terms of productivity, creativity, work enthusiasm, energy, efficiency, happiness, leading to people wanting to work at your institution, and stay – is undeniable.'

The cult of wellbeing

I am not a fan of the 'wellbeing' industry. Wellbeing is a word that's plastered everywhere (but is especially present on labels for expensive products or on saccharine Instagram posts) and it makes me suspicious. The problem with the cult of wellbeing is not just commercialization that trades on you feeling inadequate and improvable (although that is a problem) but that it manages to make 'me time' and 'self-care' seem more hard work than work itself. And that doesn't make sense to me. It's a different kind of pressure but it's still pressure – with an implied threat that if you're not committed to doing loads of wellbeing then you're not well. That's not true. You're doing fine.

So my advice is, before spending your hard-earned cash on alkaline supplements or Skype-enabled reiki healers – try to take a broader (I hesitate to type 'holistic') view. Real wellbeing is actually all about balance. Sometimes you'll work late, other times it's sunny and a Friday and the office is quiet and you'll bunk off and walk home through the park. It didn't cost you anything. One week you might enjoy yoga and benefit from thinking clearly afterwards, another week you might spend the class writing angry lists in your head or worrying you left the oven on and your flat is about to explode. Both types of yoga coexist, and so does the kind where you get dressed to go and then can't be bothered and order a Deliveroo instead. In fact, that's my favourite type of yoga.

Don't punish yourself for not living the most optimized, most impressive, most 'well' version of your life outside office hours. In the end, there's no Judgement Day where you win points for extra lunges, or a Lifetime Love of Kale Award. Wellbeing is about noticing what works for you and about being a bit careful or thoughtful with your time, energy and effort. And sometimes it's about doing nothing at all.

Overwork

Some professions have a reputation for overworking people and often it's the new staff members that bear the brunt of that. Adam Kay's book *This is Going to Hurt* recollects the brutal hours and colossal impact being a junior doctor had on his life: 'Reading back,' he says, 'it felt extreme and unreasonable in terms of what was expected of me, but at the time I'd just accepted it as part of the job.'

In some careers, you'll know in advance that you're signing up for long hours (sometimes that comes with financial compensation, sometimes it doesn't) and in others you'll have periods of pressure and fallow stretches of boredom.

In *How to be Human*, Ruby Wax reflects on the changing nature of work and how it is affecting our mental health: 'People used to leave the office behind when they went home. Now thanks to emails and smartphones, we never leave the office. The Japanese have come up with a whole new fatal illness *karōshi*, death from overwork.'

Before you freak out, please note that the following are *not* signs you're dying from overwork:

- You sometimes have to eat your lunch at your desk
- Some emails are unanswered some days
- You don't get round to everything on your to-do list by 6 p.m.

But if you're surprised to find yourself suddenly swamped, overwhelmed or working round the clock then there might be a problem. Ask yourself:

- Is my workload genuinely too big to manage?
- Is this an organization/time management problem and can I rearrange my working style and fix it myself? (See Section 3 for practical advice on how to organize your time.)

- Do I have enough resources to tackle all this (human, budget, time)?
- What are the structural barriers, such as heavy administration or lack of planning, that are causing additional work?
- Do I have the skills I need to tackle these tasks?
- Am I supported by my boss and my team?
- Is my working environment difficult, either the physical environment (e.g. is it regularly very noisy) or the personal environment (e.g. regular verbal abuse)?

And then decide what to do about it:

- Write lists of your workload, check it against your job description, raise it with your boss and talk about how resources could be allocated temporarily to support you and agree feasible workplans
- Be fair on yourself – you won't get it all done; prioritize urgent work that only you can do, and consider how you might be able to share out some commitments (be aware that this exchange goes both ways and that you may be asked to share someone else's burden in the future)
- Break down large projects into smaller ones that feel more achievable; try to balance out and vary the tasks
- Discuss possible actions to reduce any challenges in the environment such as distractions or noise; discuss a change in

working practice – a desk move might make
all the difference

This advice can be applied to most settings, but some jobs are going to be more flexible than others. As Adam Kay says about the reality of working as a doctor, 'it's a system that barely has enough slack to allow for sick leave, let alone something as intangible as recovering from an awful day'. While Kay recalls the balance of the good days (the colleagues, helping people and the feeling of having done something worthwhile), he also recounts the unspoken understanding was that he was always expected to return for work the next day, no matter how gruelling a time he had had. For junior doctors there's no recovery time.

Good people quite often feel overworked because they deliver their best performance and create opportunities within organizations. Because of this it can sometimes feel like it's your own fault. But resist this judgement. You just need to find a home in a place that can support and reward you and can harness that altruism and entrepreneurialism, rather than one that punishes you for it by draining you.

Work/life balance

If you're passionate about what you do then work is so much a part of your life that to categorize it separately would be like cutting off an arm. But that doesn't mean it should be all-consuming either; even the most hard-core, committed, visionary individuals need to take time off.

Some work requires a single-minded focus, but relentlessly working one thing can make you a joyless workaholic. Equally, if you're watching the clock every minute until you can slope off, you're probably in the wrong job. Sometimes you have to do jobs that you won't love, because it's about paying the bills. You won't always be able to find a fulfilling role wherever you are.

What's important is that, whatever you do, you are able to give your time and attention to all the parts of your life that matter. If you find them frequently cutting into each other, you're regularly skipping personal commitments, or waking at midnight thinking about what was said in the last meeting, it's time for some rebalancing. However, this may feel like it's easier said than done when the deadline is looming and you're still in work at 8.30 p.m. and your family and friends are waiting in a nearby restaurant to blow out the candles on your birthday cake.

Here are some tips on how to manage your time:

- Categorize your work into time chunks, rather than run multiple pieces of work concurrently throughout the day; shorten tasks to the necessary minimum amount of time needed to complete them
- Set expectations by being honest about your availability with your boss and team; you're creating greater cognitive load if you're checking your emails while you're running late for your evening class.

- Leave work surely and swiftly, rather than running the gauntlet of everyone trying to catch you just before you leave
- Plot out your play time just as much as you plot out your work time, giving it due credit as a structured part of your life, rather than thinking of it as an absence of work

New opportunities are emerging that reflect more networked and interpersonal ways of working. See Section 6 for more on these.

Burnout

In one of its most extreme manifestations, work-related stress can lead to burnout. The concept was first coined in the 1970s by psychologist Herbert J. Freudenberger to characterize the effect over time of factors that lead to total mental and physical exhaustion. Often beginning with people who set very high standards for themselves, burnout occurs when people work harder to meet those high standards while neglecting their own needs, avoid conflicts for fear of increasing their already unmanageable stress, and compromise the things that used to be important to them like friends and family time. Ultimately they become withdrawn, distant, detached and depressed. It's a warning to keep a check on ourselves before it's too late.

Knowing yourself well enough to know when to take a break (and how to manage that conversation with your employer without sounding like a snowflake)

As you gain experience in work, you'll start to understand more about what conditions you thrive in and what makes you feel strung out or stricken. And eventually you'll use this knowledge to help you make decisions about your career trajectory and the shape you'd like your life to take.

To use a very personal example: I now recognize that I can do about five weeks of intense, around the clock deadlines, pressure and performance. Within those five weeks I can juggle multiple projects and responsibilities and produce work at a certain quality level while also remembering to pick my child up from school and feed him occasionally. I don't enjoy this kind of regime, but it's doable, and if there's a clear end point I can knuckle down and deliver. But at week six, I become bad at everything. It's like a Cinderella deadline, the midnight moment where everything falls apart. I'm tired, and bored of the momentum. I become slapdash and my attitude starts to suffer. I know this because it's a theory I've tested over years of various kinds of working patterns. So I know that for those shifts to be effective I have to clear my social diary, go to bed early nearly all the time and plan something nice as a reward for getting through those five weeks. I'm big on rewards. And now, I try to never say YES to anything in week six.

Over time you'll learn your optimal working patterns. You might thrive at shift structures or crave flexible working.

There's a freedom that comes from knowing yourself well enough to protect your output *and* yourself. You don't need to share this knowledge with anyone, it's a sort of secret sense that you can nurture over time and use to help ration or rally your energy. We don't have to be high octane, top speed at all times. Be clever. If you know you've got a period of full-on work ahead of you, plan a long weekend after that deadline and have it there in the diary to look forward to. Rest.

As writer Matt Haig says in *Notes on a Nervous Planet*, where he lists 'Ten Ways to Work Without Breaking Down': 'Aim not *to get more stuff done*. Aim to have *less stuff to do*. Be a work minimalist. Minimalism is about doing more with less. So much of working life seems to be doing less with more. Activity isn't always the same as achievement.'

Or if you've run yourself ragged and you need a break, be honest with your employer. Say, 'I've worked really hard these last few weeks, it's been long hours and high stress and I need a break. I'd love to take Friday off . . . etc.' (NB say it on Monday, not Thursday). You're entitled to your leave, so use it. And it's always better to plan your time wisely than to disappear off sick when you're needed.

Importantly, you can only credibly do this if you've pulled your weight and worked your sorry arse off. 'Snowflake' is a stupid term and I don't believe in demonizing sensitivity, but be aware that some of your bosses may mistakenly believe that everyone younger than them is weaker or wussier. That simply by being youngish, they assume you lack stamina.

It is up to you to define your relationship between work life and the rest of your life. Your boss may have merrily sacrificed their personal life for the sake of the company, but you may want to choose to do things differently. Be aware that everyone has a different perspective and that it might be wise to reflect an understanding of their view, even if you don't subscribe to it yourself.

Final Days

Resigning (to the tune of Dolly Parton's '9 to 5')

Never resign when you're furious. Never resign when you're emotional. Never resign when you've just had enough. Never resign to get a pay rise, or a promotion (that's a begging letter or a crap kind of blackmail). Never resign out of malice. Because all these feelings pass . . .

Some people can feel trapped in their jobs and their financial situation can mean that they would find it hard to leave. But ultimately you can ALWAYS walk away, even if it puts you under pressure to get a new job the following day.

Resigning is the beginning of the end so you must be absolutely certain it's what you want before you pull the trigger. And if you've interrogated all your reasons, you're sure it's time to go, and you have a plan for what comes next, then it's time to write the hardest letter of your life.

Letter writing is, of course, a dying art. But it is still an art and your letter of resignation should be given enough consideration, drafting and refining to reflect that. How many letters have you written up until now? If you've only really dashed off a few notes to Santa then it might be time to seek inspiration from the greats. Shaun Usher's *Letters of Note* and *More Letters of Note* are perfect collections of the best examples of the genre from throughout history. They'll make you laugh and cry, they'll fire you up and are an important reminder that more can be said in a few carefully crafted sentences than in a lifetime of WhatsApp waffle.

Tips for resigning:

- Address the letter to your boss and copy it to HR if appropriate
- Start with the purpose of your letter e.g.

    'It's with great sadness that I tender my resignation.'
    'After much thought, I've decided that I've reached the end of my contribution to this organization.'

- Say that you are giving notice of your resignation from your current role as [insert job title] at [insert employer]
- Go back to your contract and set out your notice period and confirm the date of your final day of employment
- Thank your employer for the experience and wish the team the best of luck in the future e.g.

'I'm proud of the X and X achieved while
working in this role . . .'
'I have learnt so much about X during my
time here.'

● State your willingness to finish up and hand
over your work in a responsible manner

Beyond the basics, this is a chance to own the narrative of your departure and you can do that without it
being an exercise in vitriol. If you have a grievance you
can elegantly allude to it here, but this is not the place to
get all poisonous. Beware of venting your feelings, you
might think you're leaving in a blaze of glory, but you're
really just burning bridges.

Handing in or emailing your letter of resignation is a
big moment and you might need to psych yourself up for
it. Whatever the circumstances of your departure you
might feel like you're betraying your colleagues, or let-
ting the side down. Reassure yourself that this isn't the
case and that change is natural and necessary. Then listen to Dolly Parton's '9 to 5' loudly on your headphones;
it's very motivating.

It's a good idea to tell your boss in person or over the
phone you are resigning before handing in the letter. It's
much more personal and suggests that you are taking
responsibility for the impact leaving will have by giving them a heads-up; they'll need to consider what this
means for the team. When you say it out loud, don't
expect a gushing eulogy – that's for the leaving party.
Your boss may have seen it coming, in which case you
can expect calm acceptance. Equally, it may come as a

shock and they could respond negatively. Either way, keep the conversation brief, be prepared for the obvious questions: where are you going next and why have you chosen to leave. You don't have to answer those questions – sidestep them if it's awkward. And if the response is negative, don't feel you need to shoulder their emotion – you've got every right to resign with the appropriate notice whenever you choose.

What happens after you resign?

Your resignation needs to be accepted, usually through a letter or email in response confirming your end date and any relevant information about the terms of your departure. Expect it to feel businesslike and factual. Even if they are devastated you're leaving, there won't be teardrops on the paper.

During your notice period remember to retain a good work ethic and focus your time on transitioning contacts, closing things down and preparing a comprehensive handover. Don't talk too much about your new role – be modest, your colleagues don't want to feel bad they're not moving on too. And be discreet about your reasons for leaving – your colleagues are bound to ask you about it. Prepare a positive story and keep it brief; don't feel you need to confess all. A simple 'I felt ready for something new' is banal enough to deflect any unwanted quizzing.

Clear out your personal items from the building, go through files and make sure everything you leave behind is in good order. In some cases, your contract may limit your time left at work, because it terminates very quickly on handing in your notice. When your work is sensitive or if you are in a competitive environment you may be escorted from the building and asked to take 'gardening leave', during which you continue to be paid but no longer have access to your job, in order to protect the interests of your organization. So make sure you are prepared before you announce your resignation.

It may be the case that your employer tries to persuade you to stay, either by making a strong case about the benefits to your career or with a financial offer. Be prepared for this and try not to get caught up in the flattery of being courted. Consider your reasons for deciding to leave in the first place – money alone is seldom the root problem when people leave an employer or role. However, until you are contracted by your new employer you have no obligation to move, so if you are undecided, consider what is being put on the table and whether you want to negotiate. If you do choose this route, try to bear in mind the long game and avoid messing people about, especially if you work in a small industry. If you're open and honest, give reasonable timescales and help make sure everyone gets the right person for the job, even if that's not you, you can help protect your reputation and keep open the potential for future offers.

Going for an interview before you've resigned

It's an awkward truth that you'll probably need to interview elsewhere before you resign. That inevitably involves a bit of cloak and dagger so that it's not obvious to your employer that you're exploring your options elsewhere. The smartest thing to do is to take the day/morning/afternoon off. That means you don't have to lie about your absence or create a phantom dental appointment.

If you can carve out the time without feeling like you're bunking off then it takes another layer of stress out of the interview process and allows you to fully concentrate on that conversation.

If that's not a possibility, then you may have to fib. It's awful, I hate it, but sometimes it's a necessary part of the process.

Being Made to Leave

It may be that you're not delivering work to the standard expected of you. Or it may be that the way in which you approach external partners or prospective clients isn't how your organization wants it done. It may be that you've become seen as a 'problem' because you are not felt to be contributing to the team, acting rashly or as a lone wolf, being negative or disruptive or are known for stirring malicious office gossip. Or you could have broken the terms of your contract.

Performance management

Many organizations have a formal process to manage performance. Alongside this, some organizations set out behaviours about what is expected in terms of the way the work is delivered. Formal performance management systems help track learning needs, give regular feedback on how well an individual is performing in a role and encourage conversations about improvements. But while this is commonplace in large companies, it is by no means the norm everywhere; 84 per cent of businesses in the UK don't have any kind of performance management system,[30] and even in those that do, they vary widely.

Before someone gets shown the door, an attempt is usually made to improve performance. This mostly takes the form of individual meetings between an employee and their manager to give feedback on how they are doing. These meetings are held with the best of intentions: to identify where skills are lacking or an aptitude is found wanting in the hope that the employee will take on board feedback and improve.

It used to be common practice to give feedback in the 'praise sandwich' format, i.e. here's some good feedback, here are some areas for development, and here's some more good feedback. The aim was for everyone to leave the room feeling good, with a balanced view of what's going well and what is not and a commitment to improve. However, the human mind is tuned to overestimating criticism,[31] and in practice the broad feedback given to the individual wasn't always that instructive.[32] No wonder then that the format became known as the 'shit sandwich'.

The process of performance management can be upsetting and difficult, especially if you can't understand why it's happening or feel that it's a personal attack. Here are a few tips for coping if it happens to you:

- **Take it seriously, but try not to take it personally**

  This isn't about whether you are a good person or not, it's about whether you are able to deliver the requirements of the role. If you really aren't delivering what's required then start to focus on practical steps to improve your skills, rather than engage in self-criticism. Keep a log of positive feedback, so you can challenge your negative emotional reactions.

- **Try not to argue the point, justify your actions or shift the blame**

  Of course, don't feel you need to shoulder the responsibility for something you didn't do, but bear in mind that your boss's views could be quite entrenched and they'll want to see positive engagement and personal responsibility being taken. Demonstrate the spirit of cooperation by trying to deliver the recommended improvements.

- **Get specific**

  Rather than puzzle about what your boss meant when they said you need to improve how you communicate, ask for good examples to follow, ways to learn, and take time to consider how different approaches in the past might have worked better.

- **Make progress**
  Work together to address the challenges and
  show evidence of how you are learning and
  adapting to the feedback.

Dismissal

*I have been fired five times, and each
time my career took a step forward.*

PAUL ARDEN, *IT'S NOT HOW GOOD
YOU ARE, IT'S HOW GOOD YOU WANT TO BE*

Mostly, being fired (or dismissed, as it's more formally
known) is horrible. It's a brutal rejection and sometimes
comes as a shock.

People can be dismissed for repeated minor conduct
issues like consistently bad timekeeping, being incapa-
ble of meeting the required standard of performance or
being unwilling to do a job properly. The dismissal is
usually at the end of the performance management process, when insufficient progress has been made.

In extreme cases of gross misconduct, which can include
possession of drugs, aggressive behaviour towards a colleague or wilful damage to property, an employee might
be dismissed with immediate effect.

Any type of dismissal can be very unsettling. If you
are dismissed, it's important that it is done fairly, and in
some cases you may feel able to appeal the decision.

It's best to be open with a future employer about the

fact you have been dismissed and have a clear and factual statement prepared to explain why this is the case. They may not choose to recruit you as a result, but it is a lot better than the truth coming out later.

Redundancy, severance and layoffs

Redundancy takes place when an organization changes the structure of its teams. Unlike dismissal, this is not about the employee as an individual, but their role in the business. It may be that a major contract has been lost and the work no longer needs to be done or a new direction is being sought and job descriptions are being changed to better deliver this. Again, if it affects you, it's important to establish that the decision making is fair. Employees facing redundancy may be entitled to compensation or redeployment elsewhere in the organization.

The exit interview

Every organization has a different style for exit interviews. You might wonder why they bother at all. It's usually an opportunity for your current organization to gain feedback about their performance as an employer, get your suggestions about how they can improve and plug you for a bit of information about your new employer. An exit interview isn't something to be nervous about – you're not going to be grilled on your decision to leave or anything as cringeworthy as this.

Good exit interviews are conducted with someone from the HR team (not your immediate bosses) and they are refreshing conversations designed to help the organization learn from your experience as an employee within it.

Here are some of the questions you might be asked:

- What made you start looking for a new job?
- What areas do you think we could improve on as an employer?
- Did you have the management support, access to training and resources you needed to deliver your role effectively?
- Do you have any concerns about your time working here that you would like to raise?
- Did your job description reflect your role?
- Did you find your job changed during the time you were working here?
- What skills and qualities do you think we should look for in your replacement?

Just as with your letter of resignation, it's not wise to thrash out all your criticisms here. Sure, be honest, but remain professional and reasonably formal throughout. If you are asked something you feel is controversial or uncomfortable, it's OK to say 'I don't feel it's my place to comment on that' or an equivalently noncommittal sentence of that nature. Conversely, if you do need to raise a major concern, do so succinctly and with minimum drama. If there are things you think should be done differently to make sure future or existing staff are more fulfilled, more productive or more engaged – then you should say so now.

What happens next and how best to style out your notice period

Great, you've resigned but they still have to pay you. You may as well start rolling in at midday and taking long, frequent vaping breaks, right?

No. It might feel like the end, but most industries are claustrophobically small, so you are guaranteed to meet some of these people again (perhaps in a future job interview) and it's wise to leave with the same amount of professionalism that you'd like to be remembered by. Even if you've been a dedicated employee till now, your reputation won't survive a period of slacking off. So stay sharp until the very last contracted hour – it's self-preservation. Don't snooze through your final stint.

Long notice periods (anything longer than a month) are particularly hard. You've mentally moved on but you're trapped in the drudge of your old job. Use this time to close one chapter and prepare for another. Don't volunteer for new responsibilities. Make sure you take what's useful (and legal) from your current position (i.e. gather the materials to showcase a portfolio project, or have a final session with your mentor). Preserve the time to say goodbye and thank you to your colleagues.

Make sure you write personal notes to your major contacts, it's very likely that you'll be calling on them soon in
your new role and some of these people will be lifetime
friends, advisers and door openers. Introduce them to
your successor or colleague. Be careful about the rules
of engagement – trying to tempt your contacts to follow
you over to your new employer, for example, will be seen
as disloyal and may be a breach of contract. Similarly, be
aware of your contractual requirements regarding intellectual property and confidentiality.

Exiting elegantly is a cathartic experience. Do it properly and you'll be remembered as a class act.

Handing over

Most of your notice period will be spent laying the foun-
dations for the next person who assumes your role. Of
course, as soon as you resign you start thinking about
new things, and handing over can seem like a Herculean
(and hideous) task. But hopefully you've been writing and
receiving handover notes for holidays etc. so think of it as
just a more detailed version of that exercise. Your handover should include systems, forecasts, procedures, diary
planning and any other nuance that someone box fresh to
the job would need in order to pick it up and run with it.

Dedicate a good amount of time to your handover note.
An effective one covers:

- An overview of the role in practice
- The status of current work, including any issues
  that need urgent attention

- A list of contacts internally and externally, their contact details and short notes about how they relate to the work
- Where to find information and any necessary documents
- Key dates and upcoming meetings

In an ideal world you'll have the luxury of crossover time with your successor (but this doesn't always happen). You're there to teach them and to give them the best chance of success. Be kind rather than territorial – sometimes people react strangely in this situation, a sort of 'I don't want this job but I don't want them to have it either' mentality. That doesn't help anyone. Be open, engaging and supportive.

Depending on your relationships, you might want to say 'call me' if there's a question that you could help answer in the first few weeks. In practice people rarely do but it's a nice gesture and a generous offer and sets the tone for you wishing your team the very best of luck as they continue without you.

Leaving parties

Do not misbehave at your leaving party. Stay sensible. Eat something large at 5 p.m., nurse one drink from 6 to 8 p.m. and then take it sensibly until taxi time. You'll regret every other version of this evening.

Further Resources

Dave Alred, *The Pressure Principle: Handle Stress, Harness Energy, and Perform When It Counts* (Portfolio Penguin, 2016)

Paul Arden, *It's Not How Good You Are, It's How Good You Want to Be* (Phaidon Press, 2003)

Jim Collins, *Good to Great: Why Some Companies Make the Leap . . . and Others Don't* (Random House, 2001)

globalgoals.org

Matt Haig, *Notes on a Nervous Planet* (Canongate, 2018)

Adam Kay, *This is Going to Hurt: Secret Diaries of a Junior Doctor* (Picador, 2017)

Chelsea Kwakye and Ọrẹ Ogunbiyi, *Taking Up Space: The Black Girl's Manifesto for Change* (#Merky Books, 2019)

Christine Porath, *Mastering Civility: A Manifesto for the Workplace* (Grand Central, 2016)

Jon Ronson, *The Psychopath Test* (Picador, 2011)

Sheryl Sandberg, *Lean In: Women, Work, and the Will to Lead* (W. H. Allen, 2015)

Paul Schmitz, *Everyone Leads: Building Leadership from the Community Up* (Jossey-Bass, 2011)

Robert L. Sutton, *The Asshole Survival Guide: How to Deal with People Who Treat You Like Dirt* (Portfolio Penguin, 2017)

Robert L. Sutton, *Good Boss, Bad Boss: How to be the Best . . . and Learn from the Worst* (Piatkus, 2010)

Greta Thunberg, *No One is Too Small to Make a Difference* (Penguin, 2019)

Shaun Usher, *Letters of Note: Correspondence Deserving of a Wider Audience* (Canongate, 2013)

Shaun Usher, *More Letters of Note: Correspondence Deserving of a Wider Audience* (Canongate, 2017)

Matthew Walker, *Why We Sleep: The New Science of Sleep and Dreams* (Allen Lane, 2017)

Ruby Wax, *How to be Human: The Manual* (Penguin, 2018)

Sarah Wilson, *First We Make the Beast Beautiful: A New Story About Anxiety* (Bantam, 2018)

Sources of advice and support on sexism and discrimination:

ACAS: www.acas.org.uk

Department of Labor (US): https://www.dol.gov/

The Equality Advisory and Support Service: https://www.gov.uk/equality-advisory-support-service

Everyday Sexism Project: https://everydaysexism.com/

Section 6
Business is Personal

Whatever anyone might say – business is deeply, intimately and excruciatingly personal. It doesn't make sense to 'bring your whole self to work' and then tell that self to sit on the sidelines while another version of you does the business.

Whole selves at work are inclined to be sensitive to what's going on around them and to the way they're treated. But they're also more likely to approach things with empathy, thoughtfulness and energy. It's impossible to be committed to what you're doing for eight to ten hours a day and be emotionally detached from it. Or rather: it is possible, but that's a pretty divisive and difficult way to live your life.

So now that we've got that out of the way and have given ourselves permission to take things personally . . . what happens next? Having an understanding of how you interact with others, where you get your kicks from and what kind of teams bring out the best in you are all central to our happiness at work. These relationships are often intimate, deeply human and complex. Research by Gallup found that people with a best friend at work are *seven times* as likely to be engaged in their jobs, are better at engaging customers, produce higher-quality work, have greater wellbeing, and are less likely to get injured on the job.[1] That doesn't mean you MUST make a new BFF to sit at the desk next to you, but it does mean you might want to relax your preconceptions about what constitutes friendship and how you might adapt the concept at work.

In this section we'll look at how to operate as part of a team, how to deal with obstruction and collaboration techniques. We'll explore how to work with friends, enemies, family or in solitude.

Collaborating

One of the great myths of my working life is that I do everything alone. Actually, so much of the best of what I'm credited as the author of is collaborative work. I work with extraordinary designers, wonderful sound engineers, with fabulous assistants and producers. In fact the Brazilian Human Atlas work Somos Brasil has a credit list of 250 people in the back of the book.

MARCUS LYON, ARTIST AND FORMER JACKAROO

Isn't it true that if you want something done you're better off doing it yourself? The honest answer is, no. You can't do everything on your own. And great minds often don't think alike. That's why, when you come together with other humans, you pool your resources and scale your ambition. Every day, in workplaces all over the world, amazing things are achieved by shared endeavour.

Being part of a smart, diverse, talented, trusting and driven team is a feeling like no other. A legal high that will have you running to work and leaving after lights out. You're bound together by common purpose and your working days are elevated by a group momentum. You win together and fail together. You whistle while you work. You're part Avengers, part Secret Seven, part *West Wing* season one (if you don't get that last reference, put this book down and go and binge watch it all now).

Google's Project Aristotle set out to explore what makes an effective team. After extensive research they found that it's not about who is *on* the team, but how the team works *together*. The key qualities they found were:[2]

- **Psychological safety**
  Each member of the team feels that they can take risks and that no one will embarrass or punish anyone else for admitting a mistake, asking a question, or offering a new idea

- **Dependability**
  Members of the team complete work to a high quality and on time

- **Structure and clarity**
  Members of the team are clear about what's expected of them and how they will achieve what they are asked to do

● **Meaning**
The work delivers a sense of purpose to each member of the team. What this sense of purpose is will be personal to each member: self-expression, flexibility to have time with their family, increasing their financial security with better pay

● **Impact**
A sense of personal achievement and contribution to achieving the organization's goals

When you're looking at a team, notice how it's led and who by. Look for team leaders who are setting clear objectives, the right tone and high standards, explaining how each team member's work contributes to the overall goals. And look for teams that are asking questions without fear of seeming stupid.

Collaborating is fun but it ain't easy. It's rare to experience idyllic synchronization for a sustained period or more than occasionally throughout your career. But you can improve your chances by understanding the dynamics central to being a good collaborator and behaving like one, even if the circumstances aren't optimal.

Why people don't collaborate and how to force them

Well, all right, maybe not 'force' exactly. Coerce perhaps? Or even better, persuade. Look, not everyone is a team player. So it's hard if you find yourself in a team with someone who'd really rather that you weren't there at all. Sometimes you'll get off on the wrong foot and sometimes you frankly just don't like a person you have to work with.[3] How can you gain someone's trust and start to function well together?

Not all conflict is bad. In their book *No Hard Feelings*, Liz Fosslien and Mollie West Duffy talk about navigating two types of conflict: task conflict (the clash of creative ideas) and relationship conflict (personality-driven arguments). Done well, the former is the lifeblood of good collaboration: a space to refine, grow and develop each other's ideas. The latter can be the cause of misunderstanding and misery. Relationship conflict does not always come from other people. Check that the source isn't you. Are you showing people how to get the best out of you? Do you support others to learn when they make mistakes? Do you build on ideas or undermine them?

Here are a few tips:

- **Work out what you need from the collaboration and how you will approach it**
  Sometimes it's the case you won't delight in working with a person, but you'll need to have them onside to get a job done. While it's nicer to be liked, it's not always necessary. Work with them only as much as is needed, hold your tongue and be civil, agree clear tasks and expectations of each other, and when the work is done, move on. Tonally, keep it clean, brisk and businesslike.

- **Try to understand the cause of the tension**
  While you may be working hard and are keen to work together, you're receiving an inexplicably frosty reception or even outright hostility. Consider how you could be contributing to the problem: you might be a perceived threat or they have perhaps taken a dislike to you for a myriad of reasons. If you can, start an open and honest conversation. And don't be afraid to show vulnerability, it can often help to overcome preconceptions.

- **Seek to understand your own style and how it clashes with theirs**
  Your frustration at them being exhaustive and slow might mirror their frustration at your rushed and ill-considered actions. Or the other way round. Once you accept different routes to the same destination, you can start to identify strengths and distribute the work so that you add up to more than the sum of your parts. This is about acknowledging your weaknesses alongside their talents and each playing to your advantage.

- **Always deliver high quality work on time**
  Feeling demotivated at work stinks. But don't compromise your own standards because of dysfunction around you. It will only make you feel worse and may limit your chances for future, more enjoyable, more collaborative, opportunities.

- **Get some advice or ask for help from your boss or colleagues**

  Never moan about a colleague, no matter how much they piss you off – whoever you're talking to will only think you're equally critical about them behind their back, or they'll judge you for being bitchy. Frame it as a team challenge or a barrier to working together effectively instead. It is OK to admit that you are struggling with a relationship, but couch it in terms like 'the way we communicate' or 'different professional styles' to avoid making it feel like a personal attack. Almost always your boss will be able to read between the lines, but it's much more elegant to use the language of suggestion as opposed to accusation.

Credit: giving and taking

One of the important things about collaborating is to be honest and generous about credit. Ideas can and do spring from anywhere, but in a collaborative process it's essential and right to credit the individual who started something or who implemented it. Just because something is a joint enterprise doesn't mean that you can't identify the people whose contribution is specific and spectacular. You're a team, not an amorphous lump.

And if *you've* been the champion who had the moment of inspiration or breakthrough then be sure to make a note of that – and to raise it in your performance review or appraisal. There's nothing wrong with claiming credit where credit is due.

When it comes to who owns the idea, in most cases your contract will set out creative ownership and intellectual property rights. Usually the contribution you make becomes the property of the company you work for. It's important to check your position regarding intellectual property rights and to know how to avoid infringing the rights of others if you work in a creative industry where ideas are your currency.

Creativity and collaboration

Beware of situations where someone says 'there's no such thing as a bad idea'. There are plenty.

Most organizations talk about the need for innovation – whether improving practice, finding a new angle or identifying emerging markets. And one of the key benefits of collaboration is the ability to bring different points of view together to create new perspectives. The challenge is to generate the ideas you NEED. And to give feedback in a way that doesn't make people cry.

There are plenty of situations that demand new ideas, but work can be one of the worst places to create them. It's a mistake to assume that people are capable of developing ground-breaking thinking by merely asking them to. Another mistake is to assume that creativity in teams comes through some kind of free-for-all splurging session. From Edward de Bono's *Six Thinking Hats* to the Design Council's 'Double Diamond' model,[4] creativity comes through structure. Teams need to create environments for divergent thinking where bad ideas are less likely to be tabled, where good ones are understood and where new ones flourish. And the great news is there are lots of tools to help.

Playing to your strengths and supplementing your weaknesses with other warm bodies

If you're not a charmer and you're creative, it's useful to surround yourself with charmers. If you can put your ego aside enough to think 'they're going to take a bit of credit for this', if they're the ones who get you over the line, they deserve it and you should let them have it.

DAN GILLESPIE SELLS, LEAD VOCALIST AND PRINCIPAL SONGWRITER IN THE ROCK BAND THE FEELING AND COMPOSER OF THE MUSICAL *EVERYBODY'S TALKING ABOUT JAMIE* AND FORMER MUSIC SHOP ASSISTANT

In school we're taught to be all-rounders. And beyond the subjects you're passionate about, educators and parents are usually big fans of the notion of 'having something to fall back on' – as if you're ever likely to fall back on that dual award science GCSE you scraped a D grade in.

I was so consistently bad at maths from the age of five through to sixteen that as an adult I have deliberately removed all numbers from my brain to make room for things I prefer. And yes, sometimes that's problematic, but mostly I just use the calculator on my phone and don't stress about it. We don't all have to be good at *everything*. And one of the great things about work is that no one expects you to be.

Of course, you do need a solid, broad skill base to get along well at work – but in most professions, very quickly you'll start to become a specialist. Careers like the civil service encourage people to be generalists, able to work across a wide range of subjects and teams, while others like medicine encourage specialism to begin early during training.

Even if your workplace doesn't formalize the specializing process, you'll notice that by demonstrating what you're good at you'll start to be given more responsibility in the spheres you shine in and less in the areas you're likely to mess up. You can't fake this development, so there's no point thinking, 'If I'm terrible at this spreadsheet no one will ever ask me to wash up again.' It doesn't work like that. Instead focus on excelling in the areas you enjoy, feel challenged by and want to improve upon.

And what to do about the bits you're bad at? To start with, there are always parts of any job that are less enjoyable than others. I'm not telling you to cherry pick here, that will make you extremely unpopular. But if you genuinely have a blind spot, or you struggle with something, the solutions are very simple. In the beginning:

- **Ask for help**
  Don't hide. Instead take advice from someone who's been around longer than you. Scope out the hacks, or ask for support (anything from more training, to more time).

- **Even if you can't get good at it, at least try to understand it**
  The temptation when we fail at something is to dismiss it altogether. This is a mistake. It might not be your thing but it's almost certainly someone else's and it exists for a reason.

- **Find that someone else and recruit them into your team**
  This is rarely an official approach; it's about recognizing your shortcomings and making allies who are strong where you are not. All you need is one person who can balance out your gaps. And the wonderful thing is, that person will probably have a gap that you can compensate for too. It's quid pro quo.

I knew, when I started on my grad scheme, that there was very little point in trying to pretend I was a maths genius. But that job involved managing large, complex production budgets, billing and (eventually) writing important fee proposals. So I made sure I had a comprehensive knowledge of the principles behind these areas even if the figures themselves properly frightened me. And then I made sure that I only worked with people who were super buttoned down on the finances. I liked producers who were forensic about spreadsheets, account managers who loved invoicing, and when it came to fee stuff I befriended the head of finance who would patiently co-author every proposal. And I'd bribe my poor account manager 10 per cent of the overall claim to file my expenses for me (that was just laziness).

While you don't have to be good at everything, you do have to be self-aware enough to know when you need to borrow someone else's brain to get you through. And then you must be charming enough to get them to want to help you. Being honest about what you don't know makes people far more likely to bail you out. Business researchers at DePaul University in Chicago have found that self-aware teams deliver significantly better performance on factors such as decision making, coordination and managing conflict.[5]

As they put it: 'For teams to perform effectively, each member must possess a combination of technical and interpersonal skills and constantly adjust their contributions to meet the team's needs. Correctly understanding one's capabilities relative to others is therefore paramount.'

There are lots of reasons why we don't spend enough time communicating our weaknesses: pride, fear of being judged or a lack of self-awareness. But it's often the quality most valued in the workplace. So find out what you're good at and where you flounder by seeking feedback. Be specific – this isn't about whether you are good or bad at your job, it's about finding the right mix of skills in your team to get the best outcome for you and for your organization.

Like rock bands, the best teams aren't artificially manufactured – they don't answer an ad and turn up and make magic happen – they grow. The graft of rehearsals and gigs builds a sixth sense between the members. The line-up evolves with new blood and different influences coming in and out, changing the dynamic and bringing something fresh. Just because someone isn't on your organogram doesn't mean you can't work together. Seek out talent and remain close to it.

Choosing your collaborators

So how do you identify talent? Firstly, start with the people you enjoy spending time with. People you trust. People who get stuff done or who make you think. There are some extraordinarily talented individuals with great big flashy egos who have a tendency to behave like assholes and that's a whole other problem. So let's set them to one side for a moment and concentrate on the good guys.

Quentin Vicens and Philip E. Bourne, two American research scientists, set out their guidance on how to choose who to work with in their 'Ten Simple Rules for a Successful Collaboration':[6]

1. **Do not be lured into just any collaboration**
   Make sure you ask the right questions at the start, such as: Do I have the expertise required to tackle the proposed tasks? Do I have confidence to be able to deliver on time? What priority will I give the collaboration?

2. **Decide at the beginning who will work on the tasks**

3. **Stick to your tasks**

4. **Be open and honest**

5. Feel respect, get respect
This means both sides sticking to the expectations in rules 2–4

6. Communicate, communicate, communicate

7. Protect yourself from a collaboration that turns sour
If the enthusiasm wains as challenges arise, give your collaborators flexibility and the benefit of the doubt – there may be other things outside of the collaboration that are taking their attention away. If you're still not getting what you need from them after you've given them enough chances to recover, work out the minimum you need from them to get the job done

8. Always acknowledge and cite your collaborators

9. Seek advice from people with experience

10. If your collaboration satisfies you, keep it going

We all have friends who make us sparkle a bit more. The ones who you feel excited about on the way to the restaurant. The ones who listen closely and laugh loudly. The people around whom you are the best version of yourself. It's the same at work.

How to work with friends

One of the joys of working is that you make loads of new friends. You didn't need to find them, they're all sitting there waiting for you. Some industries are super matey and everyday has a party atmosphere and others have a more serious tone. But wherever you work you'll form close and often lasting relationships.

Sometimes you'll find yourself working with a very good friend – perhaps you start a business together, or maybe you're placed on a project with your flatmate. Working with friends requires a bit of discipline, you obviously have a different agenda here than when you're down the pub. But knowing someone really well can be a wonderful platform for producing great work together, so don't feel you have to fake distance or start being all aloof. Equally, take the job seriously and don't become distracted.

When you disagree or argue it's much harder than in a straightforwardly professional relationship. Conversations that are hard to have with colleagues are much harder when that colleague is someone you like, respect and treasure. And the stakes are higher because handling conflict badly can result in damage or loss that resonates far beyond the boundaries of the workplace. Approach these moments carefully and with tenderness – you must always be honest (your friend will know if you're not saying what you think anyway) but never brutal. And don't rush to react to differences of opinion; sometimes things work themselves out without massive bust-ups. Caution is key.

How to work with enemies

Some people are shits. They are. It's awful. And sometimes you look across a room in your glorious new life and there, standing in the corner, is an old shit you thought you'd seen the back of.

It's always the people you least want to see again who have a nasty habit of turning up where you don't expect them. It might be a school bully you'd forgotten about or an old girlfriend you had therapy to heal from. The shock of having a blast from your past pitch up in your box-fresh new world is deeply annoying, but it happens.

If you find yourself in a situation where you are expected to work with an enemy then consider your options:

- ~~You resolve the feud and become best friends, everything is rosy and all past crimes are forgotten. You get matching tattoos.~~ (NB we all know this is not an option).
- Can you elegantly sidestep this? Can you confess to a trusted co-worker and enlist their help? I once had to attend a meeting at a company owned by a man who had relentlessly pursued me and been a class-A creep for months. I couldn't go on my own, I had to take backup. And it was fine. I didn't see him, but my partner was prepped to be a human shield if I needed one. And I didn't spend the day looking over my shoulder.
- Total, steely professionalism. This is the most enjoyable option, the deliciously icy pleasure

of rising above it. Do your job extraordinarily well. Be archly polite. Be so good you are untouchable. Everything you do reeks of superiority (and shits hate that).

Inevitably, at work you'll meet some new shits (sadly). You might have a personality clash or you might despise a person's politics – there are lots of reasons why we don't all get on with everyone. It's not your job to be likeable or liking. As long as you remain professional and tonally neutral, you can secretly loathe someone to your heart's content. But the moment it becomes visible it opens up a whole other set of problems, so it's best not to draw attention to your feelings (even if you must wilfully restrain the eye rolls).

You don't ever have to work with someone you fear or who makes you uncomfortable. In that position, follow the guidance in Section 5 about staying safe and calling things out.

But mostly, you just have to find a way of working with the odd person you really hate, which often is not as bad as it sounds.

How to work with family

If you're able to work every day on something that you love, with people that you love, I can't really think of a better thing to do.

DUNCAN JENNINGS, TECH ENTREPRENEUR AND INVESTOR, FOUNDER OF VOUCHERCODES.CO.UK AND FORMER SANDWICH FILLER IN DEAN'S DELI

I've never worked with my family, unless you count a day in 1999 when I had to cover my sister's chamber-maiding shift at a local hotel, so she could attend an audition. I know that working with family is all about trust – you start on a firm basis, a lifetime of knowledge and shared experience.

She should not have asked me to cover that shift. I wafted about the various bedrooms, lying on all the beds like a grown-up Goldilocks. I ate lots of Elizabeth Shaw pillow chocolates and then, because I'm not completely useless, I sprayed some air freshener about and gave each loo three firm flushes. Ta da!

My sister nearly lost her job and had to work a double shift the next day to compensate for my slovenliness. This is not how you work with family.

Here's a better approach:

Our relationship is the secret to our success. There is absolute trust, respect, empathy and selflessness between us. We inspire and motivate each other every day. We challenge each other to the end to ensure we make the right decisions and those decisions are always made collectively. We keep each other in check and grounded and focused on what matters. The life of an entrepreneur can be a lonely place and there are always tough moments, and downs as well as ups. It's the strength of our relationship that has made those tough moments nothing but bumps along the road and there is never a moment you are alone in failure or success.

SIMON SALTER, CO-FOUNDER WITH HIS BROTHER
ANDREW OF THE INNOVATION STUDIO SALTER
BROTHERS AND FORMER BOX PACKER AT A SPORTS-
GOODS FACTORY

Working for Yourself

*My ambition as a child was to discover a new colour.
I remember digging and holding shells up to the light
and thinking: is there a new colour in that? If you read
my business plan in 2003, from what I wanted the office
to look like to the culture of the company, there was so
much imagination. I've definitely been imagining how
I want my life to be, and you work and rework and
rework that. And from wanting to find a new colour
and now discovering and managing amazing artistic
talent – you can see how that idea has developed.*

VICKI WILLDEN-LEBRECHT, FOUNDER OF
ILLUSTRATION AND LITERARY AGENCY THE BRIGHT
AGENCY AND FORMER FROZEN FOOD SALESPERSON

Entrepreneur is an overused word. It's often used as a
default description for anyone who doesn't have an obvious job title or a normal working pattern. But more and
more people are adopting an entrepreneurial mindset
and choosing to work for themselves.

Paul Jarvis, author of *Company of One*, spends his time
writing, creating software, podcasting and teaching online
courses with his own 'company of one' called Mighty

Small Ventures. He's connected to his purpose, maximized his work and retained his sanity. And he sees this path becoming ever more possible:

> It's getting easier and less risky to work for yourself and still make a decent living. You can outsource or hire freelancers to cover tasks that were traditionally done by an employee. And unlike a corporation, you are the boss, can't be downsized or hit a gender-based glass ceiling. As long as you're doing great work that's in demand, working for yourself has no limits.

But working for yourself is not all designer business cards and long lunches. You'll need to get smart about the practical ramifications. Things that get parcelled out to other departments in big organizations, like running the budget, checking legal documents and fixing your laptop. You'll need discipline and motivation in a world of zero structure and a thousand distractions. And resilience when the latest series of positive conversations with a potential client comes to an abrupt stop when they move roles within the company you were hoping to do business with.

It's a myth that all people who start businesses are fresh out of Harvard and hell-bent on growth. While this is definitely a type, so is the seasoned pro who has built their reputation and wants to enjoy the freedom of being their own boss, or the back-to-work parent who changes direction and starts up on their own. In all cases they have identified a niche that they want to fill that has a tangible value to others. They bring skills, ambition and tenacity to turn an idea into a success.

And when the opportunity comes to convert your idea into earning a living, get advice, scrutinize the deal and make sure you're earning and owning what you deserve. As Taylor Swift wrote in an open letter on tumblr following the sale of her masters:

> Essentially, my musical legacy is about to lie in the hands of someone who tried to dismantle it. This is my worst case scenario. This is what happens when you sign a deal at fifteen to someone for whom the term 'loyalty' is clearly just a contractual concept . . . hopefully young artists or kids with musical dreams will read this and learn about how to better protect themselves in a negotiation. You deserve to own the art you make.

For all the freedom of working for yourself, there's also the responsibility for due diligence, details and direction.

Before you start up alone:

- Work out your business goals *and* your lifestyle goals. See the example from *Pivot* in Section 4 to help 'calibrate your compass' and decide how your work and life priorities will sit alongside each other.
- Build your working capital *and* your social capital. Remember, nothing is wasted, including the occasional long lunch. Keep tracking your network, build your reputation and seek referrals.
- Build a group of trusted peers who act as your 'team' to bounce ideas off or explore new opportunities.

- Be brutal with your time. Learn how to focus on the work you need to do while managing the stream of questions and requests from clients and customers. Take a look at Section 3 for productivity tips.

- Be absolutely clear about what it is that you do. Don't overpromise or exaggerate. Be transparent and keep your promises.

- Put all the hours in. In the beginning, be prepared to devote yourself to it.

Loneliness at Work

For all its bustle and busyness, work can be a lonely place. Maybe there aren't many people of your own age around. Maybe you are feeling out of your depth. Maybe everyone has worked together for decades and they're not used to welcoming new people.

While forming social bonds can be protective in reducing social isolation and can help challenge or soften loneliness, they are not the whole answer. Because loneliness is a feeling not a circumstance. So you can't fix it just by becoming popular overnight. It's important to address the emotion as much as the situation.

Feeling lonely at work is a miserable thing. It's impossible to ignore and might seem hard to overcome. And a full working day characterized by loneliness is a VERY long day. While it may seem like knuckling down is the only answer, bear in mind that people who feel lonely at work are less engaged, their performance is lower and they are more likely to quit.[7] Research has found also that certain professions are more likely to be lonely at work because their work is often defined by long hours with limited social interaction.[8]

So, what can you do about it?

- **Say it out loud**
  It's hard to express your vulnerability, but consider – your colleagues probably have no idea how you feel. We are all very good at fronting up and seeming OK. Tell someone you trust and they'll almost always want to help you.

- **Get some perspective**
  Sometimes we feel disconnected simply because we're not getting any feedback. Approach your boss or your colleagues and put in time for an informal progress chat; it's not an appraisal but a moment to check and get their perspective on how you're doing. Even small moments of positive feedback have been shown to increase social bonds.[9] Not only is this useful for the job itself but it forges an intimacy with your colleagues because by demonstrating that you care, you'll make them more invested in helping you settle in.

- **Improve your working environment**
  Is the source of your loneliness environmental? Is your desk distant from your team? Or are you working remotely a lot? If you feel cut off,

or as if the fun is elsewhere, consider whether you can change the geography a bit and get yourself close to the action. You'll learn more in the heart of things anyway. But remember that it's completely possible to experience a sense of loneliness when surrounded by other people, so hopping desks may not be a magical fix.

● **Share what motivates you**
Open the conversation by talking about the work you are doing. Social bonds often develop at work because people share a sense of purpose about the work they are doing together.

● **Open your mind to new relationships**
Remember, friends come in all shapes and sizes, and this is especially true at work. Don't assume that just because someone is twenty years older than you they can't become a valued ally or a trusted friend. Your peer group now includes anyone you work with and that's a wonderful thing. Remain open to the idea that your new friends might be fifty-plus.

● **Make connections outside your immediate team**
Look to your 'outer circle', making links beyond your immediate team when the opportunity arises.

● **Take action**
Get involved, start things, sign up. Remember the transformative power of enthusiasm.

● **Build your resilience**
Resilience isn't something you have or you
don't have, it's something you build through
experience. Adjusting takes time. Just because
you're not regularly dancing on the tables in
the canteen does not mean you've failed at
integrating. Stick at it, and remember why you
are doing this – it's bigger than the temporary
feelings of solitude. Try to talk to yourself
positively rather than negatively and avoid self-
sabotaging (which can exacerbate feelings of
isolation). Focus on your strengths and build your
confidence in them.

This stuff is hard. And there are lots of great resources
to help you from projects who support people with their
mental health.

Further Resources

Scarlett Curtis, *It's Not OK to Feel Blue (and Other Lies):
Inspirational People Open Up About Their Mental Health*
(Penguin, 2019)

Ben Horowitz, *The Hard Thing About Hard Things*
(HarperCollins, 2014)

Sara Horowitz and Toni Sciarra Poynter, *The Freelancer's
Bible: Everything You Need to Know to Have the Career of Your
Dreams – On Your Terms* (Workman, 2012)

Paul Jarvis, *Company of One: Why Staying Small is the Next Big
Thing for Business* (Portfolio Penguin, 2019)

BUSINESS IS PERSONAL

Project Aristotle: https://rework.withgoogle.com

For support with loneliness at work:

mentalhealth.gov
mind.org.uk

Section 7
The System Will See You Now

There are a bunch of processes that happen in most jobs that you have to engage with, from clocking your hours to booking your holiday – you're not freestyling any more. So here's a rough guide to some of the systems you can expect to encounter. Each organization will have variations on these themes, but the basics remain the same.

Appraisals

Appraisals or performance management systems should be standard practice in most industries. However, this is often not the case, and your 'appraisal' might just be a conversation you have every now and again to find out how you're doing. Annual appraisals are falling out of fashion; conversations about development and performance should happen regularly. Coaching, mentoring and frequent feedback sessions provide a better structure for continual professional development. If you work somewhere where there's no official system then don't worry – put it in yourself. Start by asking your boss for feedback (from about three months in) and build from there.

Although it might feel like it, an appraisal is not the same as an end-of-term school report. Genuinely, they are essential for your progress, so try not to dread them. Instead, prepare as follows:

- Get familiar with the format if there is one. Ask to see a copy of the feedback forms/structure in advance so that you can anticipate the sorts of things you'll be asked and be ready to give thoughtful responses.
- If you're asked to nominate people to give feedback, give this proper consideration. Don't just list those characters who might quite like you. Equally, don't nominate someone you think has an irrational grudge against you or with whom you are in direct competition. Choose from different disciplines, levels of authority, perhaps include external people (clients, partners etc.). The more well-rounded a picture, the more honest the appraisal.
- This is a two-way conversation. Think in advance about what you'd like to get out of it. More direction? More training? Is there a relevant evening class you fancy and you'd like work to pay for it? Are you eyeing up a promotion? Is there something you really don't know how to handle and would like support with? Do your thinking before you enter the room, write it down as bullet points and be

prepared to adapt your demands based on the temperature of the conversation – obviously, if you get a telling off, this is not the time to ask for a wedge of extra cash, but it *is* the time to be strategic about your ambitions and to voice them with clarity and passion.

- Performance reviews are often linked to pay rises, so take this whole process seriously. It's a good time to reflect on what you've learnt and what you've achieved since you were hired (or since your last appraisal), and do not be coy about stating those achievements. Don't turn it into a bragging session, but don't be afraid, either, to point out what value you have added to the organization. Pay rises are easier to come by when you're able to cite tangible examples of your contribution. They don't happen in isolation.

- Make sure the conversation ends with a plan for what will happen next. Appraisals are no good if they're a cosy chat with no consequences. You should leave the meeting having agreed achievable goals to be completed within a realistic timeframe and with a sense that you've been heard and are better equipped to do your job well. You also need to have set a date for a follow-up meeting (and not a million months away).

Any appraisal conversation can be nerve-wracking. However cheerfully it's conducted, it's fundamentally still an assessment of you and your performance and is likely to include criticism as well as pats on the back. So consider how you respond to feedback too. I know I'm a horribly praise-driven, gold-star-seeking missile. I can't help it. If I've done well, I want someone to tell me (gushingly and repeatedly). So if I'm appraised by someone who isn't that demonstrative, I feel I have failed. This is about my ego rather than the reality of the situation. It's taken me years to realize that recognition isn't the ultimate goal. If you want praise, call your grandparents. If you want professional development, get an appraisal.

Timesheets

Being required to complete a timesheet might seem a draconian chore of a task. Accounting for your every minute isn't easy and it can feel a bit like you're being asked to justify your every move. But many businesses use timesheets as a way of managing resources and for literally accounting for working hours. It's both a record and a billing mechanism.

Filling in your timesheets properly is important because it means your work is allocated efficiently and charged out correctly. It is the data that fees are structured around and that staffing levels are planned against. Depending on the method your organization uses (which can range from Post-it notes to computer timeouts for overdue timesheets), you'll find various ways of keeping track of your time. But if you delay too long there is no chance that you'll remember accurately, if at all, what you were working on five Tuesdays ago. And if you make it up, you skew the whole system. Build this tiny but crucial piece of admin into your daily routine. Do it before you leave at the end of the day or when you first sit down at your desk.

And remember, if your time is supposed to be divided across different parts of a business but you actually spend every day on one tedious aspect, then your timesheet can help you evidence this discrepancy and renegotiate (either by getting more resources or by simplifying your way out of the doldrums).

Expenses

It's often the case that you'll be able to claim for the costs you incur as part of your doing your job. If you're self-employed, such costs may be eligible for tax relief, so check that too. Legitimate expenses might include a mileage charge for driving your own car to a site visit, buying lunch for a client or hiring specific equipment for a job. But before you present the receipts, make sure that your claim is eligible for reimbursement and submitted correctly. Be careful to not assume what is in scope: you may think that something is work related, like lunch with a colleague, local travel or a coffee with a contact, and then find that it's not, or claim twenty pounds for lunch when the company imposes a ten-pound limit, which is all a bit awkward and embarrassing. And you can't regurgitate that luxury sandwich.

If you're consistently having to fork out up front for costs incurred, while waiting for weeks to get your expenses reimbursed – bring this up with your HR department. Not everyone can afford to cover company costs even for a few days, so make your employer aware of that rather than worry about having enough money for your bus fare home.

Booking Leave

In education, you're used to taking time off between terms in a gentle, frequent and predictable structure. You're used to summers so long you go a bit feral and forget how to write your name. And you're never far from a restorative half-term break.

Sadly, that pattern is over for you. In France, for example, you'll enjoy a statutory minimum of twenty-five days' paid leave and eleven public holidays, in Japan ten days' statutory leave and fifteen public holidays and in Canada ten days' statutory leave and nine public holidays,[1] which might seem shocking compared with the generosity of leisure time you're accustomed to (let's all move to France?). On top of that, you now have to compete with your colleagues' plans and get approval from your bosses before you decide to book a week in Ibiza. It takes some getting used to.

Find out the system for booking leave in your organization. Make sure you follow it to the letter. Sometimes one person keeps the vacation calendar and is gatekeeper of the whole thing. Your boss probably needs to sign off your request and there may be forms or formalities around that. And you must personally ensure that everything is agreed and confirmed before you book that round-the-world trip on a credit card.

How to be clever with your vacation planning:

- Tag your time off to a public holiday. This will effectively gain you an extra day of your trip.
- Plan ahead. If you know you need to attend a festival or a wedding, or you must see Japan in blossom season – get these dates in early. Big trips needs to be secured in the diary well in advance to avoid the disappointment of a clash with someone else's plans.
- Avoid school holidays. If you don't have kids, go away in term time. It's cheaper, it won't be full of children and your parenting colleagues will love you because you'll be working in the school holidays and they usually don't have as much flexibility about when to take time off.
- Find out how much leave you're entitled to, whether it accumulates with years served, if you can buy extra days or sell them in return for more money in your pay cheque and if you can carry any unused time forward into a new 'holiday year'.

OOO

Oh, the Out of Office. A phrase so cheerful it even features on T-shirts and cheap bikini bottoms.

But before you start hashtagging OOO everywhere – you have to actually set an OOO reply on all your devices. So what's the best wording?

Primarily there are only two things people need to know when they receive an automated alert that you are not in the office.

1. How long will you be away for? (Or, more accurately: AARGH!! WHEN ARE YOU COMING BACK???)
2. Who should they contact in your absence if they can't wait until then? (Remember to ask that person before you namecheck them on your autoreply.)

Anything else is extra. We don't need to visualize you in a sarong. We don't need to know the details of your vacation destination. Or that Paris is beautiful in springtime. Just keep it simple.

The creative OOO notification has enjoyed fame in recent years, with some outrageous examples going viral. But honestly, the time it takes to type that witty wording is time you could be packing. And mostly, attempts at comedy versions just wind people up, especially if they're contacting you with an urgent message. Yes, you are on holiday and we are not. Try to be a bit gracious in your absence.

If it's appropriate and you want to go beyond the standard information, then consider the following add-ons:

- Can you direct people to information that they might need in your absence?
- Is there something about your team's latest work you'd like them to watch/engage with? A news story about the company? Include the link at the bottom of your 'away' message.
- Are there key things someone might want to know about urgently? Are there other people they can contact to answer their question? The more you can help the person receiving the auto response to solve their own problem, the fewer things you'll need to follow up on your return.

As a side note, I think the most artful use of the OOO function is actually not when you're on holiday but when you're really ON duty. If you have a whole afternoon in a meeting or a two-day conference, or you're travelling across the country – say so. It's helpful to know that 'I'm unavailable for most of today at a summit meeting/on a train/in a bunker and I won't be regularly checking my emails. If your message is urgent, please text me on X or contact Y in my absence'. Doing this gives you permission to pay attention in the room and to be properly present, rather than trying to write stealth emails under the table. And it's a responsible way to manage your colleagues and partners – they won't sit around waiting for your reply and they won't think you're ignoring them. We are all so used to reactive, super-quick response times that it's sometimes essential to give yourself permission to spend time away from your email, doing a different kind of working.

As a general rule, if you're on vacation, you're on vacation. The law varies by country, however: for example in the UK workers cannot be made to work more than forty-eight hours a week and are entitled to at least one day off in seven. Recent legislation in France made it obligatory for companies with more than fifty workers to set out a charter of good conduct, specifying the hours during which staff are not expected or obliged to send or answer emails.[2] But you might experience a culture that expects you to monitor your inbox from your sun lounger. For the most part you have a choice, but you might find some liberal interpretations of the standard contract clause 'be willing to work flexibly when the job requires'.

If you work in a culture that doesn't switch off (or if your team are not organized enough to work without contacting you every five minutes), try the following:

- Set aside some time before you leave to compile a status report for your team; the better your handover notes, the less likely you'll be interrupted while on holiday
- Put your work in order so that it's clear for whoever needs to pick it up; for each area of your work, set out what its status is and what needs to happen while you are away
- Set some clear rules before you leave about what you can be contacted for and what can wait

- Agree set times you'll catch up on emails or set up a regular time for a call with your team or boss
- Tell people how to contact you, e.g. by phone if it is urgent and by email if it can wait
- If you do need to do a task on holiday, communicate with your boss about what needs to be done, complete the urgent task, delegate the next steps and then go back to your holiday
- If you're away with a partner or friends, tell them what you are doing and how long it will take, rather than leave them wondering if/ when you'll ever be able to get back to the pool – they're on holiday too, after all

When you return to work, have a set of brief, informal meetings with relevant people. These conversations are great for quickly getting on top of what's happened and what needs to happen next, and your recharged perspective can help problem solve and invigorate the work.

Try to avoid getting sucked into dealing with every single email or missed task on your return. You'll lose two days, new work will stack up and you'll undo all the benefits of your break. Instead, scan for anything urgent, start up a separate file and build in some time each day to process the backlog alongside your daily tasks.

Remember, time away from work is important. Our brains need to read bad thrillers and have afternoon naps sometimes. And poolside pina coladas genuinely make you a better employee. Holidays help you manage stress, rejuvenate and fuel creativity. Yet in the UK only 12 per cent of young people take their full entitlement.[3] So plan properly and then protect your time off. 'All work and no play' is a miserable way to live, and that's why you've never seen it printed on a T-shirt or bikini bottoms.

Section 8
Staying Awake and Thinking Craftily

A lot of the advice in this book is about how to do a decent day's work. But that's not the whole picture. Being good at turning up is important, but so is knowing when to stop doing that. When to start looking around and scoping out new possibilities. How to progress from one environment to the next. And what to do when you want to change direction entirely . . .

This book is designed to help you be comfortable at work – calm, confident and curious. But I don't want you to get *too* comfortable.

Each of us has their own version of ambition. Some people want to run massive corporations. Others want to retire at thirty-five. You might want to make millions. Or to live quietly and read a novel a day. But each of these choices requires the imagining of a future, the idealizing of a lifestyle and a solid plan to turn that into a reality.

Ambitious people all share one quality – not a definition of success (because everyone's version of success looks so very different) but a sense that they are always paying attention and thinking about what comes next. Not much happens by accident; most significant events result from the accumulation of lots and lots of everyday decisions. Some will be acute and instinctive, others need agonizing over, but it's better to make those decisions with even a vague sense of where you'd like to end up and what the shape of *your* success looks like. Even if you want to stay at home making animals out of upcycled felt, you're definitely going to need a plan to execute that very particular lifestyle.

I'm not talking about rigid, frightening five-year plans. In fact, kind of the opposite – this is about staying wide awake wherever you are, however comfortable you've become. And sometimes it's about being a bit crafty.

How to be Crafty

What do I mean by 'crafty'? I don't want you to become scheming or manipulative. I just want you to think of sideways-in, unexpected approaches or ways to create opportunities where there seemingly are none. When actor Phoebe Waller-Bridge felt frustrated at the sort of parts on offer, she didn't give up, she created, wrote and starred in the sensation that is *Fleabag*.

Sometimes you might want to get somewhere (for example – break into an industry, understand the way a business works, or attract the attention of someone you admire professionally) and there's no obvious route. Don't be put off. Instead, get creative.

I am a huge believer in finding an elliptical way in. It's especially useful when you have no links to an industry, no one who can introduce you or hook you up. When I wanted to be a columnist, I knew that as an unknown writer I stood very little chance of being given a gig by any newspaper or popular magazine. I was no one, and I'd never written anything before. But I had a good idea and I was confident it had legs, so I wrote a few sample pieces and approached the venerable institution that is *The Lady*. Launched in 1885 and widely respected as England's longest-running weekly magazine, it was not the most natural choice. It had, and still has, a readership of charming, elderly women who enjoy gardening and reading adverts for domestic staff. But it also had a new editor, Rachel Johnson, whom I guessed would be looking for fresh voices. And in this context, what could feel fresher than a twenty-eight-year-old writing for the first time?

I guessed her email address, took a punt and pressed Send. She called me in for a fifteen-minute meeting. Then she gave me a full-page column for a year. With pictures.

I could have spent months being rejected by a long list of familiar, flashy titles. But what I needed was my first opportunity – the space to prove I could do the job. And at the end of that year I had a portfolio of published work, a box of fan mail from women in their nineties (which I will always treasure) and the confidence to think I might want to do more writing in the future. Result.

So often, all you need is the one move that will unlock all the other moves. That move is rarely an obvious one. It's not going to come and find you, you have to plot it. Once you've had that entry-level experience or elegant segue, you can repackage and refer to it when you level up elsewhere.

Make approaches, write letters, reach out. If you make yourself visible, available and credible and if your work is good – you will find that people will give you a chance.

Finally, a note on approaching people. Of course, social media has made everyone seem accessible, or at least contactable. But DMs are easy to ignore and the speed and quantity of our tech correspondence means that lots of it gets overlooked or ignored. Don't dismiss the value of a proper handwritten letter. In a brutally modern world, a letter is a surprisingly refreshing thing.

Are Life Goals a Good Idea?

Having goals can be a valuable way to get to where you want to be. As David J. Schwartz says in *The Magic of Thinking Big*, 'A goal is an objective, a purpose. A goal is more than a dream; it's a dream being acted upon. A goal is more than a hazy "Oh, I wish I could." A goal is clear "This is what I'm working toward." ' The act of setting goals links your intention to the action you take to achieve them.[1] To be effective they need a defined plan that sets out how they will be delivered, accompanied by regular monitoring of progress. They'll need to be specific, measurable, realistic and able to be delivered within a set period of time. And they need to align with your strengths or be within reach of your existing skills. So, if you are lucky enough to have clarity on what you want to achieve and how to achieve it, go wild with the goals.

But what about those of us who don't have that sense of purpose or ambitions that can be easily articulated? Here are a few tips on how to set some goals for people who aren't sure:

- Sketch out what you'd like to see in 'the future' vs a specific number of years (it sometimes helps to draw rather than list them) and prioritize a few key things in that picture (remember, this is an exercise, not a contract, so use your imagination)
- Keep to between three and five ambitious goals
- Make them about what *you* want, not what you think others would like you to achieve
- Describe what will happen when you reach these goals, not how you'll get there
- Describe new things rather than what you're doing already
- Set out a plan – it doesn't matter if it starts vague, you can refine it over time
- Share your goals with people you trust and discuss your plans with them

If you've been visualizing an outcome for a long time, sometimes the actual working towards it can feel like a bit of a slog. When that happens, I find it helps to imagine a weird, tangential aspect to the project. Embarrassing though it is to admit, when I've had moments of struggle while writing these eighty-odd thousand words, I've allowed myself a daydreaming session about who I'd like to voice the audiobook version (fantasy casting includes Jennifer Lawrence and the Duchess of Sussex, but I'll happily settle for Stephen Fry as he seems to read everything else).

Beware of losing yourself in the pursuit of your goals.

A narrow focus on end results can dampen your creativity or too easily lead to risky, unethical behaviour.[2] Your career may take many unexpected turns and opportunities will present themselves along the way, so being too rigidly driven by a predetermined set of ambitions can mean that you miss these moments. Because traditional career ladders aren't as prevalent as they used to be, a core of knowing what you want, while being open to what presents itself is a really good strategy.

And if you still have no idea what you want, embrace it, and be open to inspiration. It might be just round the corner.

Don't Assume the Traditional Path is the Only Path

I wish I'd known when I was younger that you don't need to conform. You can build your own version of the story. I set up a business, even though I thought I never would because I'd lost my home. I didn't go to university, but I feel I went back and got educated much later in life. And those things have served me well. So it doesn't matter if you don't take the traditional obvious route, you can take a different one and that adventure might serve you even better.

KATHLEEN SAXTON, CEO, THE LIGHTHOUSE
COMPANY, SPECIALIST EXECUTIVE SEARCH COMPANY
AND FORMER ICE-CREAM SERVER

It's tempting to believe that the organized, familiar and established routes to employment are the only routes. They're certainly the most visible. But there are lots of other ways to get a foot in the door or a rung up the ladder. As Rosalind Jana says in 'Rites of Passage', in *Rife: 21 Stories from Britain's Youth*:

> What frustrated me then, and interests me now, are the very specific messages we absorb about the order we're meant to do things in. I was miles ahead in some areas, given I'd turned up at uni with an imminent book deal in the wings and a blog that had seen me featured in publications around the world. But I'd still been swayed by this idea that I was incomplete until I'd ticked off everything else on the 'growing up' checklist.[3]

Don't feel that you need to do everything according to some predetermined order. If you don't fancy, or aren't eligible for higher education, or a graduate or apprentice scheme, don't feel defeated. Just find alternative ways in. Here are some people who famously didn't take the obvious routes and reinvented themselves in the process:

- **Arnold Schwarzenegger:** body builder, Hollywood actor and Governor of California
- **Vera Wang:** figure skater, editor and fashion designer
- **Tim and Nina Zagat:** lawyers and restaurant critics
- **Marie Forleo:** entrepreneur, writer, TV host and life coach

You could dismiss the list above for being famous first and therefore able to do what they please. But really, each of them took their skills and applied them to a new pursuit, and then worked incredibly hard to make a success of their new career (often working even harder to overcome preconceptions).

The difference between a lifetime of reinvention and a career rut in ten years' time is about being clever about what you learn along the way. And that means investing in transferable skills that can get you from where you are to where you want to be, even if you're not sure where that is yet. Think of them like a pension – they may not feel like today's priority, but you'll thank yourself later for the foresight in investing in them.

So what are these skills? Broadly, they fall into the following categories:[4]

- Knowledge – what you know (markets, products)
- Attitudes – how you approach things (enthusiasm, motivation)
- Character – your personality/personal qualities (sense of humour, diplomacy)
- Strengths – things you are naturally talented at (public speaking, numeracy)
- Experience – what you have done (work experience, qualifications, training, voluntary work)

In each role you do, think about the transferable skills you're gaining. Note down how you learnt them, perhaps how you prepared for a big presentation or the process you used to solve a new technical problem, and anticipate how you might apply that to a new challenge.

Take a look at the jobs you want to do in the future and identify the skills required that you don't yet have – it might be team leadership, industry expertise or influencing people – and find opportunities to incorporate these traits in your current role. Most job adverts ask for examples where you've demonstrated your skills or aptitudes, so documenting how you learnt those skills is great preparation for your next job application.

It is nerve-wracking trying to break into any new situation, especially if you're taking a new approach. But the most important thing to remember is that people want to be impressed. In fact, they are waiting to be impressed. It's completely joyful to meet someone and be excited by them. Having interviewed tons of people over the years I can tell you that there's an irrepressible pleasure in an encounter during which an individual makes you laugh, says something surprisingly insightful, or livens up the room with their smile. That moment when you think, 'This person is interesting . . .'

In contrast, it's not at all enjoyable to watch someone flounder and fail.

Hiring and keeping talent is a nightmare for most organizations. It takes time, costs money and is fraught with risk. So if you are clever and crafty and you find an unusual route in, if you appear as if by magic, then everyone is delighted. Without a recruitment fee? Bonus.

Shark out opportunities, hustle for introductory conversations. It takes guts, but if you remember that people are on your side it's easier to take a risk and try to be brilliant.

How to Create Opportunities Where There are None

There will be wonderful times in your life where you can say 'yes' to (almost) everything, hit some dead ends and still make many big leaps.

During your career you'll face decisions between choosing the better paid but less exciting job or taking a chance on the more risky opportunity. It's often a question of whether you want to learn or earn. If it's the former, shore up your defences – time, money, support network – and give it a whirl. Because equally, there are periods when your priorities will be elsewhere – whether it's a young family, an interesting point in the development of your side hustle or a time when you'll need to put someone else in your life first and you might want to take the less thrilling but doable job for a bit.

Even if you have all the options to choose from, there are pros and cons in any choice of role: sometimes a stable job in a great company is better than a snazzy title at an unknown organization. In the former you'll learn a lot about how a great organization delivers and in the latter you'll learn a lot about yourself. And then there will be times when you'll consider whether to take a chance and create a role that hasn't been thought of before.

Embracing opportunity means being prepared to challenge your thinking about what your limits are.

Stanford professor Carol Dweck contrasts two ways of thinking in her book *Mindset: Changing the Way You Think to Fulfil Your Potential*: the fixed mindset, which believes our skills and intelligence are innate and the growth mindset that invites challenge and learning.

As Sam Conniff Allende says in his book *Be More Pirate* we can make great leaps by being prepared to break the accepted rules and create something new: 'there's power in stepping outside anachronistic structures and challenging broken systems that benefit the few with new ideas that can benefit and inspire the many'.

Remember that opportunity doesn't pop into existence. You may be lucky enough for the Muse to speak to you on occasion, but mostly opportunity is created for you by someone or will come from a sequence of events that evolved around you.

Here are some tips on how to create opportunity at work:

- Take a look at your strengths and weaknesses, using a framework similar to that in Jenny Blake's *Pivot* and choose areas you would like to bolster
- Offer to assist on new-wave projects or volunteer for pitches
- Talk to your friends or colleagues who do very different jobs; discover what's good about what they do, what's missing and develop new ideas together that can help solve these problems

- Get involved in projects that are looking to deliver change and can benefit from your talents
- Become an expert in a specific aspect of your work, gaining the most knowledge or developing an advanced skill
- Express an interest in mentoring schemes if your employer has one or find someone to act as a mentor; mentor someone younger than you as soon as you can, it's rewarding and enlightening
- If you are in a large organization, look into opportunities to work with new teams or work abroad

Spend more time preparing and less time thinking about who knows who or how you might be able to hook yourself up. Instead be the absolute best option and that will shine through. The culture of your workplace will determine what this looks like, so it's worth reading 'Company Culture' in Section 3 first to help you identify the qualities your organization values and to make sure that you're standing out for the right reasons.

Try not to look like you're spending all your time waiting for the next opportunity rather than getting on with the job in hand. Remember, that opportunity is often already there, where you are and among the team you're in – don't miss what's right in front of you. Keeping focussed and delivering a great job, even when it gets dull, is often a very good signal to others about your perseverance and means you'll be front of mind for them when something interesting comes along.

The 'Hype Cycle' of a New Job

During your career you'll no doubt encounter the 'hype cycle'. It was coined by the firm Gartner to describe the difference between excitement about new technology and the reality of whether it delivers what's hoped for it. It applies equally well to people.[5] This occurs in four stages:

- The exciting period between being offered a job and the first few weeks in it, which are filled with inflated expectations
- Followed by a trough of disillusionment, when you realize that there are shortcomings in the role/environment
- Followed by the slope of enlightenment where you stretch and test your abilities
- And then the plateau of productivity where you've got to grips with everything, and you're delivering, learning and earning all in equal proportion

After a few cycles of doing the work competently in the plateau of productivity, you'll have made a good enough impression on the key people for them to trust you to get on with the job. For a while this might feel good – the day-to-day runs like clockwork and you've got plenty of time to focus on other areas of your life. But soon, the fact you're not learning anything new may make the hours drag and you'll find your motivation waning.

Now is the time to investigate new opportunities either within or outside your current role.

Always Think Beyond Local

Unlike any previous generation, your job market is truly global. Two generations ago there were jobs for life with local employers. One generation ago the growth of technology meant that international outsourcing became even more commonplace. Today radical outsourcing connects millions of willing freelancers all over the world with a colossal range of tasks.

Over the next few decades the impact of climate change is likely to lead to new patterns of migration and, crucially, more jobs creating innovative, sustainable solutions to meeting our needs. Already, much-criticized millennials are running their organizations in new ways that require new skills and approaches. And if all this tech-enabled, globalized future feels far too intimidating and exhausting, we can also hope that many traditional jobs will be revived as makers are able to find new markets well beyond their own communities.

That said, the local job market still shapes ambition and reality. Not every city has a 'silicon roundabout', not every community wants an enterprise hub. But whether you like it or not, your future will be as daunting and as exciting as the shifts of previous generations. So don't limit your ambition to the size of your village.

Making Progress

In the course of writing this book and recording the supporting podcast, many of the amazing people we've spoken to have been keen to promote the same, simple piece of advice: DON'T RUSH. Which makes this section on progress pretty hard to write. Because it's almost impossible to progress in your career without wanting the next thing and being a bit impatient.

It's easy (and sometimes enjoyable) to drift. To pay the bills and go on holiday and coast along. And that's fine too. But if you do feel urgent, if your version of ambition requires you to press ahead, then still: *don't rush.*

One of the most useful things I've ever been told, when I was being petulant and needy about wanting to publish a novel I'd written, was from a novelist who said, 'Lucy, calm down – nothing is wasted.' That turned out to be more true than I could have ever imagined. Nothing is wasted because whenever you are learning in the world you are banking experience. You can't always or obviously translate that experience into immediate results. Sometimes it feels like you're being distracted from your overall aims. I was grizzling because I wanted my novel to be snapped up and printed quickly and on everyone's beach reading list that same summer.

But my novel was rubbish.

It took me ten years to realize I am not a fiction writer. And in those ten years I've drafted the book you are now reading, in my head, while working on other things. I've thought about it when I've been in factories or on buses and while giving speeches in schools. And all that thinking meant that turning it into a publishable thing was a pleasurable and, dare I say, straightforward task. Because I'd practised. And refined stuff. And because nothing is wasted.

Also, MY GOD am I glad no one ever read that novel. No beach is nice enough to make that experience a good one.

I want to tell you all this because sometimes it takes years for things to come to fruition. You might have to take the circuitous route even if you'd prefer instant flashy success. And there's no shame in this. Take stock regularly. That's not the same as being comparative or judgemental; you don't need to be 'achieving' every day. Often the periods when you learn the most don't feel that productive while you are in them; it isn't until afterwards that you can see clearly what you made while you thought you were looking elsewhere. Most learning materializes when you are too busy to notice. However far you feel from your passions, as long as you are working hard, you will reap some sort of reward. Eventually. But don't panic if it isn't apparent at the time, if the money isn't rolling in or you feel fed up in a fallow period. You don't need to feel anxious about what you're missing out on. Just keep working.

Promotion

Look sharp, deliver your work on time and to a high standard, get a strong internal profile, wait until your boss gets a new job, put your hand up, and the promotion is yours. Right? Well, not always . . .

There's an old adage called the Peter Principle that goes, 'People get promoted to their level of incompetence'. What this means in practice is that those who perform well in their current job are given more and more responsibility until they are promoted to a role that is beyond their ability. Rewarding great performance with higher pay and more responsibility doesn't always deliver the best outcome: the salesperson with the best sales figures doesn't necessarily make the best team manager; the skilled engineer who can drive the quality on the shop floor doesn't naturally morph into the best setter of business strategy. And yet this is all too often how promotion works.[6]

If you want to be promoted up the ranks, the best thing to do is to find out what the job you want entails and learn how to do it. Sure, have the conversation with your boss about your desire to be a manager, but also find out about what really makes a good manager of people, speak to experienced colleagues and offer to take on management responsibility. Similarly, if you want to run a whole project rather than deliver part of it, take a project management course and ask to shadow someone at a higher level. You shouldn't expect promotion to happen straight away, but if you prepare for it, you'll be ready when the opportunity comes.

Progress and promotion are important but don't get hung up on your job title. In my experience, there's a direct correlation between people who care deeply about what they are called and the people who aren't that good.

You can't hide behind a title but oh so many people try to. The only thing that matters is what you actually do, how you spend your days and the hours you put in to produce work you are proud of. Because it's those things that make a reputation. Who cares about a senior VP in a company consisting of thousands of senior VPs? It's far better to have a title that means something and which reflects the reality of your contribution than something that sounds impressive when you say it out loud at parties.

That said, it's important to distinguish between good and bad job titles. Here's a helpful, unscientific table:

Good:
    CEO
    First Lady
    Secretary General
    Nurse

Bad:
    Top Banana (as one new-business director
        I knew had emblazoned on his card)
    The time I tried to be called 'Head of Larks'
        and no one was that up for it
    Dream alchemist (or anything that involves
        the words Genius, Wizard or Rockstar)

Status is made up of far more factors than just your job title, so don't obsess over it.

Sometimes you need to leave an organization in order to move up. If you've been overlooked, or under-supported, or if you fear someone is unfairly blocking your progress, then you need to look elsewhere. If you don't you'll end up feeling trapped and bitter. Research by the UK's Chartered Institute of Personnel and Development found that at any given moment, almost a quarter of employees are looking for a new role, with improved pay and conditions being the leading reason.[7] And it's understandable, since pay growth has dropped to some of the lowest levels in living memory – while it depends on your job and industry, average annual pay rises can be 1 or 2 per cent.

You might hear 'rules' like 'you should only move for 20 per cent or more of your salary'.[8] But while that's good advice, it's not always possible to follow. And, for that matter, moving for a pay increase might not be the best decision in the long run. Research by Matthew Bidwell and Ethan Mollick at the University of Pennsylvania about the careers of MBA graduates found that while employers may offer pay or other incentives to attract candidates from outside their organization, they're more likely to place those new recruits into jobs that are similar to the ones they are already doing. On the other hand, the researchers found that people moving to new jobs within their existing organizations received an average increase of 59 per cent in the number of people they managed and promotion alongside pay rises.[9] Interrogate the landscape before you make any big decisions.

When to Quit

Earlier we covered toxic environments and how to exit them, but there are also other moments when you need to recognize that it's time to move on. Toxic situations are easy to identify (mostly because you feel 100 per cent wretched) but change isn't always preceded by crisis, so it's sometimes hard to know when you need to get out.

Do you feel stuck? Slouchy? Stagnating? A generalized lack of enthusiasm? A reluctance to say yes to things at work? All these are tell-tale signs that the time has come to find pastures new.

Sometimes you have an obvious epiphany, an 'I can't do this any more' day, and if that happens you should take it seriously. I know people who have resigned on the spot in the triumphant afterglow of a big pitch win, as they stare down the barrel of actually running that business thinking, 'I just can't face it.'

Knowing when to walk away is important. Of course, it's better to make considered decisions and carefully strategize your next move before you chuck it all in. But there might be a time in your career where you do flounce out or tell someone to fuck off, and while I don't recommend that as ideal behaviour, know that you can recover from it too. And there is something recklessly wonderful in walking out when you've had enough. As journalist Emily Gould puts it:

Sometimes quitting is the only appropriate response: when an employer is in the wrong, say, or when you have a valid point to make and you need to make it in a very public way. Other times, it's the right thing to do for more complicated reasons. Quitting can show co-workers or colleagues who don't quite have the gumption to get out of obviously bad situations that it can be done; it can inspire others to have the courage to change their lot, maybe in less brazen, more incremental ways.[10]

You probably get to do it once in a career, so make sure you enjoy it. Be mindful you may lose trust or be branded a loose cannon, and that could stick with you for a long time. But don't let that spoil the sensation as you swank out of the building.

When (and How) to Change Direction

The pace of technological change has had a profound effect on careers. Your great-grandparents may have enjoyed a job for life and your grandparents, and possibly parents, could have expected four or five key roles in their career. According to Jenny Blake in *Pivot*, the average tenure in a job among twenty-five to thirty-four-year-olds in the US is now only three years.

There may be times when you choose to change direction. When you get a break and are asked to rise to a new challenge, for example, or you may need to take a pay cut to open up a new path. Sometimes you'll need to take a risk. At other times what you want is right in front of you. Either way, you can't have perspective if you never look up, if your nose is always to the grindstone – so if you crave change, make sure you look all around you.

Pivoting

The old convention used to be: make sure you have at least three years in a job or your CV will look suspicious. And in some people's eyes that's still the case. Recruiters and potential employers are always on the lookout for the short tenure or strange career move that could potentially be hiding a record of poor performance or early dismissal. This is, of course, nonsense – lots of people spend many years being merrily incompetent in the same job.

Rather than time spent in one role, employers are increasingly interested in an ability to move between skillsets, get up to speed, deliver and move on. And in this new territory career planning will be less about short-, medium- and long-term goals and more about knowing how to test the waters and when to splash on in.

Guardian of the concept of pivoting Jenny Blake suggests identifying the pivot point when you need to move and:

- Plant: understand your values, strengths and interests and your vision for the future
- Scan: research, plug knowledge and skills gaps, have conversations and clarify what opportunities interest you most

- Pilot: generate ideas, test those ideas, then take small, smart risks to eventually inform decisions about what's next
- Launch: address the remaining uncertainties and determine when to move and what benchmarks you can hit to be able to transition with confidence
- Lead: take career aspirations into an open conversation and help others to get to where they want to be

And if those first two steps look familiar, it's because they're what we talked about in the opening sections about getting into work in the first place. Well remembered.

Being Sought Out

Sometimes opportunity comes knocking. It might be a tentative tap or a full fanfare. Whatever the volume, it's always quite flattering to be found.

It might be a contact wanting to build a new team and looking for you to join, or it might be a talent professional sounding you out for a new role. Either way, it means you've been identified as possibly being 'of interest'. So how do you get sought out?

Headhunters are not the same as recruiters, although the line between the two can blur. While a recruiter might advertise jobs to pools of candidates, a headhunter is more likely to actively pursue opportunities for candidates or vice versa and coach both sides through the process.

How to get headhunted:

- Find out which headhunters are working in your area of interest and at what level; they will usually focus on specific areas, for example, non-profit senior executives or the food-and-drink industry
- If you would like to propose yourself as a candidate, prepare a brief covering letter and CV, give examples of the industries and types of organizations you are interested in and ask for a conversation about identifying the key things you can bring to a prospective employer or get introduced
- Keep your online presence up to date, relevant and easy to understand; this is where you'll be found (and it's the first place they go to check you out)
- Be generous, helping them to source other candidates from your network, and try to build a long-term relationship over the course of your career
- Just because a headhunter asks if you are interested in a job doesn't mean you should be flattered into saying 'yes'; work with them to develop options and seek their advice on the opportunities and challenges of any role; use the same discipline to determine if this gig is right for you as you would if you had found it yourself

Hybrid Careers

We know that cradle-to-grave jobs are mostly a thing of the past. But what about the trend for variety within or alongside a single role?

As we touched on in a previous chapter, I'm a big fan of the concept of a 'side hustle' but I hate the name. It implies hierarchy; as if the thing you do on the side is beneath or belittled by your main job. It conjures an image of running home, ragged from a day in the office, in order to sell your beloved homemade lemonade from a table on your lawn. Not particularly appealing. And generally not very accurate.

In stark contrast to this picture, a trend is emerging of having two or more significant careers in parallel, where each strand has equal weight.

In her book *The Multi-Hyphen Method*, Emma Gannon shows how a new generation of workers are rejecting the traditional path of getting an education, chasing a job and climbing the career ladder. Instead, they're asserting a new view of work that says, 'You are not your job title, instead you move in between different jobs, alongside powerful strategic personal branding, you funnel, organize, outreach, monetize and schedule your work yourself.' This isn't a new idea: Leonardo da Vinci is a pretty good example of someone who had a multi-hyphen career in the fifteenth century, but more recently the ability to manage multiple jobs and professional identities has become a lot more accessible to everyone.

As creative and complex combinations of work become

more commonplace there's a real opportunity to design your days according to the way you'd like to live. And, of course, there's joy in being able to pursue more than one interest at any one time. As Gannon says 'This is not about having fifteen jobs that you don't like and juggling to make ends meet, tearing your hair out at night. This is an active choice to have more than one job, a career with multiple strands that suits you.'

But beware the 'slashie' trap ('I'm a model slash app developer slash Pekinese breeder. Plus, on Fridays, I run a micro brewery') . . . this is not about dabbling in stuff on a whim. And don't confuse it with having hobbies (although your interests and hobbies can sometimes morph into your work choices – how else do you think I managed to give a TED talk on the unlikely subject of fancy dress?).

And importantly, run only as many things as you can meaningfully commit to. Don't do 20 per cent of everything and call yourself a polymath. No one will take you seriously.

Sabbaticals

When I was twenty-four I took three months off to plan a wedding and that was a terrible use of a sabbatical.

With the security of a job to return to, you have a window in which to experiment and improve. Don't confuse this with a long holiday. Extended time off work (either paid or unpaid) should be used to explore experiences you couldn't otherwise have. Extensive, relevant travel.

An educational course. An international research exercise. A year doing an MBA. There are lots of options.

Think of any sabbatical as an opportunity to enrich yourself in a life-altering, career-enhancing way. Your post-sabbatical self should come back cleverer, with a broader perspective, better qualifications and a nuanced understanding of your place in the world.

Don't waste it buying a couple of bridesmaids' dresses and deciding between chicken or beef. That was a long holiday. And then I got divorced.

Dealing with Change

As you've read this chapter, the prospect of planning your career may have filled you with either excitement or raw panic. In *No Hard Feelings* Liz Fosslien and Mollie West Duffy encourage us to pay attention to these emotions: 'If the thought of becoming a marketing associate fills you with dread you might want to cross that off your list of potential positions. And if you feel a thrill imagining yourself as a data scientist, that's an equally important sign about what openings you should go after.'

You will experience many points of change in work and each will excite a wide range of emotions: from sadness or guilt about leaving a job or team to anticipation and anxiety about a new workplace. At these points, you'll need to be able to manage your emotions, sifting out the helpful feelings from the unhelpful feelings and building your resilience to the negative effects of change. Here are some tips about how to do this:

- Even if the change is not of your choosing, be gracious and make sure you're prepared. Plan out the steps from one situation to another; even if you don't want to move to another role, for instance, do a good handover and make sure you leave everything as you would want to find it.

- Mark the occasion. You might not want to have a 'leaving do' for any number of legitimate reasons, but the ritual of gathering and celebrating is important for you and your colleagues.

- Keep focussed on why you are making the change. Write it down and remind yourself of these reasons a few weeks into your new role, when reality bites and you're wondering whether you made the right move.

- List your emotions. Talk to people you trust and get advice from people who have had similar experiences.

- Challenge your negative assumptions and replace them with positive ones. Know that you'll soon find yourself with a whole new set of opportunities ahead, even if things are tricky at the beginning. That's completely normal.

- Reread the early sections of this book about starting out and apply some of that thinking to your new role.

Further Resources

Jenny Blake, *Pivot: The Only Move That Matters is Your Next One* (Portfolio, 2016)

Sam Conniff Allende, *Be More Pirate: Or How to Take on the World and Win* (Penguin, 2018)

Carol Dweck, *Mindset – Updated Edition: Changing the Way You Think to Fulfil Your Potential* (Robinson, 2017)

Liz Fosslien and Mollie West Duffy, *No Hard Feelings: Emotions at Work and How They Help Us Succeed* (Portfolio Penguin, 2019)

Emma Gannon, *The Multi-Hyphen Method* (Hodder & Stoughton, 2018)

David J. Schwartz, *The Magic of Thinking Big* (Prentice Hall, 1959)

Section 9
Your
Future

nitially I'd planned to write about retirement in these final pages. That would be the logical conclusion to a book about work. We started at the beginning, so surely we should finish at the end? But retirement is such a distant and vague concept that, actually, it has no place here. This is a book about the beginnings of things. It's about promise and potential and everything that is in store for you.

You are not racing towards retirement. Instead you are about to embark on the biggest, most meandering of adventures – you'll grow, share, travel, fall in love, age and flirt with fulfilment all against the backdrop of your working life. It's an arch of experience that is decades long, fraught with frustration and touched with triumph – it's epic. And it's all about to happen.

In your lifetime, your work opportunities will be numerous, wide and multifaceted. You can choose but you can also change. The traditional binary divisions between art and science or commerce and charity have all been blurred and your life will be richer for it. Embrace that blur – refuse to faithfully occupy one discipline, one subject, one well-trodden path.

Equally, with all that freedom, try not to be crushed by the enormity of the question 'What am I going to do all my working life?' Apart from anything else, you'll still be asking yourself that in another twenty years' time; I'm afraid it never really goes away. Instead, look at the buildings you admire, medicine you need, clothes you wear, objects you treasure, music you play, systems that keep you safe, technology in its infancy – and be inspired by them all. These things exist because people worked on them. Work is not separate from life, it's not annexed off. If it feels separate that's just because it's someone else's work.

I wrote this book because I felt that there was a failure at the heart of education and from employers to adequately prepare young adults to integrate into and enjoy work. But you don't own that failure, it belongs to them. Remember that each generation, when they get secure and successful, start to demonize the young people who follow them for being lazy, inexperienced, untrained or untrainable – conveniently forgetting that they too were once lazy, inexperienced, untrained or untrainable. It's not some new phenomenon. In 1906 the snappily titled UK government report of the Consultative Committee upon Questions Affecting Higher Elementary Schools shows us that, even then, employers believed standards were slipping: 'The belief was expressed by one witness whose long experience entitles his opinion to weight, that these moral qualities are to-day far less commonly found among the working classes than they used to be thirty years ago, in spite of a larger number of schools and an increasing demand for the qualities themselves'.[1]

Let's stop repeating the same tired untruths.

I see so much enthusiasm in young adults cowed by invented but pervading beliefs in their attitudinal deficiencies. How many pieces about millennial malaise or mean-spirited caricatures of Gen Z are published every day? I'd like this book to empower you to ignore all that nonsense and instead spend your energy on demonstrating your strength, ingenuity, grace and leadership. Because these are the real qualities that we should hand down generation to generation. These are the traits you already possess and are about to hone. Lots of this book has focussed on really practical skills, but trust me, you are about to discover, by nurturing those skills, the complete connection between attention to detail and strength, getting organized and ingenuity, dealing with difficult people and grace, and learning to listen and leadership. These are not basic things, they are foundational things; they give talent traction and turn potential into power.

It is difficult to write these closing words without resorting to grandiose statements. Some naff adaptation of 'standing on the shoulders of giants' or a budget attempt at a rousing, rallying cry. *Onwards!* And yet, actually, all the advice I wanted to impart, you've now read, so it's tempting to simply wave you on your way. With best wishes. Off you pop. Does that feel like too flat a note to end on?

We all know the truth is, you are not standing on the shoulders of giants. You've inherited a world of mess and destruction and you have to solve a whole selection of shitty situations created by the very people who tell you *your* attitude stinks? The most compelling agents of change are not patronized by their predecessors, they are enraged by them. On top of all your other challenges, as you navigate your adult life (making money, being happy, getting enough vitamins) you also need to make the world a better place, we're all relying on it. You are the most diverse and connected generation in history.[2] Now it's incumbent upon you to be the most activist generation too. You are not lazy or too late. You're bang on time and you're ready.

Stay close to people who transform your thinking and expose and enable your abilities. You might meet characters who resent your youth, or rather, your future. People who are paranoid about becoming redundant relics in the wake of your energy. Gently push past them and find the people who love what they do as much as you do. Remember that when they say you don't 'fit' the role or the organization, it's just as much the case that the role or the organization doesn't fit with you, your ambition and your purpose. So find or make something that does. Set grumbling to one side and instead listen carefully to anyone who wants to teach you.

There is so much anxiety in our lives right now. Not just collective, climate-change-sized catastrophizing, but also quieter, closet, self-flagellating worry. Be aware that opportunity and anxiety often come hand in hand and as you make your way into the world of work you might experience spikes of it. But please resist the temptation to feel bleak about your prospects. A purposeful, fulfilling job that you are proud of has a significantly positive effect on your mental health and means that working is one of the best ways to invest in your wellbeing.[3]

If you want to build new systems, save the planet or raise a family, you're going to need a job. In the course of writing this book we have spoken to hundreds of people who want to employ you and who want you to thrive. The intense cross-pollination of ideas in these conversations have really surprised us – what are the chances of a US brain surgeon and a British TV producer who have never met, both telling us on the same day about '5B', the first dedicated hospital ward for AIDS patients at San Francisco General Hospital, in the 1980s? From completely different perspectives they cross over because of a passion for ideas and human endeavour. Work. It doesn't matter what profession you're in, if you can harness ideas and passion you will form connections and bonds with people well beyond the four walls of your experience or expertise. Work is about more than just earning a crust, it's about who we are as people.

All jobs, whether they are technical or philosophical, involve craft. You have to work at it every day, refining that craft. There's something so satisfying about that, generating real personal pride. The dignity in doing a decent job well is a defining and enriching way of life. And it pays the bills.

You're about to make lots of choices about who you are and who you want to become. It isn't until we hit our working lives that we properly start to carve out our place in the world. Learn how to do something competently and then try to do it with flair. Everything is more enjoyable with a little bit of flair. Look people in the eye,

form connections, be interested. Live openly and generously and you will, I promise, have a solidly good time
most of the time.

And then, just keep going. Do your best. And that will
be enough.

Acknowledgements

This book is the result of many urgent and heartfelt conversations with friends, colleagues, clients and collaborators. We are indebted to everyone who talked it through, made suggestions and added their thoughts along the way. We have been overwhelmed by your passionate insight and the intensity of support for this idea.

Thank you to Martina O'Sullivan, our editor and champion, without whom this book wouldn't exist. And to the whole team at Penguin – Celia Buzuk, Hannah Chukwu, Matthew Crossey, Leo Donlan and Ellie Smith – and to Trevor Horwood for his work on the manuscript.

The stories, advice and reflections from our early podcast guests and contributors were generously given by Graham Allcott, Antonia Belcher, Dr Marc Bush, Mollie Case, Shane Connolly, Susan Daniels, Gabby Deeming, Rob Fitch, Marie Forleo, Nell Gifford, Dan Gillespie-Sells, Paul Gillooly, Thore Graepel, Patrick Grant, Dr Joe Grove, Felicity Hassan, Manuel Heichlinger, Dr Rahul Jandial, Duncan Jennings, Katie Keith, Marcus Lyon, Gugulethu Ndebele, Andy Phippen, Vanessa Podmore, Andy Ratcliffe, David Ruebain, Andrew Salter, Simon Salter, Suki Sandhu, OBE, Kathleen Saxton, Nikesh Shukla, William Smalley, Elizabeth Taylor, Rosie Vogel-Eades, Rob Welch, Mollie West-Duffy, Vicki Willden-Lebrecht and Jude Yawson.

ACKNOWLEDGEMENTS

Invaluable insights came from Oli Barrett, Euan Blair, Graham Briggs, Matt Bryne, Tomas Burke, Grant Collins, John Cope, Jonas Chartock, Neil Crowther, Tobit Emmens, Leonora Faggionato, Sam Friedman, Sue Glover, Teddy Godfree, Bridie Hall, Sarah Holt, Debra Jones, Rew Lowe, Enda McCarthy, David Mortimer, Victoria Pickett, Miranda Pountney, Catherine Ritman-Smith, Leanne Smith, Jess Taylor and Sam Taylor, Tom Vick and Benjamin Wild.

Thanks to all our contributors and cameo appearances for your humour and wisdom. Thank you to Mr Smith for his taste and moral support. And to Susan and Peter Marston for Xinara House (the perfect place to write many thousands of words).

We are grateful to all the young people who, at the beginning their careers, informed the writing of this book, including the Somerset House Creative Job Studio and the Youth Advisory Board at the National Deaf Children's Society. Francesca Danmole and Leon Hill, who organized a superb session with the British Youth Council Work Experience Action Group to provide feedback on the draft of this book: Max, Tolu, Diana, James, Asia, Sanah and Mun. Masuma Islam, Poppy Smith and Jake Oakes gave feedback on the manuscript. Thank you also to Catherine Havers and the Leeds University Careers Centre and the team at Speakers for Schools for the opportunity to talk to so many young people about their hopes and ambitions. And to the ERSA and their members for their dedication in supporting people into work.

Thanks to the Clayton family for being great material

ACKNOWLEDGEMENTS

and to Greg Clayton for very occasionally making a joke better. To Christopher Godfree for definitely making one joke better. With love to Kit Clayton Jennings for being a patient but surprisingly persuasive motivational speaker when our attitude occasionally stank. Thank you to Chris and Ron Haines for teaching the value of taking pride in a job well done and Pam Roberts for the best bit of interview advice ever: get a haircut.

And lastly to all our future guests on *How to Go to Work*, the podcast, for your honesty and openness. Long may it continue.

Notes

Introduction

1 De Neve, Jan-Emmanuel and Ward, George W. (2017), Happiness at Work, Saïd Business School Research Paper, http://eureka.sbs.ox.ac.uk/6319/1/2017-07.pdf
2 BBC News (2014), Young People Lack Workplace Skills, Firms Say in Survey, https://www.bbc.co.uk/news/business-29454002

1 Starting Out

1 McKnight, A. (2015), Downward mobility, opportunity hoarding and the 'glass floor', https://www.gov.uk/government/uploads/system/uploads/attachment_data/file/447575/Downward_mobility_opportunity_hoarding_and_the_glass_floor.pdf
2 http://transcripts.cnn.com/TRANSCRIPTS/1507/08/acd.01.html
3 Kanter, Rosabeth Moss (2014), Overcome the Eight Barriers to Confidence, Harvard Business Review, https://hbr.org/2014/01/overcome-the-eight-barriers-to-confidence
4 Careers & Enterprise Company (2019), State of the Nation 2019, https://www.careersandenterprise.co.uk/sites/default/files/uploaded/state-of-the-nation-2019-digital.pdf

5 *Guardian* (2014), Tesco Boss Orders Senior Staff Back to the Shop Floor, https://www.theguardian.com/business/2014/oct/01/tesco-boss-orders-senior-staff-work-shop-floor

6 Schiess, M. (2017), Three Reasons Why 'Starting at the Bottom' of the Career Ladder is the Catalyst to Getting to the Top, https://medium.com/@maddie.schiess/three-reasons-why-starting-at-the-bottom-of-the-career-ladder-is-the-catalyst-to-getting-to-the-9bf02455bb77

7 Heuberger, B., Kasman, M. and Hammond, R. A. (2018), *Recommendations for Improving Youth Financial Literacy Education* (Brookings Institution), https://www.brookings.edu/wp-content/uploads/2018/10/ES_20181001_Financial-Literacy-Recommendations.pdf

8 BritainThinks Blog (2018): Young Adults and Money Management, https://britainthinks.com/news/britainthinks-blog-young-adults-and-money-management

9 Wilcox, K., Laran, J., Stephen, A. T. and Zubcsek, P. P. (2016), How Being Busy Can Increase Motivation and Reduce Task Completion Time, https://psycnet.apa.org/doiLanding?doi=10.1037%2Fpspa0000045

10 Tessema, M. T., Astani, M. and Ready, K. (2014), Does Part-Time Job Affect College Students' Satisfaction and Academic Performance (GPA)? The Case of a Mid-Sized Public University, http://www.sciedu.ca/journal/index.php/ijba/article/download/4388/2517

11 BIS Research Paper Number 143 (2013), Learning from Futuretrack: The Impact of Work Experiences on Higher Education Student Outcomes, https://assets.publishing.service.gov.uk/government/uploads/system/uploads/attachment_data/file/251027/bis-13-1249-learning-from-

futuretrack-impact-of-work-experiences-on-higher-education-student-outcomes.pdf

12 Buzzeo, J. and Cifci, M. (2017), Work Experience, Job Shadowing and Workplace Visits. What Works? (Careers and Enterprise Company), https://www.careersandenterprise.co.uk/sites/default/files/uploaded/careers-enterprise-what-works-report-work-experience.pdf

13 British Youth Council Youth Select Committee (2018), Realising the Potential of Work Experience, https://www.byc.org.uk/wp-content/uploads/2018/11/Youth-Select-Committee-Realising-the-Potential-of-Work-Experience.pdf

14 Buzzeo and Cifci (2017).

15 Adda, J. et al. (2013), Career Progression, Economic Downturns, and Skills, IFS Working Paper W13/24, https://pdfs.semanticscholar.org/3bfb/a0e1f7dc932c7d7fe2ed929c42b5097261aa.pdf

16 Roberts, C. (2017), The Inbetweeners: The New Role of Internships in the Graduate Labour Market, https://www.ippr.org/publications/the-inbetweeners

17 British Fashion Council, Internships, https://www.britishfashioncouncil.co.uk/BFC-Initiatives--Support/BFC-Initiatives/Education/BFC-Colleges-Council/Internships

18 https://www.gov.uk/employment-rights-for-interns

19 https://www.dol.gov/whd/regs/compliance/whdfs71.htm

20 'T. W.' (2014), Are Unpaid Internships Illegal? *The Economist*, https://www.economist.com/the-economist-explains/2014/09/09/are-unpaid-internships-illegal

21 Baines, P. (2005), *Penguin by Design: A Cover Story 1935–2005* (Penguin).

22 Williams, J. (2017), Involving Young People in Volunteering. What Works? (Careers and Enterprise Company).

23 Department for Education and Skills Research report RW 103, The National Youth Agency, Young People's Volunteering and Skills Development, dera.ioe.ac.uk/6643/1/RW103.pdf

24 https://www.oxfam.org.uk/media-centre/press-releases/2017/01/employers-pick-volunteers-over-other-job-candidates-new-research-reveals

25 Williams (2017).

26 Aked, J., Marks, N., Cordon, C. and Thompson, S. (2008), Five Ways to Wellbeing (New Economics Foundation), https://neweconomics.org/uploads/files/8984c5089d5c2285ee_t4m6bhqq5.pdf

27 Lumos (2018), Considering Volunteering Abroad? Here's What You Need to Know, https://www.wearelumos.org/news-and-media/2018/09/27/considering-volunteering-abroad-heres-what-you-need-know/

2 Getting In

1 Min, Ji-A (2017), Ten Ways HR Tech Leaders Can Make the Most of Artificial Intelligence, Personnel Today, https://www.personneltoday.com/hr/ten-ways-hr-tech-leaders-can-make-artificial-intelligence/

2 http://www.careerbuilder.com/share/aboutus/pressreleases detail.aspx?id=pr464&sd=10%2f8%2f2008&ed=12%2f31%2f2008

3 Bock, L. (2014), My Personal Formula for a Winning Résumé, https://www.linkedin.com/pulse/20140929001534-24454816-my-personal-formula-for-a-better-resume

4 Suler, J. (2004), The Online Disinhibition Effect, *CyberPsychology & Behavior*, vol. 7, no. 3, pp. 321–6, https://pdfs.semanticscholar.org/c70a/ae3be9d370ca1520db5edb2b326e3c2f91rb0.pdf

5 Reed, J. (2015), *Why You? 100 Interview Questions You'll Never Fear Again* (Penguin).

6 Cialdini, R. (2016), *Pre-Suasion: A Revolutionary Way to Influence and Persuade* (Random House).

7 AAT (2015), AAT Research Reveals Brits' Awkward Interview Experiences, https://www.aat.org.uk/news/article/aat-research-reveals-brits-awkward-interview-experiences

8 Rajan, A. (2019), Response to 'How to Break into the Elite' Shows Our Frustration with the British Class System, *iNews*, https://inews.co.uk/opinion/response-to-how-to-break-into-the-elite-frustrations-british-class-system/

9 Winch, G. (2015), Why Rejection Hurts so Much – and What to Do About It, https://ideas.ted.com/why-rejection-hurts-so-much-and-what-to-do-about-it/

10 How to Fail with Elizabeth Day, season 3, episode 5: How to Fail: Raven Smith, https://podtail.com/en/podcast/how-to-fail-with-elizabeth-day/s3-ep-5-how-to-fail-raven-smith/

3 The Early Days

1 Porter, M. E. and Nohria, N. (2010), What is Leadership? The CEO's Role in Large Complex Organizations, in Nitin Nohria and Rakesh Khurana (eds.), *Handbook of Leadership Theory and Practice* (Harvard Business Press), pp. 433–74.

2 ACAS (2013), Young People's Views and Experiences on Entering the Workplace, https://www.acas.org.uk/media/3758/Young-peoples-views-and-experiences-on-entering-the-workplace/pdf/Young-peoples-views-and-experiences-on-entering-the-workplace.pdf

3 CIPD (2013), Employers are from Mars, Young People are from Venus: Addressing the Young People/Jobs Mismatch, https://www.cipd.co.uk/knowledge/work/skills/jobs-mismatch-report

4 Curtis, S. (2016), Beyond the Filter: Social Media in the Age of Anxiety, *Elle*, http://www.elle.com/uk/life-and-culture/elle-voices/articles/a31441/beyond-the-filter

5 CIPD (2015), Developing the Next Generation, https://www.cipd.co.uk/Images/developing-next-generation_tcm18-10268.pdf

6 Dell Technologies/Institute for the Future (2017), The Next Era of Human|Machine Partnerships: Emerging Technologies' Impact on Society & Work in 2030, http://www.iftf.org/humanmachinepartnerships/

7 How to Fail with Elizabeth Day, season 1, episode 1: How to Fail: Phoebe Waller-Bridge, https://podtail.com/en/podcast/how-to-fail-with-elizabeth-day/s1-ep1-how-to-fail-phoebe-waller-bridge/

8 Groysberg, B. et al. (2018), The Leader's Guide to Corporate Culture, *Harvard Business Review*, https://hbr.org/2018/01/the-culture-factor

9 Kotter, J. P. and Heskett, J. L. (1992), *Corporate Culture and Performance* (Free Press).

10 Church, A. H. and Conger, J. A. (2018), When You Start a New Job, Pay Attention to These 5 Aspects of Company Culture, *Harvard Business Review*, https://hbr.org/2018/03/

when-you-start-a-new-job-pay-attention-to-these--aspects-5of-company-culture

11 ONS (2018), Young people's career aspirations versus reality, https://www.ons.gov.uk/employmentandlabourmarket/peopleinwork/employmentandemployeetypes/articles/youngpeoplescareeraspirationsversusreality/2018-09-27

12 Brown, M. (2017), LendEDU's Class of 2017 Career Report, https://lendedu.com/blog/class-2017-career-report/; JobStreet (n.d.), Salary Demands of Millennials in Asia: Expectations vs Reality, https://www.jobstreet.com.ph/en/cms/employer/salary-demands-millennials-asia-expecta tions-vs-reality/

13 https://www.gov.uk/national-minimum-wage-rates

14 India Today (2015), Starting Salaries in India Amongst Low-est in Asia-Pacific: Study, https://www.indiatoday.in/india/delhi/story/starting-salaries-in-india-amongst-lowest-in-asia-pacific-study-261833-2015-09-08

15 Whateley, L. (2018), *Money: A User's Guide* (Fourth Estate).

16 Anne Boden (2018), Why we need to #MAKEMONEY EQUAL, https://www.starlingbank.com/blog/make-money-equal/

17 Noreena Hertz (2011), Women and Banks (Institute for Public Policy Research), https://www.ippr.org/files/images/media/files/publication/2011/11/women-banks_Nov2011_8186.pdf?noredirect=1

18 https://www.harpercollins.co.uk/978000235628/slay-in-your-lane-the-black-girl-bible/

19 Mind (2016a), Money and Mental Health, https://www.mind.org.uk/information-support/tips-for-everyday-living/money-and-mental-health/#.XDeOnjj7TIU

20 Bevanger, L. (2017), Norway: The Country Where No Salaries are Secret, https://www.bbc.co.uk/news/magazine-40669239

21 Ducharme, J. (2018), This Is the Amount of Money You Need to Be Happy, According to Research, *Time*, http://time.com/money/5157625/ideal-income-study/

22 Boren, Z. D. (2015), Talking About Money is Britain's Last Taboo, *Independent*, https://www.independent.co.uk/news/science/talking-about-money-is-britains-last-taboo-10508902.html

23 https://hbr.org/2014/04/15-rules-for-negotiating-a-job-offer

24 *Washington Post* (2018), Why Many Companies are Giving Bonuses Not Raises After the New Tax Cuts, https://www.washingtonpost.com/news/on-leadership/wp/2018/01/18/why-many-companies-are-giving-bonuses-not-raises-after-the-new-tax-cuts/?noredirect=on&utm_term=.c43577d6b81f

25 Allcott, G. (2013a), Flipping the 9–5 – Reflections, https://thinkproductive.co.uk/flipping-the-9-5-reflections/

26 Garrow, V. (2016), Presenteeism: A Review of Current Thinking, https://www.employment-studies.co.uk/system/files/resources/files/507_0.pdf

27 Kohll, A. (2018), New Study Shows Correlation Between Employee Engagement and the Long-Lost Lunch Break, *Forbes*, https://www.forbes.com/sites/alankohll/2018/05/29/new-study-shows-correlation-between-employee-engagement-and-the-long-lost-lunch-break/#56e2af1a4efc

28 Krogerus, M. and Tschäppeler, R. (2011), *The Decision Book: Fifty Models for Strategic Thinking* (Profile).

29 Ashkanasy, N. M. and Härtel, C. E. J. (2014), Positive and Negative Effective of Climate and Culture: The Good, the Bad and the Ugly, in Schneider, B. and Barber, K. M. (eds.), *The Oxford Handbook of Organizational Climate and Culture* (Oxford University Press).

4 *The Every Day*

1 https://publications.parliament.uk/pa/cm201617/cmselect/cmpetitions/291/29110.htm#_idTextAnchor078

2 BBC News (2019), 'Japan's Labour Minister Says High Heels at Work are "Necessary"', https://www.bbc.co.uk/news/world-asia-48534453

3 Stewart, G. L. et al. (2008), Exploring the Handshake in Employment Interviews, *Journal of Applied Psychology*, https://pdfs.semanticscholar.org/4ec5/2406b00a950aa5b9098ede199884d51f4507.pdf

4 Dolcos, S. et al. (2012), The Power of a Handshake: Neural Correlates of Evaluative Judgments in Observed Social Interactions, *Journal of Cognitive Neuroscience*, https://www.mitpressjournals.org/doi/full/10.1162/jocn_a_00295

5 *Independent* (2010), British Scientists Devise Guide to the Perfect Handshake, https://www.independent.co.uk/property/house-and-home/british-scientists-devise-guide-to-the-perfect-handshake-2028887.html

6 Cuddy, A. (2012), Your Body Language May Shape Who You Are, https://www.ted.com/talks/amy_cuddy_your_body_language_shapes_who_you_are?language=en

7 Caspersz, D. and Stasinska, A. (2015), Can We Teach Effective Listening? An Exploratory Study, *Journal of University Teaching & Learning Practice*, https://files.eric.ed.gov/fulltext/EJ1063823.pdf

8 Shellenbarger, S. (2013), Is This How You Really Talk? *Wall Street Journal*, https://www.wsj.com/articles/SB10001424127887323735604578440851083674898

9 Anderson, R. C. et al. (2013), Vocal Fry May Undermine the Success of Young Women in the Labor Market, *PLoS One*, https://journals.plos.org/plosone/article/file?id=10.1371/journal.pone.0097506&type=printable

10 Maltz Bovy, P., Checking Privilege Checking, *The Atlantic*, https://www.theatlantic.com/politics/archive/2014/05/check-your-check-your-privilege/361898/

11 Van den Bosch, R. et al. (2018), Authenticity at Work: A Matter of Fit? *Journal of Psychology*, https://www.tandfonline.com/doi/full/10.1080/00223980.2018.1516185

12 http://www.acas.org.uk/index.aspx?articleid=1364

13 TUC/Everyday Sexism Project (2016), Still Just a Bit of Banter? Sexual Harassment in the Workplace in 2016, https://www.tuc.org.uk/sites/default/files/SexualHarassmentreport2016.pdf

14 https://www.eeoc.gov/eeoc/publications/fs-sex.cfm

15 Wallis, H. and Lea, L. (2017), What to Do if You Think You are Being Sexually Harassed at Work, https://www.bbc.co.uk/news/uk-41524922

16 CIPD (2019), Sexual Harassment in the Workplace, https://www.cipd.co.uk/knowledge/fundamentals/emp-law/harassment/sexual-harassment-work-guide; Equality and Human Rights Commission (2018), Turning the Tables: Ending Sexual Harassment at Work, https://www.

equalityhumanrights.com/sites/default/files/ending-sexual-harassment-at-work.pdf

17 Twenge, Jean M. et al. (2010), Generational Differences in Work Values: Leisure and Extrinsic Values Increasing, Social and Intrinsic Values Decreasing, *Journal of Management*, https://www.researchgate.net/publication/228360704_Generational_Differences_in_Work_Values_Leisure_and_Extrinsic_Values_Increasing_Social_and_Intrinsic_Values_Decreasing

18 Winnick, M., Putting a Finger on Our Phone Obsession, dscout, https://blog.dscout.com/mobile-touches#3

19 Love, S. (2018), Nomophobia is the Fear of Not Being Able to Check Your Phone, Vice, https://www.vice.com/en_uk/article/vbqx8m/nomophobia-is-the-fear-of-not-being-able-to-check-your-phone

20 Cajochen, C. et al. (2011), Evening Exposure to a Light-Emitting Diodes (LED)-Backlit Computer Screen Affects Circadian Physiology and Cognitive Performance, *Journal of Applied Physiology*, https://www.physiology.org/doi/full/10.1152/japplphysiol.00165.2011

21 Sparrow, B., Liu, J. and Wegner, D. M. (2011), Google Effects on Memory: Cognitive Consequences of Having Information at Our Fingertips, *Science*, http://scholar.harvard.edu/files/dwegner/files/sparrow_et_al._2011.pdf?m=1360040510

22 Przybylski, A. K. and Weinstein, N. (2012), Can You Connect with Me Now? How the Presence of Mobile Communication Technology Influences Face-to-Face Conversation Quality, *Journal of Social and Personal Relationships*, https://journals.sagepub.com/doi/full/10.1177/0265407512453827

23 Deloitte (2018), Mobile Consumer Survey 2018: The UK Cut, https://www2.deloitte.com/uk/en/pages/technology-media-and-telecommunications/articles/mobile-consumer-survey.html

24 *New York Times* (2019), Human Contact Is Now a Luxury Good, https://www.nytimes.com/2019/03/23/sunday-review/human-contact-luxury-screens.html

25 Royal Society (2018), The Impact of Artificial Intelligence on Work, https://royalsociety.org/-/media/policy/projects/ai-and-work/summary-the-impact-of-AI-on-work.PDF

26 McKinsey Global Institute (2018), AI, Automation, and the Future of Work: Ten Things to Solve For, https://www.mckinsey.com/featured-insights/future-of-work/ai-automation-and-the-future-of-work-ten-things-to-solve-for

27 Wilson, H. J. and Daugherty, P. R. (2018), Collaborative Intelligence: Humans and AI are Joining Forces, *Harvard Business Review*, https://hbr.org/2018/07/collaborative-intelligence-humans-and-ai-are-joining-forces

28 http://www.listsofnote.com/2012/02/how-to-write.html

29 Allcott, G. (2013b), Email Etiquette: 9 Email Pet Peeves, https://thinkproductive.co.uk/email-etiquette-annoying-emails/

30 Darbyshire, M. (2018), How Slack Took Over the Office, *Financial Times*, https://www.ft.com/content/8a9a8d98-0039-11e8-9e12-af73e8db3c71

31 Burgess, K. (2018), Speaking in Public is Worse Than Death for Most, *The Times*, https://www.thetimes.co.uk/article/speaking-in-public-is-worse-than-death-for-most-5l2bvqlmbnt

5 *The Bad Days*

1 https://hbr.org/archive-toc/BR1104

2 Skinner, G. and Clemence, M. (2018), Advertising Execs Rank Below Politicians as Britain's Least-Trusted Profession, Ipsos MORI, https://www.ipsos.com/ipsos-mori/en-uk/advertising-execs-rank-below-politicians-britains-least-trusted-profession; McCarthy, N. (2019), America's Most And Least Trusted Professions, Statista, https://www.statista.com/chart/12420/americas-most-and-least-trusted-professions/

3 Pawlowski, A. (2017), 'A--hole Survival Guide': 9 Tips for Dealing with Jerks, Today, https://www.today.com/health/asshole-survival-guide-dealing-jerks-work-beyond-t116051

4 Goudreau, J. (2011), Crying at Work, a Woman's Burden, *Forbes*, https://www.forbes.com/sites/jennagoudreau/2011/01/11/crying-at-work-a-womans-burden-study-men-sex-testosterone-tears-arousal/#5400af317c6d

5 Fiona Buckland (2017), Feeling Like an Impostor? You Can Escape This Confidence-Sapping Syndrome, *Guardian*, https://www.theguardian.com/commentisfree/2017/sep/19/fraud-impostor-syndrome-confidence-self-esteem

6 BBC News (2018), Michelle Obama: 'I still have impostor syndrome', https://www.bbc.co.uk/news/uk-46434147

7 See also Casserly, M. (2010), Ten Archetypes of a Terrible Boss, *Forbes*, https://www.forbes.com/sites/meghancasserly/2010/09/21/ten-archetypes-of-a-terrible-boss/#45beadfd5f8a

8 https://www.greenpeace.org/international/explore/about/values/

9 https://www.coca-cola.co.uk/about-us/mission-vision-and-values

10 McGregor, J. (2017), 'Hustlin' Is Out. Doing 'the Right Thing' is in. Uber Has Rewritten Its Notorious List of Core Values, *Washington Post*, https://www.washingtonpost.com/news/on-leadership/wp/2017/11/08/hustlin-is-out-doing-the-right-thing-is-in-uber-has-rewritten-its-notorious-list-of-core-values/?utm_term=.b658e68cd41d

11 Dondé, G. (2018), Ethics at Work, Institute of Business Ethics, https://www.ibe.org.uk/userassets/publicationdownloads/ibe_survey_report_ethics_at_work_2018_survey_of_employees_europe_int.pdf

12 Gallo, A. (2015), How to Speak Up About Ethical Issues at Work, *Harvard Business Review*, https://hbr.org/2015/06/how-to-speak-up-about-ethical-issues-at-work

13 https://everydaysexism.com/tag/workplace

14 King, E. and Jones, K. (2016), Why Subtle Bias is so Often Worse Than Blatant Discrimination, *Harvard Business Review*, https://hbr.org/2016/07/why-subtle-bias-is-so-often-worse-than-blatant-discrimination

15 https://rework.withgoogle.com/print/guides/5721312655835136/

16 *New York Times* (2016), What Google Learned From Its Quest to Build the Perfect Team, https://www.nytimes.com/2016/02/28/magazine/what-google-learned-from-its-quest-to-build-the-perfect-team.html?smid=pl-share

17 McKinsey & Company (2015), Diversity Matters, https://www.mckinsey.com/~/media/mckinsey/business%20functions/organization/our%20insights/why%20diversity%20matters/diversity%20matters.ashx

18 King and Jones (2016).

19 Porath, C. (2016), *Mastering Civility: A Manifesto for the Workplace* (Grand Central Publishing).

20 Department for Business, Innovation and Skills (2015), Whistleblowing: Guidance for Employers and Code of Practice, https://assets.publishing.service.gov.uk/government/uploads/system/uploads/attachment_data/file/415175/bis-15-200-whistleblowing-guidance-for-employers-and-code-of-practice.pdf; US Department of Labor, OSHA's Whistleblower Protection Program, https://www.whistleblowers.gov/

21 Dobbin, F. and Kalev, A. (2016), Why Diversity Programs Fail, *Harvard Business Review*, https://hbr.org/2016/07/why-diversity-programs-fail

22 International Network on Leave Policies and Research (2018), 14th International Review of Leave Policies and Related Research, https://www.leavenetwork.org/fileadmin/user_upload/k_leavenetwork/annual_reviews/Leave_Review_2018.pdf

23 In British Social Attitudes, report no. 30, http://www.bsa.natcen.ac.uk/latest-report/british-social-attitudes-30/gender-roles/public-attitudes-to-parental-leave.aspx

24 *New York Times* (2019), Nike Says It Will End Financial Penalties for Pregnant Athletes, https://www.nytimes.com/2019/05/24/sports/nike-pregnant-athletes.html

25 Farmer, P. and Stevenson, D. (2017), Thriving at Work: The Stevenson/Farmer Review of Mental Health and Employers, https://assets.publishing.service.gov.uk/government/uploads/system/uploads/attachment_data/file/658145/thriving-at-work-stevenson-farmer-review.pdf

26 Taylor, M. et al. (2017), Good Work: The Taylor Review of Modern Working Practices, https://assets.publishing.service. gov.uk/government/uploads/system/uploads/attachment_ data/file/627671/good-work-taylor-review-modern-working-practices-rg.pdf

27 Health and Safety Executive (2019), Tackling Work-Related Stress Using the Management Standards Approach, http:// www.hse.gov.uk/pubns/wbk01.pdf

28 Wilding, M. (2018), Please Stop Telling Me to Leave My Comfort Zone, https://www.theguardian.com/us-news/ 2018/nov/16/comfort-zone-mental-health

29 Mind (2016b), How to be Mentally Healthy at Work, https://www.mind.org.uk/information-support/tips-for-everyday-living/workplace-mental-health/work-and-stress/ #.XLHqYjhKjIU; Health and Safety Executive (2008), Working Together to Reduce Stress at Work, http://www. hse.gov.uk/pubns/indg424.pdf

30 ACAS (2018), Improvement Required?, https://www.acas. org.uk/media/6055/Improvement-required-A-mixed-methods-study-of-employers-use-of-Performance-Management-systems/pdf/Improvement_required_A_mixed-methods_ study_of_employers__use_of_Performance_Management_ systems.pdf

31 *New York Times* (2012), Praise is Fleeting, But Brickbats We Recall, https://www.nytimes.com/2012/03/24/your-money/ why-people-remember-negative-events-more-than-positive-ones.html?_r=0&pagewanted=all

32 Buckingham, M. and Goodall, A. (2019), The Feedback Fallacy, *Harvard Business Review*, https://hbr.org/2019/03/ the-feedback-fallacy

6 Business is Personal

1 Rath, T. and Harter, J. (2010), Your Friends and Your Social Well-Being, Gallup, https://news.gallup.com/business journal/127043/friends-social-wellbeing.aspx

2 https://rework.withgoogle.com/guides/understanding-team-effectiveness/steps/identify-dynamics-of-effective-teams/

3 Nevins, M. (2018), How to Collaborate with People You Don't Like, *Harvard Business Review*, https://hbr.org/2018/12/how-to-collaborate-with-people-you-dont-like

4 https://www.designcouncil.org.uk/news-opinion/design-process-what-double-diamond

5 Dierdorff, E. C. and Rubin, R. S. (2018), Research: We're Not Very Self-Aware, Especially at Work, HBR ascend, https://hbrascend.org/topics/research-were-not-very-self-aware-especially-at-work/

6 Vicens, Q. and Bourne, P. E. (2007), Ten Simple Rules for a Successful Collaboration, *PLoS Computational Biology*, https://www.ncbi.nlm.nih.gov/pmc/articles/PMC1847992/

7 Ozcelik, H. and Barsade, S. (n.d.), Work Loneliness and Employee Performance, University of Pennsylvania, https://faculty.wharton.upenn.edu/wp-content/uploads/2012/05/Work_Loneliness_Performance_Study.pdf

8 Achor, S. et al. (2018), America's Loneliest Workers, According to Research, *Harvard Business Review*, https://hbr.org/2018/03/americas-loneliest-workers-according-to-research

9 Achor, S. (2016), The Benefits of Peer-to-Peer Praise at Work, *Harvard Business Review*, https://hbr.org/2016/02/the-benefits-of-peer-to-peer-praise-at-work

7 *The System Will See You Now*

1 Wood, J. (2018), People in These Countries Get the Most Paid Vacation Days, World Economic Forum, https://www.weforum.org/agenda/2018/08/people-in-these-countries-get-the-most-paid-vacation-days/

2 BBC News (2016), French Workers Get 'Right to Disconnect' from Emails Out of Hours, https://www.bbc.co.uk/news/world-europe-38479439

3 Friend, Hannah (2014), Why Taking a Holiday from Work is Good for Your Career, https://www.theguardian.com/careers/careers-blog/why-taking-holiday-work-good-career

8 *Staying Awake and Thinking Craftily*

1 CIPD (2016), Rapid Evidence Assessment of the Research Literature on the Effect of Goal Setting on Workplace Performance, https://www.cipd.co.uk/Images/rapid-evidence-assessment-of-the-research-literature-on-the-effect-of-goal-setting-on-workplace-performance_tcm18-16903.pdf

2 Ordóñez, L. D. et al. (2009), Goals Gone Wild: The Systematic Side Effects of Over-Prescribing Goal Setting, Harvard Business School Working Paper No. 09-083, https://www.hbs.edu/faculty/Publication%20Files/09-083.pdf

3 Jana, R. (2018), 'Rites of Passage', in Nikesh Shukla and Sammy Jones (eds.), *RIFE: Twenty Stories from Britain's Youth*, https://unbound.com/books/rife/

4 My World of Work (n.d.), Transferable Skills to Help You Take Your Next Steps, https://www.myworldofwork. co.uk/transferable-skills-help-you-take-your-next-steps

5 Gartner (2019), Gartner Hype Cycle, https://www.gartner. com/en/research/methodologies/gartner-hype-cycle

6 Benson, A., Li, D. and Shue, K. (2018), Do People Really Get Promoted to Their Level of Incompetence?, *Harvard Business Review*, https://hbr.org/2018/03/research-do-people-really-get-promoted-to-their-level-of-incompetence

7 CIPD (2017), Employee Outlook, https://www.cipd.co.uk/ Images/employee-outlook_2017-spring_tcm18-21163.pdf

8 Keng, C. (2014), Employees Who Stay in Companies Longer Than Two Years Get Paid 50% Less, https://www.forbes. com/sites/cameronkeng/2014/06/22/employees-that-stay-in-companies-longer-than-2-years-get-paid-50-less/#6915ce1ee07f

9 Mollick, E. (2015), Does Switching Jobs Really Help Your Career? World Economic Forum, https://www.weforum.org/ agenda/2015/11/does-switching-jobs-really-help-your-career/

10 Gould, E. (2014), Quitting Your Job in Public Feels Great. Until You Don't Get Another One, https://www. theguardian.com/commentisfree/2014/sep/23/quitting-your-job-alaskan-tv-reporter-viral

9 *Your Future*

1 The Dyke Report (1906), Report of the Consultative Committee upon Questions Affecting Higher Elementary Schools, http://www.educationengland.org.uk/documents/ dyke1906/dyke06.html

NOTES

2 Milkman, R. (2017), A New Political Generation: Millennials and the Post-2008 Wave of Protest, *American
  Sociological Review*, https://journals.sagepub.com/doi/abs
  /10.1177/0003122416681031?journalCode=asra

3 Mental Health Foundation (n.d.), How to Support Mental Health at Work, https://www.mentalhealth.org.uk/
  publications/how-support-mental-health-work

STOP PRESS

The *How to Go to Work* podcast, hosted by Lucy Clayton and Steven Haines, launches in January 2020.

Available via all good platforms, including Apple and Acast.

For further information please email
Penguinbusinesscommunications@penguinrandomhouse.co.uk

PENGUIN PARTNERSHIPS

Penguin Partnerships is the Creative Sales and Promotions team at Penguin Random House. We have a long history of working with clients on a wide variety of briefs, specializing in brand promotions, bespoke publishing and retail exclusives, plus corporate, entertainment and media partnerships.

We can respond quickly to briefs and specialize in repurposing books and content for sales promotions, for use as incentives and retail exclusives as well as creating content for new books in collaboration with our partners as part of branded book relationships.

Equally if you'd simply like to buy a bulk quantity of one of our existing books at a special discount, we can help with that too. Our books can make excellent corporate or employee gifts.

Special editions, including personalized covers, excerpts of existing books or books with corporate logos can be created in large quantities for special needs.

We can work within your budget to deliver whatever you want, however you want it.

For more information, please contact
salesenquiries@penguinrandomhouse.co.uk